TRANSNATIONAL AND IMMIGRANT ENTREPRENEURSHIP
IN A GLOBALIZED WORLD

EDITED BY BENSON HONIG, ISRAEL DRORI,
AND BARBARA CARMICHAEL

Transnational and Immigrant Entrepreneurship in a Globalized World

UNIVERSITY OF TORONTO PRESS
Toronto Buffalo London

© University of Toronto Press Incorporated 2010
Rotman/UTP Publishing
Toronto Buffalo London
www.utppublishing.com
Printed in Canada

ISBN 978-1-4426-4001-6

Printed on acid-free, 100% post-consumer recycled paper with
vegetable-based inks.

Library and Archives Canada Cataloguing in Publication

Transnational and immigrant entrepreneurship in a globalized world /
edited by Benson Honig, Israel Drori, and Barbara Carmichael.

Includes bibliographical references.
ISBN 978-1-4426-4001-6

1. Entrepreneurship.   2. Transnationalism – Economic aspects.
3. Immigrants – Economic conditions.   4. International business
enterprises.   5. Globalization – Economic aspects.   6. Economic
development.   I. Honig, Benson, 1955–   II. Drori, Israel   III. Carmichael,
Barbara Anne, 1948–

HB615.T74 2010   338'.04086912   C2010-900708-5

University of Toronto Press acknowledges the financial assistance to its
publishing program of the Canada Council for the Arts and the Ontario
Arts Council.

University of Toronto Press acknowledges the financial support for its
publishing activities of the Government of Canada through the Book
Publishing Industry Development Program (BPIDP).

Dedicated to history's millions of would-be transnational entrepreneurs, whose valiant yet unsuccessful efforts to escape war, terror, and fascism cost them their lives. May we live in more enlightened times.

For Dena, Alon, and Shanee.   B.H.

For Nili, Iddo, and Tali.   I.D.

For my husband, Bill, a migrant entrepreneur.   B.C.

Contents

Foreword

IVAN LIGHT

Thanks importantly to the research of AnnaLee Saxenian (2002, 2006), the world has realized the economic importance of transnational entrepreneurs (TEs). Once thought to start only mom-and-pop stores, which they still do (Light and Gold, 2000; Light and Bonacich, 1988), immigrant entrepreneurs, it is now realized, have recently been involved in major technical sector start-ups, including Intel, Yahoo, Sun Micro Systems, E-Bay, and Google (Richtel, 2009). Approximately half of Silicon Valley start-ups from the mid-1990s to the mid-2000s had founders born abroad. During this period immigrants were only 10 per cent of the U.S. population.

Operating in their homelands, the transnational entrepreneurs have been equally important in starting technical regions akin to Silicon Valley, the mother of all high-tech regions, in China, India, and Israel. Because they operate with equal facility on both ends of their personal trajectory, their homeland and their adopted country, these entrepreneurs have earned the sobriquet 'transnational.' They are transnational because they belong to more than one nation at the same time. As a result of their economic importance, a global bidding war has now emerged in which numerous developed countries try to attract transnational entrepreneurs with advantageous and liberal visa requirements in the hope that the transnational entrepreneurs will settle some badly needed economic development in their adopted country as well as linking their adopted country more firmly to the sending country in trade.

What exactly do transnational entrepreneurs have that others lack? Scholars must ask this question if they wish to go beyond the mere chronicling of entrepreneurial achievements to understanding them. Explaining their entrepreneurial success, Saxenian (2006: 328) turns to the

transnationals' 'shared language, culture, and professional and educational experiences.' Portes, Guarnizo, and Haller (2002) take a similar tack with respect to the mom-and-pop entrepreneurs they studied.
Such explanation is very much in order, and connects, as I have shown
elsewhere (Light, 2007), to the long-standing social science interest in
non-assimilating 'middleman minorities.' But there is probably another
unexplored dimension of equal importance. This dimension bears upon
the mental stimulation of the creative energy and vision that the transnational entrepreneurs exhibit. Writing about 'creative marginality' in
the social sciences, Dogan and Pahre (1990) showed that exceptionally
creative thinkers had frequently been fluent in the disciplinary paradigm
of neighbouring but distinct disciplines. For example, Sigmund Freud
was a medical doctor and a psychologist; not just a doctor or just a psychologist. Max Weber was an economist and a sociologist, not just one or
the other. Possibly a comparable marginality supports the creativity of
transnational entrepreneurs. The editors and contributors of this volume
think that it does.

This volume stands at the confluence and intersection of several research trends in social theory. Of these, the most conspicuous in the text
is the work of Pierre Bourdieu (1930–2002) who was, until his recent
death, the world's most influential sociologist (Wacquant, 2003). But
there is a paradox here. This volume's topic, entrepreneurship, is about
innovation and mould-breaking. However, Bourdieu's central concept,
the *habitus*, explained stasis, not change. Indeed, the word Bourdieu
coined for his concept, habitus, even contains the word habit, which implies repetition. A habitus consisted for Bourdieu (2000: 259) of socially
shared perceptions and cognitions that furnish the mental equipment of
individuals, and thus explain why those individuals systematically fail
to break out of the traps their societies impose. The habitus is 'socialized subjectivity.' In effect, society traps people in the status quo by im-
posing its conventional wisdom on them. Bourdieu's central problem
was to explain the reproduction of social classes such that the children
of the working class routinely become workers and those of the elite
become elite. This problematic explains how the status quo is repeti-
tiously re-created, not how it is disturbed and replaced.

Of course, partial answers to this question were already available.
Using the concept of human capital, which he created, the economist
Gary Becker (1993) called attention to the intergenerational transmission of human capital. This capital of vocational skills naturally tended
to reproduce the social class membership of elders in that of their youth.

Influenced by Becker, but desirous of deepening his analysis, Bourdieu introduced a number of subordinate concepts that fed into the habitus without defining it. Bourdieu (1986) called them alternative 'forms of capital,' and he thought of these alternative capitals as analogous and functionally equivalent to the economists' financial and human capital in respect, at least, to their role in assuring the intergenerational transmission of social position. Just as people more easily access the elite when they possess the right financial and human capital so, Bourdieu argued, they gain access to it as well when they have the right social capital and cultural capital. Social capital and cultural capital were the alternative forms of capital whose neglected importance Bourdieu wanted to expose without disputing or denying the role of human and financial capital. Bourdieu's task was to expand, not to reject, Becker (Light, 2005; Convert, 2003).

By social capital Bourdieu meant essentially social networks that linked individuals to the elite; by cultural capital, he meant forms of *cultural* knowledge, not vocational knowledge that permitted individuals to operate comfortably in elite social environments. Advanced accounting is vocational knowledge that links its possessor to the business elite. It represents human capital. Having social contacts in the elite helped the children of the elite to gain access to the elite on their own. This was their social capital. Knowing which fork to use at a ritzy banquet was cultural capital. This knowledge enabled the children of the elite to display their comfort in this environment, and thus to acquire a better chance at a lifetime entitlement to it. If someone had only advanced accounting skills, that person would be equipped with business skills, but not with social graces. But if that same person *also* had social and cultural capital, he or she would be *still more* likely to enter the elite than someone who only had advanced accounting skills.

We may think of social capital as the telephone line that connects people, and cultural capital as what they talk about when connected. What's the use of being connected to the elite if one has nothing to say that interests them, or vice versa? Of course, everyone has social capital and cultural capital. The elite do not monopolize these. However, the social and cultural capital of the working class links the children of the working class back to the class into which they were born, inhibiting upward social mobility into the elite. The children of the working class have the human capital, social capital, and cultural capital to land a social position in the working class just as the children of the elite have the social, cultural, and human capital that enables them to penetrate the elite. In this sense, cultural capital and social capital are parts of the habitus, the broader concept, and, like the habitus, they help explain why the social class structure systematically reproduces itself from generation to generation.

Bourdieu was never interested in entrepreneurship, immigration, or transnationalism, the subjects of this volume. Moreover, as indicated above, his outlook was wholly antithetical to the concerns that animate scholars who are interested in these topics. A volume on transnational entrepreneurs wants to explain dynamism, change, and innovation, but Bourdieu wanted to explain stasis, repetition, conventional thinking, and the intergenerational reproduction of social class standing.[1] It is at this point, I submit, that the editors and contributors to this volume make an intellectual contribution that builds on but transcends Bourdieu. In their concept of bifocality of habitus (also referred to as dual habitus) the editors ask what happens to the individual who has acquired a second habitus. Bourdieu never *asked that question*, simply presuming that everyone had one and only one habitus. In the famous expression of Harold Garfinkel (1967: 68), Bourdieu assumed 'cultural dopes.' This is a safe assumption much of the time, but not always. When, as a result of transnational immigration, people have acquired the habitus of their sending country as well as that of their receiving country, they have acquired a second habitus. It is significant that Bourdieu never used the word habitus in the plural. Latinizing the word imposes an awkward neologism, *habiti*. The term 'dual habitus' avoids the awkward Latin that Bourdieu, who quoted Latin from time to time, never employed.

The editors and contributors to this volume introduce the idea that immigrants who have acquired a dual habitus were thereby liberated from the constraints of having only one habitus, the usual situation of the cultural dope, and were in this manner outfitted magnificently to innovate in and change the international business environment. One habitus implies conformity; two implies innovation. At this point, having made such a bold if plausible extrapolation of Bourdieu's theory, the editors and contributors to this volume have rediscovered a classic line of sociological research that Bourdieu might have utilized, but did not. They may, however, need and legitimately acquire some unexpected help from the archive of social science, which provides some basis in existing literature for the legitimacy of their bold claim. This contribution is the concept of the 'marginal man.' Identified with Robert Ezra Park (1864–1944), a pioneer of Chicago sociology in the 1920s, and with Park's student, Everett V. Stonequist (1961), the concept of the marginal man ultimately derived from the prior essay by the German sociologist Georg Simmel (1921: 323) on 'the stranger.' In this essay, Simmel had called attention to the mental and perceptual consequences of living as a cultural outsider in a foreign land. The consequence, Simmel thought, was a 'peculiar composition of nearness and remoteness, concern and indifference' that fed into emotional 'objectivity' with respect to the foreign culture. Merchants were, in Simmel's opinion, classic strangers:[2] 'In the whole history of economics, the stranger makes his appearance everywhere as the trader, and the trader makes his as the stranger' (Park and Burgess, 1921: 321–2).

Park and Burgess reproduced that economic passage from Simmel in their edited textbook, but Park (1928) later crafted a derivative concept of 'marginal man' from Simmel's concept of the stranger. Then Park generalized the marginal man status to immigrants, who were, Park thought, always exposed to the juxtaposition of their sending culture with American culture, the receiving culture.[3] Out of this juxtaposition immigrants often experienced moral, legal, and social confusion in the short run. Cultures disagreed and immigrants did not know which to follow or trust. But, on the positive side, the protracted experience of marginality (simultaneous participation in two cultures) empowered immigrants and to some extent their children, as well, to think clearly about social realities without the distorting effect that arises from firm social anchorage in one or another culture. The result was often an augmented instrumental rationality that could link cause and effect into chains and then derive working action plans. In essence, Park thought that the collision of cultures, typical of the modern world, liberated the human mind whereas physical and social isolation constricted it.[4] Park (1925) even argued that differences in global economic development arose as a result of the geographical centrality of some cultures and the isolation of others.

Whereas Park had turned to immigrant acculturation, not business acumen and excellence, Park's student, Everett Stonequist, returned to Simmel's interest in the relationship between social marginality and excellence in business. Stonequist (1961: 81) proposed that the centuries-long social marginality of the Jews in Europe had imposed a peculiar objectivity upon their culture. This was a more or less permanent change in culture: '[The Jew's] group life is organized upon a marginal basis, characteristically expressed in his proclivity for living in the cosmopolitan city by means of trade and banking – "business."' Proposing this idea, Stonequist was offering a cultural explanation of how the Jewish mentality supported Jewish entrepreneurship.[5] Jews did not have this mentality in King David's time. However, in the centuries of diasporic marginality, Jews had acquired, in Stonequist's view, a characteristic objectivity that conduced very well to their success in business. Had the language been available, Stonequist might have said that Jews of the diaspora acquired a permanent second habitus, and that the bifocality of their habitus then supported their excellence in business. Had he said that he would have been at the same point as are the editors and contributors to this volume.

NOTES

1 Sewell (1992: 16) criticized Bourdieu for this rigidity: 'habitus, which [Bourdieu] conceptualizes as a vast series of strictly homologous structures encompassing all of social experience. Such a conceptualization, which Bourdieu in fact shares roughly with many structurally inclined theorists, cannot explain change as arising from within the operation of structures.'

2 Stonequist (1961: 81) agreed: '[Jewish] group life is organized upon a marginal basis, characteristically expressed in ... proclivity for living in the cosmopolitan city by means of trade and banking ... The flexible and restless nature of his mind enables [the Jew] to seize an advantage and to discount the future.'

3 For an intellectual biography of Robert Park, see Lal (1990).

4 'The emancipated individual invariably becomes in a certain sense and to a certain degree a cosmopolitan. He learns to look upon the world in which he was born and bred with something of the detachment of a stranger' (Park, 1928: 888).

5 A similar point was made about the same time but in a structural way by Max Weber's intellectual antagonist, Werner Sombart (see Light, 2010).

REFERENCES

Becker, G.S. (1993). *Human Capital* (3rd ed.). New York: National Bureau of Economic Research.

Bourdieu, P. (1986). The forms of capital. In J.G. Richardson (Ed.), *Handbook of*

Theory and Research for the Sociology of Education, 241–251. New York: Greenwood.

Bourdieu, P. (2000). *Les Structures Sociales de l'Economie*. Paris: Seuil.

Convert, B. (2003). Bourdieu: Gary Becker's Critic. *Economic Sociology – European Electronic Newsletter*, vol. 4. (March). http://www.siswo.uva.nl/ES/4-2art2.html.

Dogan, M., & Pahre, R. (1990). *Creative Marginality: Innovation at the Intersections of Social Sciences*. Boulder: Westview.

Garfinkel, H. (1967). *Studies in Ethnomethodology*. New York: Prentice-Hall.

Lal, B.B. (1990). *The Romance of Culture in an Urban Civilization: Robert E. Park on Race and Ethnic Relations*. London: Blackwell.

Light, I. (2005). Cultural capital. In M.C. Horowitz (Ed.), *The New Dictionary of the History of Ideas*, vol. 2, 511–512. New York: Scribner's.

Light, I. (2007). Global entrepreneurship and transnationalism. In L. Dana (Ed.), *Handbook of Research on Ethnic Minority Entrepreneurship*, 3–15. Cheltenham: Edward Elgar.

Light, I. (2010). The religious ethic of the Protestant ethnics. In L. Dana (Ed.), *Religion and Entrepreneurship*. London: Edward Elgar.

Light, I., & Bonacich, E. (1988). *Immigrant Entrepreneurs*. Los Angeles: University of California Press.

Light, I., & Gold, S. (2000). *Ethnic Economies*. San Diego: Academic Press.

Park, R.E. (1925). Magic, mentality, and city life. In R.E. Park, E.W. Burgess, & R.D. McKenzie (Eds.), *The City*, 123–141. Chicago: University of Chicago Press.

Park, R.E. (1928). Human migration and the marginal man. *American Journal of Sociology*, 33: 881–893.

Park, R.E., & Burgess, E.W. (1921). *Introduction to the Science of Sociology*. Chicago: University of Chicago Press.

Portes, A., Guarnizo, L.E., & Haller, W.J. (2002). Transnational entrepreneurs: An alternative form of immigrant economic adaptation. *American Sociological Review*, 67: 278–298.

Richtel, M. (2009). A Google whiz searches for his place on Earth. *New York Times*, (12 Apr.), Section 1, 1, 18–19.

Saxenian, A. (2002). Transnational communities and the evolution of global production networks: The Cases of Taiwan, China and India. *Industry and Innovation*, 9(3): 183–202.

Saxenian, A. (2006). *The New Argonauts: Regional Advantage in a Global Economy*. Cambridge, MA: Harvard University Press.

Sewell, W.H., Jr. (1992). A theory of structure: Duality, agency, and transformation. *American Journal of Sociology*, 98(1): 1–29.

Simmel, G. (1921). The sociological significance of 'the Stranger.' In R.E.
   Park & E.W. Burgess (Eds.), *Introduction to the Science of Sociology*, 322–326.
   Chicago: University of Chicago Press.
Stonequist, E.V. (1961). *The Marginal Man: A Study in Personality and Culture
   Conflict*. New York: Russell Sage.
Wacquant, L. (2002). The sociological life of Pierre Bourdieu. *International
   Sociology*, 17: 549–556.

Preface

BENSON HONIG, ISRAEL DRORI, AND
BARBARA CARMICHAEL

This work began when two colleagues (Israel Drori and Benson Honig), each working on opposite sides of the world, were introduced by a mutual friend at the Academy of Management (AOM) meeting in New Orleans in 2004. We soon realized that despite our eclectic backgrounds, we shared extraordinary similarities, including extensive economic and entrepreneurship development research in Africa and the Caribbean. As one conversation bled into another, we found ourselves embracing the study of transnational entrepreneurship (TE), mirroring in many ways our own unique transcontinental cultural experiences. Barbara Carmichael's experience with transnational tourism rounded out our team.

Our first efforts to frame the study of TE were well received, including a best paper finalist at AOM the following year. Given this warm reception, we followed this effort by hosting an international conference in 2008 at Wilfrid Laurier University, in Waterloo, Ontario, where we brought over forty international scholars together to discuss and debate the importance of this emergent field of study. Together with a special 2009 issue of *Entrepreneurship Theory and Practice*, this volume provides an opportunity to examine emergent theoretical and empirical studies in this very important and growing field of interest.

For the purpose of our current work, including this volume, we define transnational entrepreneurs (TEs) as 'social actors who enact networks, ideas, information, and practices for the purpose of seeking business opportunities or maintaining businesses within dual social fields, which in turn force them to engage in varied strategies of action to promote their entrepreneurial activities and societal changes.'

The growing impact of TE can be mainly attributed to the changing nature of international migration and diasporas and to the complex nature of international business activities. In recent years, the concept of transnational entrepreneurship as a distinctive attribute of globalization has drawn considerable attention in social science disciplines such as sociology, anthropology, economics, economic geography, and regional planning. Despite their interest in similar questions, theory-building approaches to these three questions remain discipline-based and fragmented, making the accumulation of empirical research contributions difficult to achieve. For example, sociologists view TE in terms of the process of immigrant integration and economic adaptation or in terms of social structure and network relations of immigrant communities. Sociologists have also studied demographic and social characteristics of TE, such as the propensity to become a transnational entrepreneur, the growth rate of transnational new ventures, their impact on particular industries, and their assimilation into mainstream institutional frameworks. Economic geographers and regional planners review the role of TE in influencing the creation of business opportunities, as well as its impact on the transfer of knowledge, technology, and know-how, and as a catalyst for the evolution of global production networks.

This book is specifically focused on an entrepreneurship approach that deals with mechanisms that enable a wide range of entrepreneurial activities. These include seeking and exploiting opportunities, entering markets under conditions of uncertainty, and meeting the needs of the new firm and the interests of various stakeholders who directly or indirectly support the new venture. Understanding TE from this perspective calls for taking into account the unique functioning of these mechanisms in different social situations and contexts and in varied social fields.

Yet, the phenomenon of transnational entrepreneurship – the formation and maintenance of business firms by entrepreneurs whose activities span home and host countries – is undertheorized. In particular, there is only a rudimentary understanding of such firms' bifocal contexts, structures, and practices. For example, what is their preferred bifocal modus operandi, or how do transnational entrepreneurs function within a cross-border context; how do TEs reconcile structural and cultural differences and operate businesses in home and host societies; what influences the prospects and maintenance of transnational entrepreneurship; how do varied cross-border contexts shape opportunities and ventures; how are TE conditions and activities manifested in different fields; and how do the dual cross-border contexts stimulate entrepreneurship?

In this book we have set ourselves the task of exploring the above-mentioned issues. It is roughly divided equally by theoretical and empirical studies, beginning with four theoretical perspectives, followed by four primarily empirical studies, and a concluding chapter.

We begin the volume with 'Researching Transnational Entrepreneurship: An Approach Based on the Theory of Practice,' where Israel Drori, Benson Honig, and Ari Ginsberg develop an analytical framework to study transnational entrepreneurship, the process of creating new businesses by social actors with dual cultural, institutional, and economic features. Grounded in the theory of practice, they examine: (1) cultural repertoires and social capital, (2) institutional fields and industry networks, and (3) power relations and political meanings. They suggest how this proposed framework can renew the research agenda of transnational entrepreneurship allowing for greater coherence and robustness among existing research streams.

In Chapter 2, 'Contemporary Diasporic Entrepreneurship: A Conceptual and Comparative Framework,' Xiaohua Lin examines the role of contemporary diasporic entrepreneurs (CDEs), focusing primarily on returnee Chinese migrants. He points out that despite their growing prevalence, due to global and economic shifts and new opportunities, there exists a surprising dearth of scholarly material relating to these firms in the existing international entrepreneurship (IE) literature. Lin's framework for the future study of CDEs focuses on the cultural contrasts that CDEs must manage in returning to their home countries, where they demonstrate very different norms, knowledge, and values. He provides a set of propositions that attempt to explain the emergence, development, orientation (both technological and international), and managerial processes employed by CDEs. Finally, Lin offers some interesting insight into the particularistic role of the Chinese government vis-à-vis their CDEs, who provide important technological, organizational, and social advantages to the Chinese entrepreneurial landscape.

In Chapter 3, 'Transnational Scientific Entrepreneurship: A Conceptual Framework,' Amalya L. Oliver and Kathleen Montgomery refer to a particular kind of TE, which is associated with the globalization of science and technology. They explain how the scientific communities, which span national boundaries, share similar practices and sets of institutional rules regarding standards and norms. In addition these communities, through a well-defined and diversified network, are responsible for knowledge and information sharing and transfer. The permeability of boundaries in the social domains of academia or the business domain of industrial firms that engage in state of the art research, for example, in the fields of biotechnology, nanotechnology, or electronics and computers, provides a ready impetus for transnational scientific entrepreneurship (TSE). Thus, the global environment of science is not only providing an opportunity for the acquisition and dissemination of knowledge, but also exposes the entrepreneurs to the commercialization possibilities of inventions and innovation. In their chapter, Oliver and Montgomery claim that TSE is a complex construct of the following hybrids: transnational entrepreneurship, transnational science, and scientific entrepreneurship. All three constructs point to the fact that the field of science is offering entrepreneurial opportunities that are embedded in multiple settings and materialized as a result of dynamic global processes such as the formation of scientific networks or the high exposure enjoyed by scientific advancement or inventions.

Given the complexity of the 'environment of TSE, in particular the inherited reality of operating in a dual setting, Oliver and Montgomery identify four factors that have an impact on the business prospects of TSE: scientific social capital and trust, exploratory research capabilities, exploitation and technological capabilities, and entrepreneurial culture. In addition, business opportunities of TSEs are also influenced by individual factors such as the social capital of the scientist or the previous entrepreneurial experience or position of the scientist within a 'value chain' that enhances the possibilities of commercialization. Furthermore, scientists are embedded within a normative system that stems from the nature of the scientific venture. For example, distinct laws of intellectual and property (IP) rights or norms of collaboration may under certain circumstances provide an incentive to or inhibit the founding of a business.

Transnational scientific entrepreneurship emerges as a business arena in which scientific knowledge translates into business opportunities through the exploitation of both science and transnational environments in a dual setting. The conditions under which each of the settings facilitates or inhibits entrepreneurship are closely associated with the dynamics of the context of commercialization as well as the ability of the individual scientist-entrepreneur to gain and retain the social and economic capital needed for moving from creating knowledge to founding a business.

In Chapter 4, entitled 'Building Effective Networks: Network Strategy and Emerging Virtual Organizations,' Ingrid Wakkee, Peter Groenewegen, and Paula Danskin Englis examine how emerging organizations become immersed in the global market and what the causal relationships are between networking strategies being used by the emerging venture and the venture's usage of virtual and social networks. A series of propositions is formulated regarding effective network building for emerging organizations and how these lead to more traditional versus more virtual modes of organization. A micro-level perspective of emerging venture organizational development is adopted. In relation to the networks, the full network (small world and scale free) is considered. Social networks are established as the provider of both relational ties and a structural position that contributes to the founding and maintaining of transnational entrepreneurship. Being immersed in certain networks implies potential access to resources and knowledge that greatly influences the entrepreneur's chance of survival. In particular, TEs that operate in dual settings and different social and economic spaces may be part of diverse networks, for example, ethnic, national, and global. The authors provide a conceptual framework for explaining how networks are created by organizations using the Internet as a platform that transcends physical and social boundaries. Thus, the Internet provides business opportunities that use virtual networks as drivers for immersion in the global market. The nature of virtual networks, their flexibility, and permeability enable TEs to expand their boundaries in the early days of their founding. Wakee, Groenewegen, and Englis provide a two-dimensional matrix that explains the role of networks' characteristics in the context of virtual organizations that operate transnationally. The network structure and the network strategy are both enhanced by the scope and number of virtual ties available to the TE, and consequently expand its market reach.

In Chapter 5, 'One World or Worlds Apart? Dual Institutional Focus to Enhance Venture Performance,' Pankaj C. Patel and Betty Conklin examine bifocality as an imperative component of transnational entrepreneurship. The TE is socialized into two distinct sets of roles and relationships that have evolved for the purpose of creating and growing businesses. Over time, TEs internalize a set of mental structures, or dispositions, which they employ in the course of using capital to spot and exploit opportunities in a cross-border context. Drawing on both Bourdieu's theory of practice and Kaufman's NK model, Patel and Conklin explore the dynamics of balancing the distribution of resources between the TE's dual settings. Their simulation examines the nature of balancing entrepreneurial activities in dual settings. Their finding that greater balance influences the scope and extent of entrepreneurial activities may well be grounded in the nature of operating in the dual settings. In their dual settings, TEs encounter vastly different business conditions and institutional frameworks encompassing the entire social, economic, political, and cultural systems. The observation that balancing bifocality is instrumental to entrepreneurial activities may stem from the idea that if not balanced, the asymmetrical ways that TEs accumulate, exchange, and utilize various types of capital in their home-country and host-country environments may pose a liability. For example, TEs may waste their various forms of capital by mismanaging them.

In Chapter 6, 'The Progression of International Students into Transnational Entrepreneurs: A Conceptual Framework,' Gerry Kerr and Francine K. Schlosser address the relationship between students (primarily university) and transnational entrepreneurship, by specifying the processes by which some students are either drawn into, or directed into, transnational entrepreneurship (push-pull). They summarize extant literature highlighting the roles immigrants and entrepreneurship, pointing towards the potential role of students in the creation of TE activity. As they indicate, immigrant countries such as Canada are in a particularly good position to benefit from the wealth of diversity and talent that immigrant students bring into the labour force. Kerr and Schlosser's framework provides a useful tool for public policy actors to begin examining the impact of formal education on regional TE growth processes according to both the resource pool and perceived opportunities. The authors provide a number of pragmatic policies that might be enacted in support of TE specifically for the student population.

In Chapter 7, 'The Trade and Immigration Nexus in the India-Canada Context,' Margaret Walton-Roberts provides an important (and refreshing) geographer's perspective to the study of transnational entrepreneurship. She focuses on trade patterns and immigration, with a particular interest in Indo-Canadian exchanges. Walton-Roberts examines the sometimes contradictory findings, highlighting the importance of contingency and locality in attempting to explain immigration in terms of a multiplicity of economic relationships. In the case of Canada she discusses specific localized policies, such as the non-recognition of foreign credentials and immigrant earnings discrepancies yielding transnational behaviour of necessity, rather than desire. She draws on semi-structured in-depth interviews conducted with eight Canadian trade officers in Vancouver, Delhi, Mumbai, and Chandigarh, and nine immigrant entrepreneurs/corporate employees in Vancouver who were actively involved in trade with India. Walton-Roberts provides important empirical evidence that, while acknowledging some indifference on the part of authorities, recognizes modest trade growth attributed to immigrants, with an underutilized potential TE population. Still, she points towards a number of successful TE ventures, and highlights examples of immigrants in promoting TE occurring in both directions. Using the work of Bourdieu, and symbolic capital, Walton-Roberts asserts that different discourses regarding immigrant 'quality' exist in the Canadian bureaucracy, impacting both the treatment of immigrants and the support of immigrant entrepreneurs, sometimes providing contradictory measures. For example, she finds that the vigilance by one arm of the Canadian immigration authorities restricts mobility essential to the viability of transnational entrepreneurs, many of whom are developing businesses that rely on and support Canadian export activities. While the TE literature offers us an important research agenda, we must maintain a close watch on the structure within which TEs attempt to operate as we look more closely at the grounded practice of TEs.

In Chapter 8, 'Legal and Social Institutions for Transnational Entrepreneurship: A Multiple Case Study in the Spanish Context,' David Urbano, Nuria Toledano, and Domingo Ribeiro-Soriano focus on 'transnationalism from below.' They rely on institutional economics to explore four very different, yet rich case studies of TE that they systematically examined in Spain. They found that the Spanish legal system, while possibly influencing their decision to locate in Spain, had little if any impact on their subjects' decision to become transnational entrepreneurs. Further, there was a general perception by TEs that mainstream business support mechanisms were not intended to help them, although this was not shared by the support agencies themselves. These authors use inductive techniques to develop a set of propositions that examine how the impact of institutional support, immigrant receptivity, technological and economic development, social and informal networks, informal institutions, and a 'start-up' supporting environment all led to the establishment of transnational activity. They present a model based on these propositions that highlights the importance of formal institutions that they found facilitated the emergence of TEs, and informal institutions that provide social networks essential for the emergence and development of transnational entrepreneurship. They conclude with an appeal for TE friendly public policy, including assistance with capital and mobility in order to facilitate and stimulate transnational entrepreneurship.

Finally, in Chapter 9, 'A Review of Related Streams of Immigration and Global Entrepreneurship Research,' Benson Honig and Israel Drori conclude by comparing and contrasting the fields of ethnic entrepreneurship (EE), international entrepreneurship (IE), and transnational entrepreneurship (EE), providing a context within which to anchor studies in this emergent field.

ACKNOWLEDGMENTS

The editors gratefully acknowledge the support of the Social Science Research Council, Canada, for a research grant enabling the development of this edited volume. The book publication was also supported with funding from the NeXt Research Centre (Centre for the Study of Nascent Entrepreneurship and the Exploitation of Technology) at Wilfrid Laurier University, Waterloo, Ontario.

TRANSNATIONAL AND IMMIGRANT ENTREPRENEURSHIP
IN A GLOBALIZED WORLD

1 Researching Transnational Entrepreneurship: An Approach Based on the Theory of Practice

ISRAEL DRORI, BENSON HONIG, AND ARI GINSBERG

In recent years, the concept of transnational entrepreneurship (TE) as a distinct attribute of globalization has drawn considerable attention in social science disciplines such as sociology, anthropology, economics, economic geography, and regional planning (Light, 1972; Portes, 1987; Portes, Guarnizo, & Haller, 2002; Portes & Zhou, 1996; Saxenian, 2000). These diverse approaches to the study of TE are linked by a common desire to understand how, why, and when individuals and/or organizations build new business organizations in currently adopted countries while relying on resources and opportunities that stem from maintaining business-related linkages with their countries of origin. Transnational entrepreneurs are individuals who migrate from one country to another, concurrently maintaining business-related linkages with their countries of origin and with their adopted countries and communities. By travelling both physically and virtually, transnational entrepreneurs engage simultaneously in two or more socially embedded environments, allowing them to maintain critical global relations that enhance their ability to creatively and efficiently maximize their resource base. The growing impact of transnational entrepreneurship can be mainly attributed to the changing nature of international migration and diasporas, and to the complex nature of international business activities (Zahra & George, 2002; Yeung, 2002).

A good illustration of this phenomenon is the case of a transnational entrepreneur who was a former Chinese prosecuting attorney and who is now living in a rural farming community in Northern Ireland. Initially drawn to Ireland to study English, she met and married a farmer who resided far from the existing network of overseas Chinese resident in Belfast. Responding to the curiosity of her newly acquired Irish neighbours, she soon identified business opportunities and began e-mailing friends and family in China regarding the logistics of starting a tourist business. This led to her establishing a unique enterprise tailored to the particular cultural and demographic make-up of her vacationing Irish clientele. Most of her customers were in their sixties and unable to 'keep up' with the rigorous physical demands of typical Chinese packaged tours, and uncomfortable with the diet conventionally offered to overseas tourists. Realizing that her clientele were interested in daily life in China, she designed specialized tours that included visits to ordinary Chinese in their homes and social and cultural engagements. She organized these tours by utilizing various friends and family, all the while acting as a personal guide, interpreter, and concierge. She became somewhat of a national celebrity, appearing on local television and radio programs, leading to recognition and assistance from the Irish small business support network, and the further expansion of her business activities.

The efforts of our transnational entrepreneur to translate, innovate, and modify structures simultaneously operating in two distinct cultural paradigms represent entrepreneurial activities that take advantage of a new globalized and interconnected world. Her strategy of entrepreneurial action is poorly framed in terms of theories of international or ethnic entrepreneurship, which are focused on a business trajectory emanating from a single cultural perspective.

Accordingly, we define transnational entrepreneurs as: *social actors who enact networks, ideas, information, and practices for the purpose of seeking business opportunities or maintaining businesses within multiple social fields, which in turn forces them to engage in varied strategies of action to promote their entrepreneurial activities and societal changes.*

We contend that to develop a deeper understanding of the activities of the transnational entrepreneur such as the one described above requires the use of an analytical tool capable of deciphering dual cultural perspectives. To that end, we introduce in this chapter a theoretical framework based on recent developments in the *theory of practice*, which account for the dynamic relationship between a cross-cultural actor, multiple contextual fields of activity, and the development of structure based on Bourdieu's concept of *habitus*, which forms a world view guiding entrepreneurial action (see Bourdieu, 1977, 1990, 1998; Schatzki, Knorr-Cetina, & Von Savigny, 2001).

The objective of this chapter is to adopt and develop an analytical framework that is particularly well suited to addressing the epistemological challenges reflected in the TE phenomenon that we have deline-ated. Formulating a theory of practice to the study of TE enables us to examine more deeply how the multiple cultural, institutional, and economic features of the complex, cross-national domains in which im-migrants operate influence the entrepreneurial strategies and actions they undertake. In integrating micro- and macro-levels of analysis, the practice-based analytical framework we develop provides a means by which we can better understand the dynamic nature of TE as it flows through the intersection of individual and collective meanings, per-ceptions, experiences, and practices. This conceptual gap is particu-larly evident with respect to our understanding of such firms' multiple contexts, structures, and practices (Portes, Guarnizo, & Haller, 2002). In this chapter we would like to address gaps in current theorizing about transnational entrepreneurship. The first concerns the manifold nature of TE's modus operandi, or how transnational entrepreneurs function within cross-border contexts. Second, we present the mecha-nisms through which transnational entrepreneurs develop and sustain their business activities: specifically, what influences the prospects and maintenance of TE, how varied cross-border contexts shape opportuni-ties and ventures, how transnational entrepreneurial conditions and ac-tivities are manifested in different fields, and how cross-border contexts stimulate entrepreneurship. Third, we demonstrate why transnational entrepreneurs must engage in a flexible array of practices in the course of seeking and exploiting business opportunities in response to such differences.

Transnational Entrepreneurship and the Theory of Practice

The previous discussion suggests that to develop a more robust analyti-cal framework for the study of transnational entrepreneurship, we need to look more closely at the role of the cumulative history of action and interaction, as well as multiple cultural affiliations, in generating the strategies and decisions of transnational entrepreneurs. The construc-tion of a conceptual framework in these terms leads us to propose an analytical framework derived from recent developments in the theory of practice (see Bourdieu, 1977, 1990, 1998; Pickel, 2005; Schatzki et al., 2001). The reasoning of actions, which is a continuous endeavour of so-cial actors, can be viewed as the 'range of arguments and principles of evaluation which individuals deploy in the process of trying to define what may be the most proper legitimate action or standard of action and whereby they grope for or re-establish social agreement' (Silber, 2003: 429). As we elaborate in the next section, viewing transnational entrepreneurs as resourceful actors that operate in dual changing contexts requires a 'means of transposition of schemas and remobilizations of resources that make the new structures recognizable as transformations of the old' (Sewell, 2005: 137). The search for such a range of transformation implies that research on TE should include macro-level social constructs within which the individual entrepreneurs act. Furthermore, the meaning of actions can only be understood by observing the backdrop of sociocultural and institutional processes that both enable and constrain social reality (Giddens, 1984).

The theory of practice developed by Bourdieu also calls our attention to the role of agency and practice in enabling transnational entrepreneurs to validate the social and economic characteristics and attributes of their dual contexts. In this vein, practice implies human activities that invoke aggregate sets of interactions (Schatzki et al., 2001: 2). Constructed values and interests, or consented actions, eventually shape and reshape both the individual and the institutional contexts of TE. Thus, understanding TE via the theory of practice calls for taking into account those constructs that refer to both the micro-level, that is, individual actions, cognitions, and beliefs, as well as the macro-level, that is, structural and institutional contexts.

Structuration Theory and the Theory of Practice

The basic epistemic disposition of the theory of practice is closely related to Giddens' structuration theory (1979, 1984). *Structuration theory* examines the social relations resulting from both pre-existing structures and individual agency. Structures are conceived as 'rules and resources, recursively implicated in the reproduction of social systems' (Giddens, 1984: 377), and are dual in nature in the sense that they are 'both the medium and the outcome of practices which constitute social systems' (Giddens, 1981: 27).

Recently, a few studies have made reference to structuration theory, conceptualizing the entrepreneurial process as a mutual interaction between individuals and opportunities (Chaisson & Saunders, 2005; Sarason, Dean, & Dillard, 2006). As argued by Sarason et al. (2006: 288), the individual entrepreneur and his or her social system co-evolve 'as the entrepreneur interfaces with the sources of opportunity and engages in venturing process … Similarly, the sources of opportunity and the structuring processes are constructed and reconstructed in the entrepreneur's actions.' In revealing the nature of the relationship between the entrepreneur and opportunities as a 'recursive dualistic process' and not as a mutually exclusive endeavour, structuration theory focuses on the nature of the structures themselves within which such processes occur. In particular, this work examines the duality of structures, which are 'composed simultaneously of schemas, which are virtual, and of resources which are actual' (Sewell, 2005: 136).

Similar to structuration theory, Bourdieu's theory of practice explores processes of social construction that take place within structures that are dual in nature and consist of 'mental structures' and the 'world of objects.' However, Harker, Mahar, and Wilkes (1990) identify three explanations regarding how the theory of practice provides a more dynamic view of social processes than Giddens' structuration theory. First, Bourdieu asserts that individuals rely on strategies related to social practices instead of strategies related to rules. Second, Bourdieu examines what Giddens refers to as resources, in terms of various forms of capital (e.g., cultural, social, and human) over which actors struggle. Transnational entrepreneurs are situated to accumulate, exchange, and leverage asymmetrical capital in their dual environments, which in turn provides them an advantage in their struggle. Third, and most important for the study of TE, is Bourdieu's notion of dynamic field, in which agents struggle for position and power, as opposed to Giddens' reliance upon a rather static notion of institutional field. Dynamic fields, as we will discuss later on, represent a particularly helpful conceptual device for understanding the multiple structural environments under which TEs operate.

The Concept of Habitus

According to the theory of practice, the reproduction of cognitive schema and options for action constitute the context for 'temporally durable structures' (Sewell, 2005: 138) or, in Bourdieu's terminology, the 'habitus.' Bourdieu (1990: 54) defines habitus as 'a product of history that produces individual and collective practices ... It ensures the active presence of past experiences, which, deposited in each organism in the form of schemes of perception, thought and action, tend to guarantee the "correctness" of practices and their constancy over time, more reliably than all formal rules and explicit norms.' Thus, when individuals decide to start a transnational entrepreneurial activity, they are drawing on a series of dispositions that are generated from certain cultural schemas (Mouzelis, 1995). For example, recall our opening case of the Chinese entrepreneur in Ireland and her specialized travel agency. Interpreting her experience and knowledge of both Chinese and Irish cultures, she was able to comprehend the probable Irish perceptions of China. In terms of the business opportunity, she identified the needs, and provided specialized tours to China, which catered to the Irish experience, values, expectations, and norms.

Practices are the outcomes of habitus, which provides social actors with the principles and logic that eventually guide action (Bourdieu, 1990). Habitus thus informs practices that are not planned or explicit, but that guide the individual entrepreneur in managing change and uncertainty. While it is both historically and socially situated, habitus may also be novel, adapting to new forms and actions, and responding to changes in social relations. It is a useful theoretical device to explain activities involved in the creation and development of new businesses, particularly those involved in processes of transnational entrepreneurship, which straddle multiple dispositions of social relations. Consider the testimony of an Israeli Internet entrepreneur who maintained the R&D aspects of his business in Israel and the operation and sales in New York: 'Luckily enough, I'm familiar with the American sales culture, since I have a silk ties business in San Francisco and have to manage an army of salespersons. So, I'm the bridge between these people, and their clients and the technical geeks back in Israel' (interview, 8 Dec. 2006). This suggests that the entrepreneur's habitus consists of his individual experience, as well as the collective experiences, perceptions, and norms of his employees both in the United States and Israel. These provide him a reference for action and an ability to adjust to the particular conditions of dual contexts (e.g., Bourdieu 1990: 53). We thus develop the following proposition:

Proposition 1: Transnational entrepreneurs engage in multiple relationships which are enacted in at least two different cultural contexts or habitus for business activities. Their understanding of the overlapping or dual habitus provides them with a reference for action that results in the creation of transnational businesses.

To understand how dual habitus is produced and activated, we need to discuss the notion of 'field,' which is a complementary construct to habitus in Bourdieu's theory of practice. The field consists of a network or a configuration of relations between different types of capital (social, cultural, economic, symbolic) that form relations and distributions (Bourdieu, 1993: 72–7). Furthermore, fields are subsequently marked by a tension or conflict between the interests of different groups who struggle to gain control over the field's array of capital. Following Bourdieu and Wacquant (1992), we define a field as a network of relations reflecting various kinds of capital (e.g., social, economic, cultural, symbolic) within which social actors strategize for exerting degrees of control. Social actors primarily reference the social relations, values, and perceptions shared by the members of their group. It is the role of habitus to form a link between an actor's social sphere and a structure and/or action. Thus, at the individual level, habitus interacts with the collective through the common relationship of the field. The structures within the fields that both enable and constrain action arise from the process of reproduction that is internally created in the relationship between habitus and multiple fields. Thus, the process of reproduction is framed in terms of the different economic, social, and cultural capital with which people strategically act on the basis of their habitus. The concept of habitus, along with its accompanying fields, provides a means by which we can explain an orientation towards action, at the intersection of the collective and the individual.

In examining the fields that are relevant to TE, researchers should focus on situations in which transnational entrepreneurs engage in interactions within a certain institutional context that serves as the arena for their constructed rules and the patterns reflected in their entrepreneurial activities (Bourdieu, 1977; Bourdieu & Wacquant, 1992). This field provides a structural barrier that transnational entrepreneurs must navigate in assuming their habitus. In short, while the habitus of the entrepreneur essentially represents the dispositional component of the social world, the field essentially represents the relational component, each operating in a dialectical context. For example, in the cross-nationally contested institutional fields that mark the TE realm, diverse and at times incompatible institutional norms complicate the social and economic meanings and consequences of entrepreneurs' strategies and actions. For example, one transnational entrepreneur we studied utilized his understanding of the institutional environment of a multinational telecommunications company to develop complementary products in a location not previously occupied or contested. He observed that his awareness of institutional expectations was instrumental in guiding his new activities in an innovatively synergistic way. Thus, we propose a field-related proposition as follows:

Proposition 2: Enacting strategies in dual fields for the purpose of creating and maintaining transnational enterprise requires both understanding and operating in multiple (sometimes contested) institutional environments. Therefore, transnational entrepreneurs require cognitive maps that allow them to understand and enact a variety of social and cultural resources or capital simultaneously.

The Fields that Influence Transnational Entrepreneurship

Habitus and Fields of Interaction

In the case of transnational entrepreneurs, we maintain that their habitus is implemented in one of the following four distinctive fields, by which we mean institutional contexts that serve as the arena for their constructed rules and the patterns of interaction reflected in their entrepreneurial activities: (1) cultural repertoires, (2) legal and regulatory regimes, (3) social and professional networks, and (4) power relations. Transnational entrepreneurs construct a habitus that reflects the different fields of activity that they must navigate in their reality of operating simultaneously in both host and origin countries, while objectively readjusting to particular conditions in which the enterprise is constituted. In the remainder of this section we elaborate on each of the four fields mentioned above. The relation of these fields to habitus provides the foundation for the theory of practice that informs our research agenda for the study of transnational entrepreneurship.

Cultural Repertoires

Our proposed analytical framework pays special attention to the field of cultural repertoire because the cultural contexts of transnational entrepreneurs are usually different and often at odds; they employ a variety of ideals and symbols that may influence the ability to identify and exploit opportunities or that may harness resources for TE activities. Taking into account the dual nature of TE, we follow Silber (2003: 432), who argues that repertoire theory should display both 'distinctive and systematic concern with the internal ideational contents and internal structure of cultural repertoire.' In line with our theory of practice framework, we contend that the use of culture and its conceptualization in conjunction with TE 'can be understood only in relation to the strategies of action they (cultural symbols, identification) sustained' (Swidler, 1986: 283). Of course, the cultural tool-kit of entrepreneurial action is not a static entity containing 'fixed' cultural codes and modes of behaviour from which social agents simply pick and choose. In keeping with Sewell's semiotic approach to culture, a cultural code 'means more than being able to apply it mechanically in stereotyped situations – it also means having the ability to elaborate it, to modify or adapt its rules to novel circumstances' (Sewell, 1999: 51). Cultural repertoires of entrepreneurial actions, therefore, are manifested by certain actions within dual social contexts, and in accordance with the entrepreneur's knowledge, skills, and habits.

Cultural repertoires of entrepreneurial action are not necessarily limited by existing cultures in the traditional sense. As Swidler (2001: 23) suggests, 'there are not simply different cultures: there are different ways of mobilizing and using culture, different ways of linking culture to action.' While recent studies on entrepreneurial culture dismiss culture as non-variable, we argue that certain ethnic segments within such groups are endowed with cultural resources that influence their entrepreneurial pursuit both within and without their respective groups (Drori & Lerner, 2002; Pecoud, 2004; Putz, 2003). Entrepreneurial propensity may be dependent on predisposed cultural values that favour such entrepreneurial activities and provide members with both the 'cultural tradition' and the capital and resources to start and maintain such activities. Examples include group solidarity and/or a generalized reciprocity that translates into access to resources, such as family capital, or an advantaged labour force (Putz, 2003). Therefore, while we acknowledge the possible role of 'culture,' we eschew assertions that the role of the individual entrepreneur is reliant upon independent cultural schema. Such assertions presuppose that cultural homogenization shapes the pattern and propensity of certain ethnic groups for entrepreneurship, regardless of the contextual, individual realm.

Our approach highlights the role of the transnational entrepreneurs' articulation and knowledgeable use of culture to reconstruct entrepreneurial action, since by its very nature the process of transnational entrepreneurship occurs within the global arena and transcends local cultures. We refer to the ways actors use their cultural tool-kits, which are embedded in multiple contextual settings, and symbolically facilitate strategic action.

A complementary line of argument for the action-oriented role of culture in TE is associated with the essence of transnationalism and the assertion that cultural boundaries are fluid and implicit. For example, Moallem (2000) argues that Iranian transnational entrepreneurs in London tend to mobilize various cultural frameworks: 'pre-national,' national, or transnational (both conceptually and literally) to create business opportunities. Such an approach views transnational entrepreneurs as agents who have to redraw the boundaries of their cultures in order to follow action paths and routines embedded both in practice and in diverse symbolic orders. It should be noted that conceptualizing transnational entrepreneurs as agents is particularly appropriate for studying global settings, wherein symbolic and material artefacts float across national and cultural borders. In this sense, the role of culture in TE is aligned with the logic of culture as a strategy of action (Swidler, 1986, 2001). Thus, transnational entrepreneurs adopt diverse schemas of meaning and strategizing within varied symbolic orders leading to action as a 'repertoire' of choices within certain cultural frames.

The practices of transnational entrepreneurs are both shaped by and shape the cultural repertoires in which they are embedded. For example, Mexican immigrants in the United States have been notably weak in developing entrepreneurship. Roberts (1995) suggests that this is due both to the transient nature of U.S./Mexican immigration as well as the need to send remittances home. Israeli entrepreneurs, in contrast, appear to share institutionalized beliefs that celebrate the relocation and triumph of the Israeli high-tech market in the diaspora, necessitating the development of offshore subsidiaries, typically in Silicon Valley or other high-tech locations. These cultural myths serve to enhance institutional structures including industry networks, and practices both formal and informal, such as the diffusion of knowledge, the creation of trust, and the leveraging of resources with the explicit purpose of maximizing opportunities for Israeli technical labour and contributing to the national project (Zilber, 2006). We thus derive the following cultural repertoire proposition:

Proposition 3: Transnational entrepreneurs adopt diverse schemas of meaning and strategizing within varied symbolic orders, leading to action as a 'repertoire' of choices within certain cultural frames (habitus). Therefore, dual

cultures create frames of reference that account for or are modified by entre-
preneurs' actions and enhance the ability for understanding alternative per-
spectives and activities.

Legal and Regulatory Regimes

We may assume that cross-national legal or regulatory regimes are
substantially different in many aspects, and therefore pose a varied set
of challenges to the transnational entrepreneur. For instance, the government industrial policy in one country may be best suited for foreign, direct investment-related activities, and relevant entrepreneurs
must strategize as to how to leverage such policies in accordance with
business functions across countries. Furthermore, in their attempt to
leverage their strategic advantages, transnational entrepreneurs strive
to control resources, enhance capabilities, and exploit opportunities.
These factors are largely dependent on a hospitable regulatory regime
that must be nurtured and sometimes modified. This can be done, for
example, by lobbying for favourable tax exemption policies through
local social networks or political brokers.

National variations in legal and/or regulatory regimes may influence
the ownership patterns of firms, new business formation and coordination, intrafirm management and work, and employment relations, all of
which may be relevant to the practices in which transnational entrepreneurs engage. For example, German law firms operate in a legal regime
that emphasizes civil law that is developed through formal legislation
and academic comment while English law firms operate in a legal regime that emphasizes common law as it continuously evolves through
lawyers' daily practice and judges' decisions (Morgan & Quack, 2004).
In examining work activities through which lawyers construct their
field, for example, the drafting of legal documents, observations of
senior colleagues, and negotiations of appropriate problem-solving approaches, Smets (2005) found that English and German finance lawyers
working for a cross-national law firm constructed a cross-jurisdictional
field around their shared legal practice. In contrast, Smets found that
English and German litigators working for the same firm focused on
disparate sets of legal knowledge that foster field constitution around
national legal orders. This leads to the following proposition:

Proposition 4: Variations of legal and regulatory regimes are prevalent in TE
institutional fields. The magnitude of the variations of these legal and regula-

tory regimes and their successful adoption of these legal and regularly regimes necessitates an understanding of different schemas of meaning (habitus) and the relational context associated with such regimes.

Social and Professional Networks

Social networks provide a rich stock of behaviours and resources (Hoang & Antoncic, 2003). The variety of network characteristics, their relational and structural stance, or their content and strength all impact differently the emergence and outcome of TE. For example, relational embeddedness may affect the founding rate of TE ventures, as one cohort of successful firms spawns successive generations (see, e.g., Eisenhardt & Forbes, 1984). Various and diverse firms in a network can be catalysts for the generation of new TE ventures (Florida & Kenny, 1988).

Network connections may be particularly helpful in explaining the size and scope of transnational entrepreneurs' opportunity structure and social and cultural capital (for a review, see Hoang & Antoncic, 2003). The activities of transnational entrepreneurs, which span two social spheres, expose them to both opportunities and threats. In line with network theory, their position with relation to structural holes and social spaces between network clusters may influence access to various resources (Burt, 2000). Operating within a similar network cluster may reflect dense internal relations, but it may also constrain relations with those in other clusters (Baum & Ingram, 2002). Transnational entrepreneurs may serve as 'bridges' for structural holes and, thus, they are more prone to be aware of, and exploit, business opportunities.

Transnational entrepreneurship supposes three domains for simultaneous network formation: network of origin (ethnic, national), network of destination, and network of practice. Networks of origin frequently play a role in the selection of destinations, as well as the adaptation and acclimatization to the new environment.

The history of emigration has been one of unequal opportunities, whereby increasing integration between two economies results in the development of networks of economic migrants. These network structures serve as support mechanisms linking migrants, former migrants, and non-migrants in both origin and destination communities (Massey, 1988). Thus, immigrants from certain countries and communities favour particular destinations, gradually building on established relationships and the resultant social capital available to them. However, as shown by Kyle's (1999) study of Ecuador's Otavalo trade diaspora in the United States, in-group social capital is not necessarily sufficient for grassroots transnational entrepreneurship. Both symbolic and cultural capital generated from outside the group and society at large may be necessary in order to obtain the required resources for their ventures.

Following immigration, networks of destination provide primordial affinity that yields social capital in the form of affection and trust. This enhances business possibilities and cross-national partnerships, alleviating risks and uncertainty stemming from the complexity and unpredictability of the global markets. For example, the so-called bamboo networks of loosely structured Chinese transnational businesses reflect the Confucian value system of familial affinity, which mandates solidarity, cooperation, harmony, and trust, thus providing a conducive environment and inter-network support for the members of a particular network (Fukayama, 1995; Weidenbaum & Hughes, 1996). The ensuing social capital not only lowers the barriers to emigration, but also enhances economic opportunities by leveraging resources towards the establishment of migrant-friendly businesses. These Chinese businesses are advantaged through sourcing labour from migrant pools at competitive rates; through the diffusion of critical information on markets, suppliers, technologies, and business practices; and through the provision of assistance such as credit (Light, Bhachu, & Karageorgis, 2003). Such a newly established migrant network is capable of transferring social capital and resources back to China. As well, the development of Taiwanese venture capital is partly explained through the formation of cross-national networks established through Taiwanese-U.S. relations. In many cases, Taiwanese entrepreneurs establish firms in the United States using Taiwanese capital, while leveraging the technical advantages and expertise located in the United States (Breznitz, 2007).

Within their social networks, transnational entrepreneurs make use of professional associations, including those that span geographical borders (Autio, Sapienza, & Arenius, 2005; Johanson & Vahlne, 1977). These represent another specific case of the institutional field that is empirically linked to transnational entrepreneurship. TE habitus reflects the ability of agents to adopt, advocate for, and introduce preferential scripts and world views into their institutional field. For example, one high-tech transnational entrepreneur we studied found his technology locked out of an important technical standards protocol committee in the United States. The entrepreneur then proceeded to align himself with a European firm and eventually succeeded in influencing the establishment of the U.S. protocol via the European proxy.

Entry into these professional associations may supersede advantages provided by ethnic and/or community relations, as members embrace a unique and common language and a shared culture. Barley and Kunda (2004: 271) refer to this as 'a network of practice,' crossing geographical boundaries, providing access to critical resources – including jobs, knowledge, and customers – and relying upon both trust and reputation in their occupational communities. For instance, computer programmers highly expert in a particular, esoteric language develop discrete networks by virtue of their membership in informal and formal associations, through reputation, as well as through friendship. These connections assist them in solving difficult problems, obtaining contracts, and sourcing labour. This leads to our next proposition, as follows:

Proposition 5: Transnational entrepreneurs' positions within their distinct industry networks expose them to diverse institutional settings. These industrial networks affect their capabilities to develop entrepreneurial activities within their institutional settings.

Power Relations

In addition to highlighting the role of cultural repertoires and social and industry networks, Bourdieu's concept of habitus draws attention to the importance of credentials and qualifications in mediating power relations between individuals by utilizing social relations linked to institutions. Laws and legal institutions are said to symbolically consecrate the structure of these power relations (Bourdieu, 1977: 188). This yields a legitimating environment that reproduces itself, along with its implicit social hierarchy. Individuals who experience dissonance based on a radical disparity between their relative positions of power or authority are likely to seek alternative ways of regaining their former stature. We have encountered transnational entrepreneurs whose origins provided considerable advantages that were not transferred to their destination environments, and accordingly had to find different ways to replicate their power relations.

The notion of power relations (Bourdieu, 1990) is closely associated with Swidler's (1986) conception of 'strategies of action' which may reflect that the actors' choice of strategy depends on resources available to them, either material or symbolic. Examples include professional knowledge and skills (Giddens, 1990), cultural capital (Bourdieu, 1973), and a social position in organizational, communal, and familial settings. While these factors can constrain actors' repertoire choices, they can also potentially provide them with cultural tools that increase their latitude in negotiation and their ability to manipulate business relations in their dual settings. Furthermore, transnational entrepreneurs' business-building strategies inherently bear political meanings and consequences. In particular, the fact that the entrepreneurs operate in at least two societies requires multiple strategies that reflect different social and business boundaries and contexts. Moreover, we suggest that in politically contested environments, the political meanings and consequences of transnational entrepreneurs' strategies are intensified.

The relationship between transnational entrepreneurs' strategies and their power relations is situated, contextual, and emergent. Thus, their respective meanings are to be discovered and explored empirically. We consider the scope and degree of transnational entrepreneurship, and the magnitude of power relations, to be contingent upon their changeable meaning for various participants in the dual contexts. We contend that providing an adequate account of actors' strategic behaviour necessitates a fuller understanding of the local context, the participants' positions and viewpoints, and the existing cultural repertoires of entrepreneurship available to immigrants in both host and origin country. In line with our theoretical framework, the field of power relations and the political context shape both the choice and the meaning attached to a particular form of TE. Indeed, actors' choice of strategy is both shaped by and shapes the political context, or in Bourdieu's term, the 'field of power' (1977), which is 'the source of hierarchical power relations which structure all other fields' (Jenkins, 1992: 86). By operating within a certain habitus, transnational entrepreneurs define their social relationships, demarcate social boundaries, and identify the constraints and opportunities that are determined by the power relations of their respective fields. Since power relations are the 'mediating context[s] wherein the external factors-changing circumstances are brought to bear upon individual practice and institutions' (ibid.), they are important aspects of the transnational entrepreneur's strategizing, which in turn links practice, habitus, and social arenas as fields. Thus, we propose the following:

Proposition 6: Transnational entrepreneurs utilize a field whose power relations affect access to resources resulting in structural outcomes. These power relations may allow transnational entrepreneurs to compete within a societal context operating beyond customary ethnic or institutional boundaries.

Outcomes of Field-Related Practice

The theory of practice and its emphasis on habitus encompasses elements of action, including taken for granted, common sense beliefs, social classification, and social structure. We examine transnational entrepreneurs as a specific group, using the theory of practice as a framework that consists of (1) transnational entrepreneurs' common histories and social reality, manifested in the 'objective conditions' they face (Bourdieu, 1977), and (2) their habitus, which consists of schemata of mental structures such as aspiration, dispositions or patterns of appreciation, as well as classifiable practices and strategies that utilize resources that are byproducts of schemata (Sewell, 2005). By adopting the key principles of the theory of practice to the study of transnational entrepreneurship, we are able to identify four fields of analysis, each of which illuminates a different facet of TE: cultural repertoires, institutional fields and industry networks, social capital, and power relations. In this section, we examine the three critical outcomes that are possible results of these fields. By 'outcomes,' we are referring to those processes, resources, structures, and activities that lead to the development of a unique TE habitus.

Transnational entrepreneurs are able to exercise some degree of control over their entrepreneurial activities, which, in line with the theory of practice, implies a potential for shaping their outcomes. We maintain that the analysis of TE should be viewed in a longitudinal fashion, addressing the issues of the transnational entrepreneurs' activities that produce and reproduce structures within their habitus (Bourdieu, 1977). This will provide researchers with a conceptual tool to analyse and evaluate the TE process, which influences and is influenced by the dual contexts that define the milieu of the transnational entrepreneur. In this vein, we suggest that future research should consider operating within one or more of the four general outcomes influenced by habitus – the availability of resources, social capital, knowledge, and legitimacy and control – in order to expand and analyse the scope of TE along the theory of practice.

Availability of Resources

The first outcome of TE habitus consists of the availability or resources acquired from the broader social sphere. Following Sewell (2005: 143), transnational entrepreneurs are 'empowered to act with and against others by structures: they have knowledge of schemas that inform social life and have access to some measure of human and non-human resources.' Thus, looking at TE through the lens of the theory of practice highlights the importance of schemata, which reflect and inform the nature of particular institutions and structures, and which shape the strategic action of the individual transnational entrepreneurs in new contexts. The cultural repertoire field reflects a determinant, whereby transnational entrepreneurs organize their core institutions or problems and provide the context to form a strategy of action 'within which particular pieces of culture make sense' (Swidler, 2001: 25). In conjunction with the social capital field, transnational entrepreneurs constitute the determinants of the availability of resources, providing a competitive advantage that enables transnational entrepreneurs to initiate businesses and to operate in what are frequently ambiguous environments. Here, the basic query regards the immersion capabilities of transnational entrepreneurs, mainly within their social group, for the purpose of enacting social networks (Granovetter, 1985) as well as for channelling social and cultural resources.

Scholars should consider examining issues related to culture and social capital across the multiple environments of TE activity. For example, it is commonly argued that during the founding stage the entrepreneur is embedded in a personal social network that is crucial to mobilizing key resources needed for the firm in its nascent days (Aldrich & Zimmer, 1986; Aldrich, Rosen, & Woodward, 1987; Hite & Hesterly, 2001; Saxenian, 1991). Scholars may wish to study how TE ventures leverage ties with friends and family members to secure initial financial support (Menzies et al., 2000), establishing relationships with critical actors such as suppliers or customers (Brown & Butler, 1995). This would help us understand how TEs expand the trust base of their social and business relations (Lorenzoni & Lipparini, 1999; Podolny & Page, 1998; Saxenian, 1991) providing them with critical information and advice (Hoang & Antoncic, 2003) as well as legitimacy from the reputation of their network linkages (Shane & Cable, 2002; Stuart, Hoang, & Hybels, 1999). Of course, despite the supportive role of social networks, opportunist or errant transnational entrepreneurs may face sanctions or a lack of cooperation. The social sphere also has a 'dark side,' namely, a propensity of agents who overlook efficiency or other relevant considerations regarding the well-being of their businesses, in favour of kin recruitment, nepotism, or favouritism (Shapiro, 2005). This leads us to the following propositions:

Proposition 7a: The greater the reliance of transnational entrepreneurs on ethnic (versus societal) embedded resources and network structure, the narrower their possibilities of expanding the scope of their business.

Proposition 7b: The greater the reliance of transnational entrepreneurs on societal (versus ethnic) embedded resources and network structure, the broader are their possibilities of expanding the scope of their business.

Social Capital

Recent research has shown that social capital is instrumental for resource acquisition in entrepreneurial settings and eventual new business success (Davidsson & Honig, 2003; Hoang & Antoncic, 2003; Nahapiet & Ghoshal, 1998; Shane & Cable, 2002). For example, they might leverage social capital in order to obtain financial resources in their home country, with the goal of establishing themselves in their destination country. One TE we interviewed systematically leveraged his social capital in India in order to obtain start-up resources for his activities in Canada. Once in Canada, he developed an entirely new social support network made up of sympathetic, experienced Canadian entrepreneurs.

Social capital, according to Bourdieu, is the 'sum of the resources, actual or virtual, that accrue to an individual or group by virtue of possessing a durable network of more or less institutionalized relationships of mutual acquaintances and recognition' (Bourdieu & Wacquant, 1992: 119). Bourdieu views social capital as a network attribute embedded in social relations that are in turn reflected in a variety of networks used interchangeably by the transnational entrepreneur.

Social capital is accumulated through the organization and reproduction of transnational entrepreneurs' dual (host-home) networks, and provides resources and access to those social and economic features that facilitate entrepreneurs' predicaments in business foundation, retention, and 'surplus production' (Westlund & Bolton, 2003). Bound to certain resources, the existence of social capital implies that transnational entrepreneurs may be able to convert, provide, or acquire various social, economic, tangible, or symbolic assets within particular social networks. It is their membership in dual settings, and the scope of transnational entrepreneurship, that consequently provides the social capital needed for their business enterprises. In this regard, the scope, depth, and effectiveness of social capital and social networks are associated with a power structure and practices of power. Social actors' position in the TE dual spaces may be influenced by their and others' sociocultural, political, and economic characteristics and related institutions, which are context bound. Thus, social capital, too, is bounded by both historical and contextual factors involving varied actors in social networks, or the social structure within which transnational entrepreneurs are located. This leads us to the following proposition:

Proposition 8: The more aware they are of the bounded nature of social capital, the more successful transnational entrepreneurs will be at employing social capital.

Knowledge Accumulation

The third outcome of TE habitus relates to knowledge accumulation, the result of immersion. The institutional field of analysis is a process determinant, involving the formation of habituation (Tolbert & Zucker, 1996), and focuses on the ways a problem is approached, including solving behaviours and objectification, as well as shared social meanings that interpret behaviours. It further allows for the institutionalization of rational scripts that are utilized by transnational entrepreneurs, and which form the habitus of accepted and established wisdom. Industry networks focus on the scope and extent of the connectivity determinant for actors within an institutional field, which indicates their position within the dual institutional environment and hence their prospects of establishing an enterprise and obtaining knowledge-based assets.

Transnational entrepreneurs are both subject to and creators of the industrial networks and institutional settings that cross their multiple environments, affecting knowledge accumulation and diffusion. A research endeavour that focuses on the nature of embeddedness of transnational entrepreneurs is likely to depict the various strategies of founding and conducting businesses in dual environments intrinsic to TE situations and contexts that influence entrepreneurial actions (Gorton, 2000). As indicated by various studies on transnationalism and immigrant integration (Light & Gold, 2000; Morawska, 2005; Portes, Guarnizo, & Haller, 2002; Vertovec, 2004), entrepreneurship provides particular opportunities that reinforce the prospects of community integration, while strengthening an anchor in the origin society. In this way, transnational entrepreneurs resort to an inclusive strategy benefiting from the advantages of both worlds. Issues to be investigated are those concerning, among others, the way TEs mobilize resources, acquire knowledge and information, adapt to institutional and social constraints, and develop strategies for overcoming them. This leads us to the following proposition:

Proposition 9: The more dependent transnational entrepreneurs are on their dual setting, the stronger will be their mobilization of action towards accumulating and creating effective knowledge.

Legitimacy and Control

The fourth outcome of TE habitus focuses on issues of legitimacy and control. The power relations field highlights the dependent relations whereby transnational entrepreneurs strive to establish influence over those organizations and institutions that are amenable to their dual social and economic sphere. This creates mechanisms for organizational legitimacy and control.

The ability to achieve competitive advantage over other actors (be it transnational entrepreneurs or other bona fide competitors) requires effective practices and competencies that are embedded in multiple institutional environments that transcend individual interest and motivation (Bourdieu & Wacquant, 1992). In this vein, actors utilize scripts that may become legitimated, providing a source of power and/or credibility (Barley & Tolbert, 1997). As Chaisson and Saunders (2005: 765) note: 'Entrepreneurial opportunities are considered to be both formed and recognized by the entrepreneur. Viewed in this way, entrepreneurial action involves both the acceptance and modification of scripts, guided by feedback on the legitimacy, meaningfulness/competence, and power of scripts among the various stakeholders.' Transnational entrepreneurs are in a favourable position to transfer scripts from one environment, where they might be quite common, to a new location, offering opportunities of differentiation and competitive advantage.

The power relations research agenda includes varied agency relationships such as those of competition and cooperation, as well as legal and regulatory issues that may offer opportunities or pose constraints to TE activities. Similarly, as Sewell (2005: 143) indicates, 'agents [transnational entrepreneurs] are empowered to act with and against others by structures: they have knowledge of the schemas that inform social life and have access to some measure of human and nonhuman resources.' Power relations are also likely to provide critical insights, in-

Figure 1.1: A practice theory-based framework for the study of transnational entrepreneurship

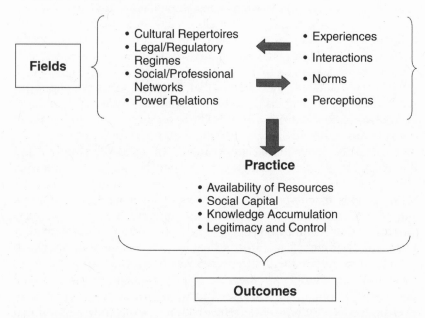

cluding the importance of professional knowledge and skills (Giddens, 1990), as well as cultural capital (Bourdieu, 1973). This leads us to the following proposition:

Proposition 10: Engaging in power relations provides transnational entrepreneurs with legitimation as a strategy for establishing influence over dual institutional and cultural resources.

Figure 1.1 provides a schema that graphically summarizes the key components and interrelationships of the practice theory-based framework we have outlined above.

Summary and Conclusion

To address the challenges involved in developing a research agenda for transnational entrepreneurship, we have offered a theoretical framework that unifies the mechanisms of adaptation to both the home and the host country spheres, contingent on how transnational entrepreneurs strategize as business entrepreneurs within two or more socio-cultural contexts.

The nature of TE indicates that transnational entrepreneurs' position in both the host and origin society is closely associated with the sociocultural, political, and economic resources at their disposal. Furthermore, business strategies, or perceived chances of success, are associated with the specific social and cultural preconditions that may supplement economic considerations. We maintain that TE implies a distinct opportunity structure that enables those immigrants who found and maintain businesses to benefit from 'two worlds' as a crucial factor for survival, a way of 'breaking out,' and/or a method for providing competitive advantage. Thus, transnational entrepreneurs are able to apply and adapt their social structures to changing circumstances and contexts (Sewell, 1992: 20).

Our proposed analytical approach views transnational entrepreneurship as a social realm of immigrants who operate in a complex, cross-national habitus (Bourdieu, 1990), consisting of dual cultural, institutional, and structural features, schemas, and resources from which actors can formulate their entrepreneurial strategies of action. The position of transnational entrepreneurs in their respective organizational fields provides them with diverse institutional interests and opportunities, as well as with resources from which they exert their cultural and social 'tool-kit' for action. Expanding on previous studies, our framework pays systematic attention to material resource environments, as well as to the mix of existing and new populations of providers and to institutional and regulatory structures. Using the resources at their disposal, transnational entrepreneurs strive to exert certain power over the organizational field at particular points in time (Bourdieu, 1986) in order to achieve both individual and societal objectives.

The actions of transnational entrepreneurs stem from their possibilities within a structural context that reflects individual decisions and motivations, as well as the respective institutional environment. In this vein, transnational entrepreneurs are not passive but active and instrumental in understanding and forming their diverse social and economic relationships and structures. Thus, these structures, their contexts and traits, are present in multilevel realms, both macro and micro, imbued with the capacity to enable or constrain human agency (Bourdieu, 2005; Ozbilgin & Tatli, 2005). Various social arenas intersect with dispositions and activities of certain actors' orientations and practices, which, in turn, (re)constitute these very social arenas.

Rather than select and utilize a single perspective of the relevant field or social arena within which struggles take place over specific resources, our framework highlights four different types of fields – cultural repertoires, legal and regulatory regimes, social and professional networks, and power relations – that are connected to habitus. While each of the four fields of activity we discuss yields insight into specific dimensions of TE, none is sufficiently broad to capture the dynamics of TE across the entire range of cross-national interactions. TE is best understood with its unique multidimensional context. While it links agency and structure, which are positioned within the relational and contextual aspects of the venture, TE is also situated within a wider cultural and business context. We have argued that the complexity of TE, distinct from international entrepreneurship (IE) or ethnic entrepreneurship (EE), as manifested by the multiplicity of social contexts and structures, calls for a conceptual framework that is based on a theory of practice. This approach, which highlights the role of habitus in helping transnational entrepreneurs advance their business ventures in both the host society and the society of origin, enables interested scholars to study: (1) the integration of multilevel organizational forms, (2) the role of reflexivity, (3) social actors as actively engaged in business practices in actual social contexts, and (4) the methodological and epistemological ways of dealing with the linkage of agency and structure (Ozbilgin & Tatli, 2005).

The theory of practice and its constructs posit a fruitful research direction into how TE orientations and practices influence the particular outcomes and institutional structures associated with international business. These effects may be intended or unintended, in the sense that transnational entrepreneurs are not on a 'guided mission' to reinforce hospitable structures and practices. The effect of their presence as a prevalent entrepreneurial phenomenon within the international business realm has appeared to contribute to the expansion of global trade, the rapid economic growth of various countries (e.g., India and China), and the dissemination of the advantages and disadvantages of globalization. Further study is necessary to better understand the occurrence of such contributions.

In conclusion, our analytical framework links the structural aspects of the theory of practice to an action-oriented one (see, e.g., Emirbayer, 1997; Emirbayer & Mische, 1998), thereby enabling us to review systematic patterns in the founding and growth of transnational entrepreneurs with their multiple contexts and situations. The theory of practice, which guides our analytical framework, focuses mainly on the multilevel dynamics of transnational entrepreneurs and the varied territorial and societal-institutional contexts in which they operate and reside. We have argued that instead of attending to the transformation of dual institutional fields as reified entities, for example, countries or ethnic groups, future research on transnational entrepreneurship needs to focus more on the micro-level processes of social construction that occur through daily practice. To that end, we have endeavoured to offer an analytical framework for the study of transnational entrepreneurship that is sufficiently robust for the investigation of a highly complex, dynamic phenomenon that crosses multiple cultural, social, economic, and geographical boundaries.

REFERENCES

Aldrich, H.E., Rosen, B., & Woodward, B. (1987). The impact of social networks on business founding and profit: A longitudinal study. In N. Churchill et al. (Eds.), *Frontiers of Entrepreneurship Research*, 154–168. Wellesley: Center for Entrepreneurial Studies, Babson College.

Aldrich, H., & Zimmer, C. (1986). Entrepreneurship through social networks. In D. Sexton & R. Smilor (Eds.), *The Art and Science of Entrepreneurship*, 3–23. Cambridge: Ballinger.

Autio, E., Sapienza, H., & Arenius, P. (2005). International social capital, technology sharing, and foreign market learning in internationalizing entrepreneurial firms. In D. Shepherd & J. Katz (Eds.), *Advances in Entrepreneurship, Firm Emergence, and Growth*, 9–42. Amsterdam: Elsevier.

Barley, S.R., & Kunda, G. (2004). *Gurus, Hired Guns, and Warm Bodies: Itinerant Experts in a Knowledge Economy*. Princeton: Princeton University Press.

Barley, S.R., & Tolbert, P.S. (1997). Institutionalization and structuration: Studying the links between action and institution. *Organization Studies*, 18: 93–117.

Baum, J.A.C., & Ingram, P. (2002). Interorganizational learning and network organization: Toward a behavioral theory of the interfirm. In M. Augier & J.G. March (Eds.), *The Economics of Choice, Change, and Organization: Essays in Memory of Richard M. Cyert*, 191–218. Cheltenham: Edward Elgar.

Bourdieu, P. (1973). Cultural reproduction and social reproduction. In R. Brown (Ed.), *Knowledge, Education and Social Change*. London: Tavistock.

Bourdieu, P. (1977). *Outline for a Theory of Practice*. Cambridge: Cambridge University Press.

Bourdieu, P. (1986). The struggle for symbolic order. *Theory, Culture and Society*, 3: 35–51.

Bourdieu, P. (1990). *The Logic of Practice*. Stanford: Stanford University Press.

Bourdieu, P. (1993). *Sociology in Question*. London: Sage.

Bourdieu, P. (1998). *Practical Reason*. London: Polity Press.

Bourdieu, P. (2005). *The Social Structure of the Economy*. Malden, MA: Polity Press.

Bourdieu, P., & Wacquant, L. (1992). *Introduction to Reflexive Sociology*. Chicago: University of Chicago Press.

Breznitz, D. (2007). *Innovation and the State: Political Choice and Strategies for Growth in Israel, Taiwan, and Ireland*. New Haven: Yale University Press.

Brown, B., & Butler, J.E. (1995). Competitors as allies: A study of entrepreneurial networks in the U.S. wine industry. *Journal of Small Business Management*, 33: 57–66.

Burt, R. (2000). The network structure of social capital. In R. Sutton & B. Staw (Eds.), *Research in Organizational Behavior*, 22(3): 45–124.

Chaisson, M., & Saunders, C. (2005). Reconciling diverse approaches to opportunity research using the structuration theory. *Journal of Business Venturing*, 20: 747–767.

Davidsson, P., & Honig, B. (2003). Role of social and human capital among nascent entrepreneurs. *Journal of Business Venturing*, 18: 301–331.

Drori, I., & Lerner, M. (2002). The dynamics of limited breaking out: The case of the Arab manufacturing businesses in Israel. *Entrepreneurship and Regional Development*, 14: 135–154.

Eisenhardt, K.M., & Forbes, N. (1984). Technical entrepreneurship: An international perspective. *Columbia Journal of World Business*, Winter: 31–37.

Emirbayer, M. (1997). Manifesto for a Relational Sociology. *American Journal of Sociology*, 103: 281–317.

Emirbayer, M., & Mische, A. (1998). What is agency? *American Journal of Sociology*, 103: 962–1023.

Florida, R., & Kenny, M. (1988). Venture capital, high technology and regional development. *Regional Studies*, 22: 33–48.

Fukayama, F. (1995). *Trust: The Social Virtues and the Creation of Prosperity*. New York: Free Press.

Giddens, A. (1979). *Central Problems in Social Theory: Action, Structure and Contradiction in Social Analysis*. Berkeley: University of California Press.

Giddens, A. (1981). *A Contemporary Critique of Historical Materialism*, vol. 1, *Power, Property and the State*. London: Macmillan.

Giddens, A. (1984). *The Constitution of Society: Outline of a Theory of Structuration*. Berkeley: University of California Press.

Giddens, A. (1990). *The Consequences of Modernity*. Cambridge: Polity Press.

Gorton, M. (2000). Overcoming the structure–agency divide in small business research. *International Journal of Entrepreneurship Behavior Research*, 6: 276–292.

Granovetter, M. (1985). Economic action and social structure: The problem of embeddedness. *American Journal of Sociology*, 91: 481–510.

Harker, R., Mahar, C., &Wilkes, C. (Eds.). (1990). *An Introduction to the Work of Pierre Bourdieu: The Practice of Theory*. London: Macmillan.

Hite, J., & Hesterly, W. (2001). The evolution of firm networks: From emergence to early growth of the firm. *Strategic Management Journal*, 22: 275–286.

Hoang, H., & Antoncic, B. (2003). Network-based research in entrepreneurship: A critical review. *Journal of Business Venturing*, 18: 165–187.

Jenkins, R. (1992). *Pierre Bourdieu*. London: Routledge.

Johanson, J., & Vahlne, J. (1977). The internationalization process of the firm: A model of knowledge development and increasing firm commitments. *Journal of International Business Studies*, 8: 23–32.

Kyle, D. (1999). The Otavalo trade diaspora: Social capital and transnational entrepreneurship. *Ethnic and Racial Studies*, 22: 422–446.

Light, I. (1972). *Ethnic Enterprise in America*. Berkeley: University of California Press.

Light, I., & Gold, S. (2000). *Ethnic Economies*. San Diego: Academic Press.

Light, I., Bhachu, P., & Karageorgis, S. (2003). Migration networks and immigrant entrepreneurship. In I. Light & P. Bhachu (Eds.), *Immigration and Entrepreneurship*, 25–49. New Brunswick, NJ: Transaction Publishers.

Lorenzoni, G., & Lipparini, A. (1999). The leveraging of inter-firm relationships as a distinctive organizational capability: A longitudinal study. *Strategic Management Journal*, 20: 317–338.

Massey, D. (1988). Economic development and international migration in comparative perspective. *Population and Development Review*, 14: 383–413.

Menzies, T., Brenner, G., Filion, L.J., Lowry, L., Perreault, C., & Ramangalahy, C. (2000). Transnational Entrepreneurship and Bootstrap Capitalism: Social Capital, Networks and Ethnic Minority Entrepreneurs. Paper presented to the Second Biennial McGill Conference on International Entrepreneurship, Aug., Montreal.

Moallem, M. (2000). 'Foreigners' and belonging: Transnationalism and immigrants' entrepreneurial space. *Comparative Studies of South Asia, Africa and the Middle East*, 20: 200–216.

Morawska, E. (2005). Immigrant transnational entrepreneurs in New York: Three varieties and their correlates. *International Journal of Entrepreneurial Behavior and Research*, 10: 325–348.

Morgan, G., & Quack, S. (2004). Global Networks or Global Firms? The Organizational Implications of the Internationalisation of Law Firms. Paper presented at IESE/DMU conference on Multinationals and the International Diffusion of Organizational Forms and Practices, July, Barcelona.

Mouzelis, N. (1995). *Sociological Theory: What Went Wrong?* London: Routledge.

Nahapiet, J., & Ghoshal, S. (1998). Social capital, intellectual capital, and the organizational advantage. *Academy of Management Review*, 23: 242–266.

Ozbilgin, M., & Tatli, A. (2005). Book review essay: Understanding Bourdieu's contribution to organization and management studies. *Academy of Management Review*, 20: 855–877.

Pecoud, A. (2004). Entrepreneurship and identity: Cosmopolitan and cultural competencies among German-Turkish businesspeople in Berlin. *Journal of Ethnic and Migration Studies*, 30: 3–20.

Pickel, A. (2005). The habitus process: A biopsychological conception. *Journal for the Theory of Social Behavior*, 35: 437–461.

Podolny, J., & Page, K. (1998). Network forms of organization. *Annual Review of Sociology*, 24: 57–76.

Portes, A. (1987). The social origins of the Cuban enclave economy of Miami. *Sociological Perspectives*, 30: 340–372.

Portes, A., Guarnizo, L.E., & Haller, W.J. (2002). Transnational entrepreneurs: An alternative form of immigrant economic adaptation. *American Sociological Review*, 67: 287–298.

Portes, A., & Zhou, M. (1996). Self-employment and the earnings of immigrants. *American Sociological Review*, 61: 219–230.

Putz, R. (2003). Culture and entrepreneurship: Remarks on transculturality as practice. *Royal Dutch Geographical Society*. 94: 554–563.

Roberts, T. (1995). Socially expected durations and the economic adjustment of immigrants. In A. Portes (Ed.), *The Economic Sociology of Immigration*, 42–86. New York: Russell Sage Foundation.

Sarason, Y., Dean, T., & Dillard, F. (2006). Entrepreneurship as the nexus of individual and opportunity: A structuration view. *Journal of Business Venturing*, 21: 286–305.

Saxenian, A. (1991). The origins and dynamics of production networks in Silicon Valley. *Research Policy*, 20: 423–437.

Saxenian, A. (2006). *The New Argonauts: Regional Advantage in a Global Economy*. Cambridge, MA: Harvard University Press.

Schatzki, T., Knorr-Cetina, K., & Von Savigny, E. (Eds.). (2001). *The Practice Turn in Contemporary Theory*. London: Routledge.

Sewell, W. (1992). A theory of structure: Duality, agency, and transformation. *American Journal of Sociology*, 98: 1–29.

Sewell, W. (1999). The concept(s) of culture. In V.E. Bonnell & L. Hunt (Eds.), *Beyond the Cultural Turn: New Directions in the Study of Society and Culture,* 35–61. Berkeley: University of California Press.

Sewell, W. (2005). *Logic of History: Social Theory and Social Transformation.* Chicago: University of Chicago Press.

Shane, S., & Cable, D. (2002). Network ties, reputation, and the financing of new ventures. *Management Science,* 48: 364–381.

Shapiro, P.S. (2005). Agency theory. *Annual Review of Sociology,* 31: 263–284.

Silber, I.F. (2003). Pragmatic sociology as cultural sociology: Beyond repertoire theory? *European Journal of Social Theory,* 6: 427–449.

Smets, M. (2005). *Micro-Processes of Field Construction: Evidence from a Global Law Firm.* Working Paper No. 7. Oxford: Oxford University, Clifford Chance Centre for the Management of Professional Service Firms, Said Business School.

Stuart, T.E., Hoang, H., & Hybels, R. (1999). Interorganizational endorsements and the performance of entrepreneurial ventures. *Administrative Science Quarterly.* 44: 315–349.

Swidler, A. (1986). Culture in action: Symbols and strategies. *American Sociological Review,* 51: 273–286.

Swidler, A. (2001). *Talks of Love: How Culture Matters.* Chicago: University of Chicago Press.

Tolbert, P., & Zucker, L.G. (1996). Institutional analysis of organizations: Legitimate but not institutionalized. In S.R. Clegg, C. Hardy, & W. Nord (Eds.), *Handbook of Organization Studies,* 175–190. London: Sage.

Vertovec, S. (2004). *Trends and Impacts of Migrant Transnationalism.* Working Paper No. 04-03. Oxford: Oxford University, Centre on Migration, Policy and Society.

Weidenbaum, M., & Hughes, S. (1996). *The Bamboo Network.* New York: Free Press.

Westlund, H., & Bolton, R. (2003). Local social capital and entrepreneurship. *Small Business Economics,* 21: 77–113.

Yeung, H. (2002). Entrepreneurship in international business: An institutional perspective. *Asia Pacific Journal of Management,* 19: 29–61.

Zahra, S.A., & George, G. (2002). International entrepreneurship: The current status of the field and future research agenda. In M. Hitt, D. Ireland, D. Sexton, & S. Camp (Eds.), *Strategic Entrepreneurship: Creating an Integrated Mindset,* 255–258. Oxford: Blackwell.

Zilber, T. (2006). The work of the symbolic in institutional processes: Translations of rational myths in Israeli hi-tech. *Academy of Management Journal,* 49: 281–303.

2 Contemporary Diasporic Entrepreneurship: A Conceptual and Comparative Framework

XIAOHUA LIN

Contemporary diasporic entrepreneurs (CDEs) are skilled immigrants who have returned to their country of origin in the pursuit of entrepreneurial activities, most commonly in knowledge-intensive, technological sectors (Lin, 2006). As CDEs are closely associated with migration, they therefore differ from the conventional international entrepreneurs, who do not share the experience of immigration. Despite their immigrant background, however, CDEs are also different from the classic ethnic entrepreneurs (EEs), who are limited to conducting business within their country of residence. When moving their businesses beyond the country of residence and into the international arena, ethnic entrepreneurs have a tendency towards their country of origin, a business approach referred to as transnational entrepreneurship (TE) (Portes, Guarnizo, & Haller, 2002; Drori, Honig, & Ginsberg, 2006). Contemporary diasporic entrepreneurs, as discussed in this chapter, have emerged from an immigrant community in the diaspora community and turned to focusing their business in their country of origin. Although they may continue to draw resources from the adopted country, they may or may not involve the adopted country in their current entrepreneurial endeavour. In other words, they may be part of the transnational entrepreneurial phenomenon but are not necessarily so. The position of CDEs in relation to other 'branches' of entrepreneurship is portrayed in Figure 2.1.

The incidence of CDEs has been noted in several emerging or fast-developing markets such as Taiwan, Israel, Ireland, and India (e.g., Saxenian, 1999, 2002), but their most observable presence is in China, the largest emerging market that is also experiencing a transition towards a market-based economic system (Financial Times, 2007; Wright et al.,

Figure 2.1: Contemporary diasporic entrepreneurs (CDEs) and other entrepreneurship branches

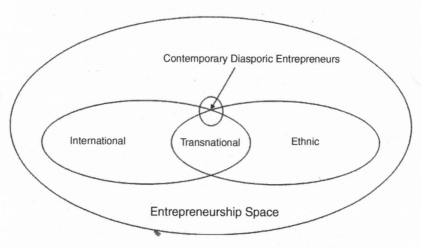

2008). In Zhongguancun, often referred to as China's Silicon Valley, approximately 2,300 technological ventures existed by 2007 that involved more than 5,700 returnees; through knowledge-transfer and innovation, the CDEs have helped boost China's efforts to transform its technological capability from its formerly lagging state to an improved state, bringing it into step with the global scientific-technology community (Wang & Zweig, 2008). Arguably, CDEs have become a distinctive and formidable force alongside domestic private firms and foreign-funded enterprises in China's high-tech industries (Xia, 2004). However, while there is a growing body of anecdotal evidence in the business press and a burgeoning literature on transnationalism in ethnic and immigration studies, management scholars have been less attentive to this newer emerging phenomenon. In the scholarship on international entrepreneurship (IE), which has maintained a focus on technology-oriented industries and emerging entrepreneurship in transition economies, there is rarely a mention of its existence. There is little knowledge about the propensity for an immigrant to become a CDE, or about how the new ventures run by CDEs differ from those of international entrepreneurs who do not have experience with the CDEs' home market, or from those run by domestic entrepreneurs who have no experience of migration (Vanhanocker, Zweig, & Fung, 2006).

The objective of this chapter is to present a novel conceptualization of the phenomenon to guide further empirical investigation. I treat contemporary diasporic entrepreneurs as a distinct segment of immigrant entrepreneurship. Compared with traditional modes of immigrant businesses in the form of enclave economy or trade mediation, CDEs can be seen as a unique way by which immigrants make economic adjustments (Portes, Guarnizo, & Haller, 2002). Using Aldrich and Waldinger's (1990) terminologies, I address three important questions: What opportunity structure is responsible for the emergence of CDEs? What characteristics are observed in CDEs? And what unique businesses are adopted by CDEs? I take a comparative approach in addressing these questions. In light of the different rates of engaging CDEs across countries, it is necessary to ascertain factors that distinguish more successful countries from those that are less successful, such as the sub-Saharan states (Patterson, 2006). It is also important to compare CDEs with their indigenous and foreign counterparts competing in the same markets. While the CDE phenomenon has not been subject to serious scholarly attention in the management literature, anecdotal observations suggest that CDEs should be considered a formidable economic force in emerging markets such as China (Financial Times, 2007).

In the next section I establish the theoretical foundation of the proposed framework. Although CDEs are an immigration-associated phenomenon, they have developed as a result of multiple forces at the intersection of immigrant/ethnic economy, international entrepreneurship, and economic transition in formerly more regulated countries. Following this, I define CDEs and position them in relation to other entrepreneurship sectors. Consistent with Aldrich and Waldinger (1990), and drawing on the experiences of Chinese CDEs, I conceptualize the CDE phenomenon in terms of opportunity structure, group characteristics, and business strategies, and offer a set of testable propositions. I conclude the chapter by discussing implications for research and practice and offer suggestions for future studies.

Theoretical Foundation

Immigrant and Ethnic Economy

Diaspora is a phenomenon associated with the process of migration and immigration and thus diasporic entrepreneurship should be informed by the literature on immigrant/ethnic economy, which has taken various forms in Western societies. According to Aldrich and Waldinger

(1990), the business strategies of ethnic minorities emerge from the interaction of their access to opportunities (e.g., market conditions) and group characteristics (e.g., resource endowments). In much of Western history, immigrant and ethnic minority groups have turned to self-employment, often because of disadvantages in the labour market and the lack of available resources for them within mainstream society (Light, 2004). As a result, they have looked for opportunities in co-ethnic communities or niches in non-ethnic markets. They have, of course, had to be industrious, but their entrepreneurship has often been facilitated by the cultural norms available in an immigrant/ethnic group and always by ethnic resources centring on co-ethnic networking (Aldrich & Waldinger, 1990). In ethnic enclaves, arguably the most visible presence of the ethnic economy, minority entrepreneurs take advantage of niche markets arising primarily within the immigrant community and mobilize resources from co-ethnic members in business ventures confined to geographically concentrated urban districts (Light, 1972). Strong ethnic ties, while often celebrated as an essential source of ethnic resources, tend to discourage ethnic entrepreneurs from accessing opportunities and resources beyond their ethnic communities (Portes & Landolt, 1996). As a whole, although ethnic businesses offer a possible avenue out of disadvantage, they by and large are associated with poor working conditions and marginal financial positions (Light, 2004).

Diaspora refers to immigrants who have maintained a subjective, dual identity (Radhakrishnan, 2003) and a longing to return home (Skeldon, 2003). Middlemen minorities, another major type of ethnic economy alongside ethnic enclaves, are mostly found in liquid occupations due to their expectation of returning to their homeland (Bonacich, 1973). The engagement of diaspora with the homeland is not new. Historically, diasporic communities have been engaged with their countries of origin in the economic arena, including the sending of remittances, mediating trade, or even investing in productive projects (Carana Corporation, 2004). The recent resurgence of scholarly attention to diaspora is associated with global economic and political shifts that have significantly transformed the notions of nation and national identities, accompanied by advances and changes in economic and technological infrastructure (Braziel & Mannur, 2003). What is new about the contemporary diasporic community is the combination of higher levels of education, skills, and professional knowledge; in other words, the contemporary diaspora is a result of skilled migration and can be viewed as a feature of globalization (Brinkerhoff, 2006). While a selection bias always exists among migrants, the contemporary source of 'positive selection' is largely made by institutions in economically advanced receiving countries (e.g., universities, employers, and immigration officials), who want to make sure they get the brightest talents from immigrant-sending countries (Kapur & McHale, 2005). On the other hand, the purpose of emigration for the high-potential individuals is to acquire additional human capital. Further education, training, and work experience in Western advanced economies offer the opportunities not only to upgrade technical knowledge, but also to acquire new sets of skills and resources that enable future entrepreneurship, such as financial capital and business contacts (McCormick & Wahba, 2003). When the skilled and resource-rich diaspora is met with the unprecedented opportunities in the former country of origin, a new breed of ethnic entrepreneur emerges.

Also riding on the wave of globalization and associated with the process of immigration, but not limited to technological industries nor to both host and home country markets (Portes, Guarnizo, & Haller, 2002), transnational entrepreneurship (TE) has gained recent attention among management scholars, as is evidenced in this edited volume. By definition, transnational entrepreneurship involves at least two different social and economic arenas, including the immigrant's former country of origin (Drori, Honig, & Ginsberg, 2006), but CDEs are returnees and tend to focus their businesses on the homeland market. Thus, although CDEs could remain intensely engaged overseas (Vanhanocker, Zweig, & Fung, 2006), they are characteristically different from transnational entrepreneurs. As evidence shows, the entrepreneur's home base makes a difference (Lin, Guan, & Nicholson, 2008).

International Business and Entrepreneurship

The process of contemporary diasporic entrepreneurship consists of a technological diaspora creating new businesses in a cross-national context, and thus can be validated by the existing international business and entrepreneurship literature. While mainly dealing with large multinational corporations (MNCs), mainstream international business theories suggest that firms go after structural discrepancies between home and host countries when entering a foreign market. By investing overseas, firms can exploit their core competencies developed at home. For example, a firm may be able to enter a foreign market wherein indigenous firms enjoy home court advantages because they possess superior competitive advantages in information-based capabilities (Acs, Dana, & Jones, 2003). Foreign investment allows firms to explore location-specific assets including market structure, government regulations, and other aspects of institutional environments (Dunning, 1988). Indeed, China has topped the world as a target of foreign direct investment (FDI) by offering an untapped market and low-cost manufacturing during the past two decades, and it has now started attracting knowledge-intensive activities from MNCs for its commitment to technological innovation and its vast pool of talents.

To a certain degree, the above exploitation-exploration perspective also applies to 'born global' entrepreneurs. For example, evidence shows that new international ventures are more likely than new domestic ventures to operate in knowledge-and-technology-intensive industries characterized by high degrees of global integration (McDougall, Oviatt, & Shrader, 2003) and by diminished national-cultural mandates (Dana, Korot, & Tovstiga, 2003). However, the international entrepreneurship literature has a greater emphasis on the resource-based view because international entrepreneurs are more likely to be resource-constrained in comparison with large MNCs emerging from an incremental internationalization process (McDougall, Oviatt, & Shrader, 2003). To meet cross-cultural management challenges, for example, an MNC could have a variety of options, ranging from global hiring and rotation of experienced expatriates to internal or outsourced training programs, but these options tend not to be available at smaller entrepreneurial firms. To investigate this resource deficiency, researchers have focused on the profile of the founder and founding team within a new venture, such as their level of international experience (Oviatt & McDougall, 2005). Research into skilled returnees being used by international entrepreneurial firms to bridge the cross-cultural gap has not yet been conducted, although skilled diaspora individuals have been found to use their indigenous knowledge and special links to the homeland to serve as expatriates for MNCs (Saxenian, 1999). Since firm internationalization is a continuing process of organizational learning, and effective cross-cultural management determines the fate of these new ventures (Barkema & Vermeulen, 1998), it is intriguing to question whether returning diaspora individuals might help manage the process more effectively, in light of their knowledge and experience with both cultural environments.

Conceptualizing CDEs: A Comparative Framework

Contemporary diasporic entrepreneurs (CDEs) are individuals who
have returned from the diaspora and are engaging in entrepreneurial
activities in their country of origin. Entrepreneurship means the creation of a new business, which usually requires a person to physically
engage in developing and managing the business. CDE thus differenti-
ates itself from purely 'virtual' engagement as old as remittances and
as new as electronically mediated involvement (Portes, Guarnizo, &
Haller, 2002). CDE is also different from 'return migrant microenter-
prises' in traditional business sectors such as restaurants and retail enterprises (Landolt, Autler, & Baires, 1999). Although ventures created
by CDEs are not limited to technology-intensive industries, their occurrence is most common and promising in such industries, and this
gives them a contemporary character. The term *diaspora*, indicator of
the immigrant/diaspora imprint in such technology ventures, suggests that CDE could be viewed as a special type of the ethnic economy,
which is defined by either ownership or control by co-ethnics (Light,
2004). Ethnic enclave, probably the most noticeable type of ethnic economy, represents those immigrant entrepreneurs who would employ a
significant proportion of the co-ethnic labour force, rely on co-ethnic
suppliers, and maintain a geographical presence in a co-ethnic neighbourhood (Zhou, 1992). To a large degree, enclave businesses maintain
an inward, co-ethnic orientation and do not need to interact with either
the larger society in the host or the home country. In contrast, wage
employment represents a cosmopolitan way of economic adaptation,
which embeds the immigrants in the host country's general labour
market. Immigrants in this category are able to avoid or overcome barriers to occupational opportunities, probably because they emigrated
at a younger age and subsequently acquired the necessary human and
social capital through schooling in the host country. With transnational
entrepreneurship, enterprising immigrants simultaneously engage in
two or more socially embedded environments and maximize their resource base by doing so (Drori, Honig, & Ginsberg, 2006). Originating
from immigrant communities but being able to master national as well
as ethnic resources, transnational entrepreneurs conduct business beyond the boundaries of the co-ethnic environment and host country.
Finally, CDEs are returnees and thus focus their business in their home
country. While returning diaspora individuals may maintain personal
and professional ties with the host country and a business orientation

towards the international marketplace, they are categorically different from a typical transnational entrepreneur who keeps his or her primary home in the host country (Lin, Guan, & Nicholson, 2008).

According to Aldrich and Waldinger, ethnic entrepreneurship should be conceptualized as strategies that 'emerge from the interaction of opportunity and group characteristics' (1990: 114). Recognizing CDEs as a special case of ethnic economy and following the above authors' three-part model (i.e., opportunity structure, group characteristics, and entrepreneurial strategies), I address the following three questions: (1) Why have CDEs emerged in countries like China – and why now? (2) What are the key characteristics of CDEs? and (3) What are the typical strategies CDEs use in their homeland ventures? My initial conceptualizations, including related points of comparison, are summarized in Table 2.1.

Access to Opportunities

A comprehensive examination of the opportunity structure accessible to CDEs will have to take into account the conditions in the host country. For example, I take it for granted that skilled migrants travel to host countries for opportunities to further enhance their skills and knowledge (Meyer, 2001). Instead, I focus my discussions on the opportunities that may exist across host and home countries and the factors that have made such opportunities available to individuals who have returned from the diaspora. I have to recognize CDEs as a historically contingent phenomenon.

Structural Discrepancies and Economic Readiness

It is widely recognized that emerging market opportunities have produced flocks of successful Chinese entrepreneurs returning from overseas, especially from Western industrial economies. However, a closer examination reveals that CDEs have mostly emerged in industries where there is a clear gap between the host and home countries. In China, a majority of successful CDEs are found in information technology (IT), biotechnology, and new materials, which are all considered new and high-technological sectors as well as the sectors of top interest to China given the opportunity of 'leapfrogging' (Niosi & Reid, 2007). However, such opportunities may be bypassed by indigenous Chinese entrepreneurs and conventional overseas Chinese investors who lack

Table 2.1
Contemporary Diaspora Entrepreneurship (CDE): A Comparative Framework

Research Questions	Propositions	Points of Comparison
Opportunity Structure What are the historical contexts shaping the prospects open to CDEs?	1a Sufficient structural discrepancies between host and home countries 1b Home country readiness for economic development	Cross-country economic environment
	2a Home country commitment to entrepreneurship 2b Home country acceptance of participation of CDEs	Cross-country institutional environment
Group Characteristics What are the key characteristics of CDEs in terms of psychological profile and resource endowment?	3a High entrepreneurial spirit 3b Intense homeland sentiments	Cross cultures
	4a Rich in host country resources 4b Rich in home country resources	Indigenous/international entrepreneurs
Business Strategies What are the entrepreneurial strategies emerging as an interactive consequence of the above two?	5 High technology focus 6 International orientation 7 Hybrid management style	Indigenous/international entrepreneurs

the necessary skills and knowledge, or conventional overseas Chinese investors or large MNCs that have little interest in helping China keep up with the technology frontier. Only CDEs are in a position to perceive and subsequently seize such an opportunity. This is because of their education and training in these cutting-edge fields, and their highly regarded work experience gained through involvement in the emerging high-tech industries in the United States and other developed countries. Looking in from the outside, they understand what works in the West but is lacking in China. For those with work experience in China and/or personal ties in the Chinese technology industry, identification of the structural discrepancies has proved to be particularly easy (Xia, 2004). It is suggested that CDE-led new ventures have helped China fill technological gaps in numerous areas (Wang, 2007).

Successful entrepreneurs do not live solely on a dream, but set their feet on a possibility. In the case of Chinese CDEs, structural discrepancies alone do not bring them back home; the time also has to be right when all necessary infrastructure is in place for them to capitalize on the opportunities. For Western-educated CDEs, one particular concern is the technology infrastructure in the home country. In the early years of China's ongoing economic restructuring, professionals who returned from diasporic communities were rare and, after a short period of repatriation, a returnee might well have left China again, as the country lacked sufficient research facilities at the time. More importantly, the would-be CDE would need to see the emergence of market demand accompanied by an adequate build-up of indigenous R&D activities, as captured by the notion of absorptive capacity (Lane & Lubatkin, 1998). When micro-processors and related IT technologies first emerged, many Chinese professionals in the diaspora, who were part of the technological revolution spreading in the United States and other Western countries, immediately realized the possibility of bringing these technologies to their home country and the wealth-creation potential that a technology venture could bring to it. However, the dream to 'bring the Internet to China' did not materialize until the late 1990s for most Chinese professionals working in the IT field in the West, as they waited for the country to build a basic industrial infrastructure. During this period, significant groundwork was accomplished in building China's technology infrastructure. When CDEs entered the Zhongguancun Science Park around the late 1990s, they were embraced by an industrial cluster that conferred legitimacy, enabled networking, and provided infrastructure for essential R&D activities (Tan, 2006). The charge of international entrepreneurs can be summarized as the discovery, enactment, evaluation, and exploitation of cross-border opportunities (Oviatt & McDougall, 2005). In China's case, successful CDEs will not only have to identify emerging opportunities in the home country but also they will have to arrive at the opportunities at a time when supporting infrastructure is readily available. For other countries, it seems that opportunities have long existed but the professionals in the diaspora have been deterred by a perceived gap between what is needed for their entrepreneurial undertakings and what is available in the homeland (Ite, 2002). This suggests:

Proposition 1: The emergence of CDEs is positively associated with (1) structural discrepancies between CDEs' home and host country and (2) development readiness in CDEs' home country.

Entrepreneurship Climate and Diaspora Acceptance

A ready business environment for a diasporic entrepreneur homecoming is not limited to an adequate economic infrastructure, but includes a supportive institutional context in terms of economic policy and management, and legal and regulatory frameworks, which tend to be ideologically driven (Gevorkyan & Grigorian, 2003). While entrepreneurial research in Western industrial countries has emphasized the characteristics of entrepreneurs (Baker, Gedajlovic, & Lubatkin, 2005), CDEs have to be understood in a broader institutional context if the focus is on diasporic individuals whose countries of origin belong to the developing world, wherein fundamental changes in the institutional environment have been taking place. Indeed, the Chinese have been known for their indigenous entrepreneurial tradition, but entrepreneurs emerged in contemporary China only after the government allowed for a national entrepreneurial climate by lifting the restriction on free enterprises (Tan, 2002). It is not a coincidence that the CDE-established new ventures increased significantly after 1999, when the China's law recognized the legitimacy of private enterprises (Wang & Zweig, 2008). Note also that many returnees have chosen to set up their businesses in the more than 100 science parks in major cities. An important reason for this is that, guided by purposely designed policies and incentives, science parks offer the best protection for property rights and a culture that encourages risk-taking entrepreneurship (Tan, 2006).

Essentially, the homecoming diaspora individual has to overcome additional hurdles to cross the geopolitical boundaries that have historically separated diasporic communities from their home countries by way of territorial identities (e.g., citizenship) and other regulatory measures. Until very recently, in many nations, the returning diaspora individual was regarded as 'the bastard child of the nation – a disavowed, inauthentic, illegitimate, and impoverished imitation of the original culture' (Gopinath, 1995). Historically, overseas Chinese who are accepted and become successful in other countries are denied the same opportunities back in China, and suspicions have always accompanied the relationship between the individual who has returned from the diaspora and his countrymen at home (Wang, 1993). The Chinese government has apparently taken measures to avoid making the same mistakes in its recent campaign to attract CDEs. Today, governments are more welcoming towards diasporic individuals and are adopting policy initiatives that enhance diasporic ties with the homeland and facilitate return. To explain their aspirations for homeland entrepreneurial undertakings, many CDEs recall the direct involvement of high-level government officials that facilitated the creation of their business ventures. On the surface, CDEs enjoy some favourable treatments (e.g., tax holidays and start-up loans) similar to those given to foreign firms. What is not shown in these written policies is the autonomy and special care that the the CDE might have received from the government. In China's current environment, the mistreatment of domestic private firms and MNCs is inevitable. However, abuse of CDE-created ventures in Zhongguancun, for example, is almost unheard of. Investment is an act of faith. Silicon Valley-based Chinese professionals considered 'factorable government treatment' an important item in their decision to return (Saxenian, 2002). To understand such faith and confidence, one only needs to review the message of Deng Xiao Ping, the grand designer of China's contemporary economic reforms, when he spoke with individuals who had returned from the diaspora during his famous South China tour in 1992.

Proposition 2: The emergence of CDEs is positively associated with homeland readiness for (1) entrepreneurial undertaking and (2) returnees' participation.

Group Characteristics

Who are the CDEs in China? What qualities have enabled them to succeed in a country wherein indigenous entrepreneurs are still subject to mistreatment? Is their engagement with the country of origin because of their patriotism or because of their entrepreneurial zeal? What has enabled the contemporary individual in the diaspora to break out of the trap of classic enclaves? In this discussion, China's experience may be informative to other nations, as Chinese migrants are historically known for their significant presence in the traditional ethnic economy, and this presence is once again proving its ability to mobilize community resources through cultural identity.

Entrepreneurial and Homeland Sentiments

Why do some ethnic groups have a greater propensity than others to engage in entrepreneurial pursuits? Busenitz and Lau (1996) found that start-up intentions are significantly affected by entrepreneurial cognition, which in turn is influenced by cultural values, social context, and other personal variables. According to their cross-cultural cognitive model of new venture creation, Chinese immigrants' tendency towards venture creation is due to the Chinese cultural tradition that values future-oriented activities, thriftiness, and persistence, and which is conducive to entrepreneurship. Indeed, privately owned Chinese companies, most of which are located outside mainland China, make up the world's fourth largest economic power, after North America, Japan, and Europe (Kao, 1993). Despite a four-decade anti-free-enterprise Communist regime, entrepreneurship has emerged and developed in China at a pace and scope that clearly exhibits the entrepreneurial zeal of the Chinese people. Comparing the different outcomes of economic reforms in China and Russia, for example, researchers have cited greater entrepreneurial tradition as one reason why China has outperformed Russia (Tanzer, 1996). Exploring the reasons why overseas Chinese far outperformed their Indian counterparts in homeland investment, Kapur (2001) finds that the Indian diaspora comprises largely professionals, while the Chinese diaspora has more entrepreneurs. In engaging the skilled individuals in the diaspora, even the Chinese government has recognized the necessity of such an entrepreneurial drive and started reframing its outreach accordingly (Biao, 2006).

Having said that, what distinguishes diasporic entrepreneurship from international entrepreneurship without the experience of migration is the very nature of the diaspora. People in the diaspora are migrants who maintain a memory or myth about their original homeland, are committed to the maintenance or restoration of this homeland, and maintain a continuing relationship with it (Safran, 1991). Compared with non-diaspora international entrepreneurs, CDEs are more likely to harbour motivations beyond economic returns in their homeland ventures. In other words, the aspirations behind diasporic entrepreneurship cannot be reduced to economic or technological flows as '[this type of entrepreneurship] remains, above all, a human phenomenon' (Braziel & Mannur, 2003: 8). Because of their continuing connection to homeland roots, diasporic entrepreneurs often maintain an interest in matters related to the development of their homeland, whether it is for the social and economic well-being of remaining family members and friends, humanitarian concerns, business interests, professional aspirations, or even a desire to return home some day. For many returnees from the diasporia, engaging in business with their home countriy implies giving back – psychologically as well as physically. To a certain extent, the giving-back motivation entails a great deal of altruism and patriotism, as exemplified by the early Jewish diaspora investment in Israel in its initial building period (Gillespie et al., 1999), and more recently in the Dominican Republic, in several initiatives undertaken by individuals from the Dominican diaspora across the globe to reverse their country's declining economy (Shillingford, 2003). It should be noted, however, that homeland sentiments are not limited to altruistic patriotism. A survey of Chinese professionals in Silicon Valley suggests that 'culture and lifestyle' are important factors in decisions to return home (Saxenian, 2002). Finally, homeland sentiments among individuals in the diaspora vary in intensity and scale across diasporic groups from different countries of origin (Burrell, 2003). The emotional attachment that a particular diasporic community feels towards the homeland is associated with factors such as migration history and the physical and sociocultural distance between the country of origin and the destination country. Such emotions can be strong enough to compensate for the financial loss in a CDE's homecoming. Why has the sub-Sahara not been successful in engaging its overseas diaspora community? According to Patterson (2006), the vast majority of people in the African diaspora in the United States are unable to point to any single country as their homeland.

Summarizing the above discussions, both the overall entrepreneurial propensity of a diaspora community and its emotional attachment to the homeland can help explain cross-country differences in the rate of CDE.

Proposition 3: The emergence of CDEs is positively associated with (1) the entrepreneurial spirit of the individuals in the diaspora and (2) their emotional attachment to the homeland.

Host and Home Country Resources

The ethnic economy literature has been focused on ethnic advantages derived from personal networks within the ethnic community. In homeland ventures, diasporic individuals also enjoy such ethnic advantages. When a market is characterized with imperfect information, relationships may be used to deal with uncertainty. Clearly, personal ties with the home country give the returnees an edge over other international players and serve as entry points in their entrepreneurial endeavours (Saxenian, 1999). In a recent survey, 83 per cent of Chinese diasporic professionals became associated with homeland institutions through personal connections (Biao, 2006). CDEs' advantages are also embedded in their indigenous knowledge about the homeland including its market, language, and cultural protocols (Gillespie et al., 1999), as an incomplete understanding of the local environment or practices is considered a major disadvantage of international entrepreneurs in a foreign market (Oviatt & McDougall, 1994). The language ability is particularly advantageous when a cross-border business venture involves tacit or non-codified knowledge. In such a situation, diasporic entrepreneurs should be especially adept at transferring technology because they can avoid language and cultural barriers to the diffusion of knowledge (Rauch, 2003). Finally, CDEs may face a lesser degree of 'liability of foreignness' associated with international firms, including large MNCs and smaller entrepreneurial firms, because of their shared cultural identity with the locals. In certain cases, they may even be able to turn their dual-identity into a competitive advantage in transition economies such as China, where the government remains suspicious of both indigenous private entrepreneurs and MNCs in terms of technological capabilities and incentives to transfer advanced technologies, respectively. There is evidence that government agencies treat CDEs favourably in research funding procurement processes involving technologies considered to have a bearing on national security. One example involves a returnee who set up an IT company focusing on firewall technology (Xia, 2004: 285–90).

However, to create technological ventures back in their home country, returning professionals need more than just ethnic resources. In all cases, the CDEs are also rich in host country resources. They are educated and/or trained in Western universities and sometimes have professionally established themselves in the host societies. This is the situation in Zhongguancun, where 83 per cent of returnees possess either a doctoral or master's degree from a Western university (Xia, 2004). In a way, these are not ordinary returnees but 'part of the elite in their respective communities in terms of education and legal standing' (Portes, Guarnizo, & Haller, 2002: 293). Working experience in the host country may also make the diasporic entrepreneur more innovative and creative – the essential qualities required for an entrepreneur. For example, immersion within a U.S. setting, in which creativity is valued to a greater extent than within an Asian setting, may make an Asian returnee more creative (Farmer, Tierney, & Kung-McIntyre, 2003). Personal and professional ties within the host society, both within and outside the ethnic community, also give a diaspora individual the ability to secure partnerships with Western organizations. While indigenous Chinese entrepreneurs often encounter difficulties in financing (Peng, 2001), CDEs are normally able to start up and sustain their business with funds from Western venture capital firms. Especially for those listed on the NASDAQ and other overseas markets, all have been involved with foreign venture capital firms. Western venture capital firms favour returnees because they have had overseas education and work experience and they can communicate with the investors easily (Wang & Zweig, 2008).

Proposition 4: The emergence of CDEs is positively associated with diasporic individuals' endowment of both (1) home country resources and (2) host country resources.

Entrepreneurial Strategy

The literature on both international entrepreneurship (e.g., Oviatt & Mc-Dougall, 2005) and ethnic entrepreneurship (e.g., Aldrich & Waldinger, 1990) considers venture strategy as the result of interaction between opportunity structure and founder characteristics. Three distinct business strategies – focusing on a technological niche, having an international orientation, and employing a hybrid management style – are identified from the experience of Chinese CDEs. These strategies are unique relative to those commonly practised by indigenous Chinese entrepreneurs or international entrepreneurs of non-diaspora background.

High-Technology Niche

Market selection plays a central role in CDEs' entrepreneurial strategies, as they have to deal with an environment characterized by irregularity and overcome resource constraints within the firm. Facing a similar situation, Western entrepreneurs entering an international market would adopt a niche-focused strategy by offering differentiated products or services (Rialp, Rialp, & Knight, 2005). In China, most returnee entrepreneurs have focused on high-tech industries. Among a group of 300 successful CDEs, for example, 77 per cent were engaged in high-tech enterprises (Wang & Zweig, 2008). From the CDEs' point of view, involvement in these industries offers the best chance to go public in a global market. However, the very reason for their success in these industries is twofold. First, to the returnees they offer better opportunities than traditional industries. High-tech industries are relatively new and thus have less competition from domestic firms. When contemporary diaspora entrepreneurs return with cutting-edge technological skills and knowledge, they enjoy a clear competitive advantage. It is not surprising that Chinese returnees have been concentrated in IT and related sectors, which offer vast opportunities for individual entrepreneurs because of their unintegrated industry structure (Saxenian, 1999). By focusing on a carefully selected technological niche, a CDE-led firm can also avoid head-to-head competition with powerful MNCs, a fearful force in China's emerging technology fields. Second, the returnees are more likely to be successful in high-tech industries because they tend to be subject to a lesser likelihood of government interference but greater likelihood of government support. More than in traditional business sectors such as manufacturing, CDEs are likely to gain autonomy and support from national governments because of their knowledge and experience at the international technology frontier. In China, skilled returnees have been invited to give seminars to top government officials on high-tech subjects, to participate in the development of national or industry-specific technology strategies, and to lead government ministries with direct responsibility over science and technology issues (Wang, 2007). Thus, the reason CDEs enjoy a more favourable opportunity structure in the high-tech industries in comparison with that facing domestic private entrepreneurs is also dependent on their access to various 'power resources' (Brinkerhoff, 2006), in terms of legitimacy and influence as well as more tangible resources such as tax incentives resulting from coordinated efforts across different government agencies.

Proposition 5: CDEs are more likely to focus on high-technology niche industries.

International Orientation

CDEs are likely to adopt an international orientation in strategizing their new ventures. On the defensive side, such an orientation is used to deal with market uncertainty. A higher degree of turbulence and uncertainty typifies high-tech industries, and this is especially the case in emerging markets such as China (Tan, 2006). Li and Atuahene-Gima (2002) find that Chinese technology ventures tend to involve the marketing and distribution of the products of foreign firms, and they attribute this agency behaviour to environmental uncertainty in China. Bruton and Rubanik (1997) describe how a Russian high-tech start-up company relied on an international strategy to compensate for weak domestic demand in a period of financial crisis. Similarly, most Chinese CDEs have tried to ensure survival by orienting their new ventures towards the international marketplace, using their global networks. Case studies show that returnee-led Chinese companies have often successfully turned themselves around by shifting business to international markets when their Chinese business encountered difficulties (Xia, 2004). Many private Chinese entrepreneurs have made attempts to participate in the international market but have not been successful – primarily because of resource constraints, including a lack of international connections.

One the offensive side, an international orientation allows CDE-led new ventures to leverage the integrative nature of the marketplace – the high-tech industries they serve. Research shows that many Indian CDEs, for example, started off by outsourcing work from Silicon Valley. While developing-country-based international firms have a tendency to focus on the low end of the global value chain with a possibility for moving up later (Craig & Douglas, 1997), start-ups created by returned professionals may set higher goals at inception. It is the Chinese government's belief that many CDE-created ventures have been able to keep up with technological advancements in the Western world and that some of them have even achieved a leadership position in their respective niches (Xia, 2004). Previous research has emphasized the central role of the entrepreneur in developing international business opportunity. Compared with indigenous Chinese entrepreneurs, CDEs can be better able to explore international opportunities because of their connections with the global network, which is gaining increased importance in the internationalization of firms (Rialp, Rialp, & Knight, 2005). While evidence is scant, limited research has shown that, due to necessity as well as capacity, CDEs tend to be more extensively engaged internationally than their indigenous counterparts – in terms of overseas networks, business volumes, and affiliated operations (Vanhanocker, Zweig, & Fung, 2006).

Proposition 6: CDEs are more likely to adopt an international orientation.

Hybrid Management Style

Cross-cultural challenges are widely recognized in international entrepreneurship research (e.g., Oviatt & McDougall, 1994). However, when referring to such challenges, the researchers have usually referred to issues related to the initial process of the new ventures, such as opportunity scanning and identification in foreign markets. In the current study, the notion of national culture became prominent because CDEs figure importantly in an underexplored issue in the international entrepreneurship literature: the ongoing management of new ventures. Western education and work and life experience have, to various degrees, acculturated the diasporic professionals. When returning to China to set up a technology venture, they inevitably carry cultural baggage that does not conform to local management practices. As the creators, owners, and/or managers of the new venture, they will have to deal with a workforce that may see and do things differently, a problem they apparently share with expatriate managers from multinational companies. However, because they are born and raised in the motherland but educated and trained in the country of settlement, diasporic entrepreneurs tend to have a clearer understanding of the need to integrate the two different management systems and to be better able to practise a hybrid management style for effective functioning. Indeed, 'combining Oriental wisdom and Western methodology' has been cited by many CDEs as key to managing a successful new venture in China (e.g., Xia, 2004).

As indicated in earlier studies, private Chinese entrepreneurial firms may be burdened by indigenous practices such as overreliance on personal relationships or *Guanxi* (Fu, Tsui, & Dess, 2006). On the other hand, foreign-invested firms, especially those from the United States, have a tendency to impose home-grown, formal systems in coping with complexities in the host environment (Tung, 1993; Boisot & Child, 1999). A consistent theme that emerged from interviews is the ability of the CDEs to integrate these seemingly contradictory approaches. Besides the convergence effect of a 'transnational techno-culture' (Dana, Korot, & Tovstiga, 2003), there seem to be other factors that contribute to the CDEs' ability to incorporate both native and foreign elements in their management practices. For example, CDE-led firms could be expected to be different because of their diaspora status. Compared with their foreign counterparts, on the other hand, CDEs tend to have a greater appreciation for and ability to implement local enculturation, for instance, by combining selected local practices in management. For returning entrepreneurs, such local enculturation is necessary not only because they are 'pressured' by institutional norms, but also because knowledge activities (e.g., diffusion, re-creation, and utilization) within their ventures require a resocialization process, which in turn has to be enabled by locally approved management practices (Meyer, 2001).

Proposition 7: CDEs are more likely to implement hybrid management.

Discussion and Conclusion

Contemporary diasporic entrepreneurs have emerged in the growing, globalizing knowledge-intensive industries wherein connectivity is rapidly becoming the norm. CDEs have been most visible in transition economies that have undergone significant changes in economic and institutional infrastructure. Parallel to its extraordinary growth records, China has witnessed an influx of professionals returning from the diaspora whose high-tech ventures have helped the country to effectively build up indigenous technological capabilities by engaging international knowledge transfer, and have arguably created a type of business that is characteristically different from both domestic entrepreneurial firms and foreign-funded firms as well as state-owned enterprises (SOEs). Diasporic professionals returned at a time when the initial development of technological infrastructure allowed them to fill some of the substantial gaps in the existing economic structure and when the reshaped institutional environment started to embrace and encourage entrepreneurial activities and the participation of returnees in such activities. Successful CDEs are unique psychologically and resource-wise: they are opportunity-driven and rich in both host and home country resources. To a certain extent, returnees' dual identity helps them overcome the 'liability of foreignness' (Zaheer & Mosakowski, 1997), often suffered by conventional international entrepreneurs. These qualities, combined with the historical opportunities presented, have resulted in a set of start-up strategies including a focus on technological niche markets, a stronger international orientation, and a hybrid management approach, in contrast with other players in China's burgeoning entrepreneurial sector.

Theoretical Implications

High-tech industries have been the most visible venue for international entrepreneurship (Oviatt & McDougall, 1994) and have attracted the most empirical research on the subject (Burgel & Murray, 2000). It is thus surprising that the IE literature has largely ignored the CDE phenomenon, and that research on emerging markets-based entrepreneurs has not even recognized the CDE as a distinctive force alongside domestic entrepreneurial firms and foreign direct investment in technology. Perhaps China remains an extreme case in that no other country has witnessed CDEs in the same magnitude. However, given China's size and therefore its importance to the world economy and given China's influence among emerging markets as an institutional-change and economic-development model (Tan, 2005), a systematic examination of Chinese CDEs offers a unique opportunity to advance our understanding of emerging markets and their newly developed entrepreneurial sector.

The findings, while limited, suggest that the CDE phenomenon cannot be fully explained by existing theories of either the ethnic economy or international business. As shown in Figure 2.1, there is an intersection between international entrepreneurship and ethnic entrepreneurship: part of the international entrepreneurship involves ethnic entrepreneurs and part of the ethnic entrepreneurship is involved in international markets. However, CDEs direct their entrepreneurial activities at their country of origin, thus differentiating themselves from broadly defined transnational entrepreneurs (Portes, Guarnizo, & Haller, 2002; Drori, Honig, & Ginsberg, 2006), whose international ventures could locate them in a third country, for example, Taiwanese entrepreneurs operating IT businesses in Germany (see Leung, 2001).

In this chapter, I have considered CDE as a mode of immigrant economic adaptation. If the classic ethnic economy for the most part can be said to be necessity-based, CDE is by and large opportunity-driven. Returned diasporic entrepreneurs are contemporary by virtue of both the high-flying opportunity that they can capitalize on in the homeland and the resources that they can draw from both their homeland base and Western experience. The literature has started looking at the possibility of globalization as an equalizer that will help recently developed countries to catch up. Could the same process also make it possible for immigrants of minority status to move upward economically by leveraging opportunities in their countries of origin? Figure 2.1 also suggests that CDEs be conceptualized as a branch of international entrepreneurship. However, until we know more about their activities as knowledge disseminators and integrators across their countries of origin and residence, we will not be able to comprehend fully what may be gained from research on CDEs as a distinct branch of IE. Finally, I have mentioned the possibility of the substantial involvement of CDEs in the 'destination' country, in those cases in which the CDEs fall into the category of transnational entrepreneurship. At a time when the notions of nation-state and civic identity have become increasingly fluid, a change in home base is no longer difficult to make. However, the extent to which ethnicity and its associated sentiments remain influential is a question worth further investigation.

While examining the CDE phenomenon in the intersections of the ethnic economy, international entrepreneurship, and institutional change, the usefulness of the institutional perspective has become especially prominent, as suggested by recent literature (Ahlstrom & Bruton, 2002; Bruton, Ahlstrom, & Obloj, 2008). As this work claimed, the social and economic consequences of contemporary diasporic entrepreneurship could be intensified by institutional diversity in globally contested institutional environments (see also Drori, Honig, & Ginsberg, 2006). The institutional perspective has helped previous research to identify some common strategies employed by entrepreneurs in emerging markets. According to Phan and Foo (2004), any framework dealing with technological entrepreneurship may have to take government involvement into consideration. What is remarkable about China is that the government apparently has treated returnees from the diaspora differently from either domestic private firms or foreign entrants. The state not only implements policies that give professionals from the diaspora greater autonomy but is also in many cases directly involved in the business ventures created by the CDEs. In a sense, the returnee's dual identity does not carry a 'liability of foreignness' but a discriminating advantage against both private and foreign rivals. Our framework emphasizes the impact of both national culture and government, a perspective that deviates from much of the Western scholarship resting on an individual approach (Lee & Peterson, 2000). Hybrid management style is a prominent example of how CDEs carefully establish a 'third place' that allows Western 'systems' and Oriental 'wisdoms,' each time-honoured in its own right, to complement one another.

Practical Implications

Apparently, CDEs have been the new players in China's high-tech sector that, until recently, included only domestic private and joint-venture firms (Ahlstrom & Bruton, 2002). The entrance of CDEs has brought about both challenges and opportunities for domestic private firms. Already weak in status due to continued regulatory discrimination and public scrutiny, the private entrepreneur usually lacks dynamic technological capability. However, network-oriented CDEs may need domestic partners who carry certain location advantages such as market knowledge and established distribution networks (Xia, 2004). If domestic private entrepreneurs can effectively demonstrate such advantages and subsequently ally with CDEs, they have the opportunity to enhance their competitive positions and legitimacy. The current study also offers lessons for Western multinational corporations and other foreign entrants. Up until this point, Western businesses have focused their attention on domestic private firms and state-owned enterprises, with the importance of the latter decreasing steadily. CDEs have evolved into a new competitive force in China, at least in contemporary high-tech industries, for their resource advantages discussed in the preceding section. Importantly, the CDEs may also be more inclined and better able to form alliances with domestic private entrepreneurs (Xia, 2004) and thus alter the competitive balance between indigenous and foreign players. On the other hand, as suggested earlier, the entrepreneurial strategy employed by CDEs may also bring about collaborative opportunities for interested Westerners. For instance, since CDEs are likely to have an international orientation, Western firms involving technology, manufacturing, and distribution may serve a role in CDEs' international strategies.

While home countries have apparently benefited from brain gain through repatriated diasporic professionals, host countries in the Western world have yet to fully understand the implications of the CDE phenomenon. With growing numbers in countries such as the United States and Canada, people have started wondering to what extent the repatriation of CDEs or returnees from the diaspora in general impact the respective country's national or diplomatic policy, tax revenues, and civic identity, but the foremost concern is the loss of talent and intellectual property to the diasporas' home countries. However, it is important to note that CDEs are a product of the globalization that has increasingly made the borderless flows of ideas and humans a reality. My initial research has shown that CDEs may travel back and forth between China and their adopted country on business, especially when they keep a home there. This suggests that, instead of trying to reverse the inevitable trend of interconnectivity in high-technology industries, host countries may need to consider ways to better capitalize on potential and ongoing brain circulation (Meyer, 2001). Indeed, emerging economies such as China and India are no longer always at the receiving side of global production networks, but are also being used by many multinational companies as a source of innovation. With properly designed policies and strategies, host countries may be able to take advantage of CDEs in enhancing their positions in high-technology development and economic internationalization.

Limitations and Future Research Directions

Conceptualizations advanced in the current study are preliminary and have to be expanded to fully capture CDEs as a complex social phenomenon. I addressed my research questions using the opportunity-group characteristics-strategy framework (Aldrich & Waldinger, 1990). However, other conceptualizations of ethnic entrepreneurship (EE), for example, the push-pull framework (Light, 1972) and the theory of practice (Bourdieu, 1990; Drori, Honig, & Ginsberg, 2006), should be considered in enriching the current theorizing. The methodology employed in the study is also limited. While information from in-depth interviews is insightful, future research should use a quantitative design to ascertain causal relationships and generalize the ideas (Chen, 2007).

Due to the current study's context, it is not clear whether the findings can be generalized for other countries, such as India, that have also reported phenomenal entrepreneurial undertakings by returnees from the diaspora, or Central and East Europe, where research has not reported the same level of entrepreneurship among highly skilled returnees (Tung & Lazarova, 2006). However, the conceptualizations presented here can serve as a framework for comparative studies across countries or within a nation. As an initial step, research can be carried out in countries where a significant number of CDEs can be identified. The researchers can ascertain commonalities in, for example, the economic and institutional readiness that facilitates the involvement of CDEs. By comparing countries with sizeable diaspora communities but different rates of diaspora involvement, the researchers can test the effects of, for example, entrepreneurial culture and homeland sentiments (Proposition 3). As suggested in previous studies, countries may differ in such dimensions (e.g., Busenitz & Lau, 1996; Burrell, 2003). Other propositions advanced in this chapter suggest contrasting CDEs with private entrepreneurs and/or foreign firms, particularly with regard to entrepreneurial strategies. For example, the stronger networking ability of CDEs invites comparison with domestic private entrepreneurs (Proposition 6), and their hybrid management approach is distinguished from the practice of foreign-funded firms (Proposition 7). Such comparisons should help in the further development of international entrepreneurship theory.

ACKNOWLEDGMENTS

The author acknowledges financial support from the Asia Pacific Foundation of Canada, the Social Sciences and Humanities Research Council of Canada (grant no. 864-2007-0288), and Ryerson University.

REFERENCES

Acs, Z., Dana, L., & Jones, M. (2003). Toward new horizons: The internationalization of entrepreneurship. *Journal of International Entrepreneurship*, 1(1): 5–12.

Ahlstrom, D., & Bruton, G.D. (2002). An institutional perspective on the role of culture in shaping strategic actions by technology-focused entrepreneurial firms in China. *Entrepreneurship Theory & Practice*, Summer: 53–69.

Aldrich, H.E., & Waldinger, R. (1990). Ethnicity and entrepreneurship. *Annual Review of Sociology*, 16: 111–135.

Baker, T., Gedajlovic, E., & Lubatkin, M. (2005). A framework for comparing entrepreneurship process across nations. *Journal of International Business Studies*, 36(5): 492–504.

Barkema, H., & Vermeulen, F. (1998). International expansion through start-up or acquisition: A learning perspective. *Academy of Management Journal*, 41(1): 7–26.

Biao, X. (2006). Promoting knowledge exchange through diaspora networks: The case of the People's Republic of China. In C. Wescott & J. Brinkerhoff (Eds.), *Converting Migration Drains into Gains: Harnessing the Resources of Overseas Professionals*, 33–72. Manila: Asian Development Bank.

Boisot, M., & Child, J. (1999). Organizations as adaptive systems in complex environments: The case of China. *Organization Science*, 10(3): 237–252.

Bonacich, E. (1973). A theory of middleman minority. *American Sociological Review*, 38(5): 583–594.

Bourdieu, P. (1990). *The Logic of Practice*. Stanford: Stanford University Press.

Braziel, J.E., & Mannur, A. (2003). Nation, migration, globalization: Points of contention in diaspora studies. In J.E. Braziel & A. Mannur (Eds.), *Theorizing Diaspora*, 1–22. Malden: Blackwell.

Brinkerhoff, J.M. (2006). Diaspora mobilization factors and policy options. In C. Wescott & J. Brinkerhoff (Eds.), *Converting Migration Drains into Gains: Harnessing the Resources of Overseas Professionals*, 127–153. Manila: Asian Development Bank.

Bruton, G., Ahlstrom, D., & Obloj, K. (2008). Entrepreneurship in emerging economies: Where are we today and where should the research go in the future? *Entrepreneurship Theory & Practice*, 32(1): 1–14.

Bruton, G., & Rubanik, Y. (1997). High technology entrepreneurship in transitional economies: The Russian experience. *Journal of High Technology Management Research*, 8(2): 213–223.

Burgel, O., & Murray, G.C. (2000). The international market entry choices of start-up companies in high-technology industries. *Journal of International Marketing*, 8(2): 33–62.

Burrell, K. (2003). Small-scale transnationalism: Homeland connections and the Polish 'community' in Leicester. *International Journal of Population Geography*, 9: 323–335.

Busenitz, L.W., & Lau, C.M. (1996). A cross-cultural cognitive model of new venture creation. *Entrepreneurship Theory & Practice*, Summer: 25–39.

Carana Corporation. (2004). *Diasporas, Emigrants and Development: Economic Linkages and Programmatic Responses*. Washington, DC: USAID Trade Enhancement for the Services Sector (TESS) Project.

Chen, W. (2007). Spinning Transnational Webs: Ethnic Entrepreneurship and Social Networks in the Internet Age. Unpublished manuscript, University of Toronto.

Craig, C., & Douglas, S. (1997). Executive insights: Managing the transnational value chain – strategies for firms from emerging markets. *Journal of International Marketing*, 5(3): 71–84.

Dana, L., Korot, L., & Tovstiga, G. (2003). Toward a transnational techno-culture: An empirical investigation of knowledge management. In H. Etemad & R. Wright (Eds.), *Globalization and Entrepreneurship: Policy and Strategy Perspectives*, 183–204. Northampton: Edward Elgar.

Drori, I., Honig, B., & Ginsberg, A. (2006). Transnational entrepreneurship: Bridging dual socio-cultural affiliations. Unpublished manuscript, Wilfrid Laurier University.

Dunning, J. (1988). The eclectic paradigm of international production: A restatement and some possible extensions. *Journal of International Business Studies*, 19: 1–31.

Farmer, S.M., Tierney, P., & Kung-McIntyre, K. (2003). Employee creativity in Taiwan: An application of role identity theory. *Academy of Management Journal*, 46(5): 618–630.

Financial Times. (2007, 5 Jan.). The dragon's lab – how China is rising through the innovation ranks, 13.

Fu, P.P., Tsui, A.S., & Dess, G.G. (2006). The dynamics of Guanxi in Chinese high-tech firms: Implications for knowledge management and decision making. *Management International Review*, 46(3): 277–305.

Gevorkyan, A., & Grigorian, D. (2003). Armenia and its diaspora: Is there a scope for a stronger economic link? Working Paper No. 03/10. Washington, DC: Armenian International Policy Research Group.

Gillespie, K., Riddle, L., Sayre, E., & Sturges, D. (1999). Diaspora interest in homeland investment. *Journal of International Business Studies*, 30(3): 623–634.

Gopinath, G. (1995). Bombay, U.K., Yuba City: Bhangra music and the engendering of diaspora. *Diaspora*, 4(3): 303–322.

Ite, U.E. (2002). Turning brain drain into brain gain: Personal reflections on using the diaspora option. *African Issues*, 30(1): 76–80.

Kao, J. (1993). The worldwide web of Chinese business. *Harvard Business Review*, 109: 24–36.

Kapur, D. (2001). Diasporas and technology transfer. *Journal of Human Development*, 2(2): 265–286.

Kapur, D., & McHale, J. (2005). *Give Us Your Best and Brightest: The Global Hunt for Talent and Its Impact on the Developing World*. Washington, DC: Center for Global Development.

Landolt, P., Autler, L., & Baires, S. (1999). From 'Hermano Lejano' to 'Herman Mayor': The dialectics of Salvadoran transnationalism. *Ethnic and Racial Studies*, 2: 290–315.

Lane, P.J., & Lubatkin, M. (1998). Relative absorptive capacity and interorganizational learning. *Strategic Management Journal*, 19: 461–477.

Lee, S., & Peterson, S. (2000). Culture, entrepreneurial orientation, and global competitiveness, *Journal of World Business*, 35(4): 401–416.

Leung, M. (2001). Get it going: New ethnic Chinese businesses – the case of Taiwanese-owned computer firms in Hamburg. *Journal of Ethnic and Migration Studies*, 27(2): 277–294.

Li, H., & Atuahene-Gima, K. (2002). The adoption of agency business activity, product innovation, and performance in Chinese technology ventures. *Strategic Management Journal*, 23: 469–488.

Light, I. (1972). *Ethnic Enterprise in America*. Los Angeles: University of California Press.

Light, I. (2004). The ethnic ownership economy. In C.H. Stiles & C.S. Galbraith (Eds.), *Ethnic Entrepreneurship: Structure and Process*, 3–44. Oxford: Elsevier.

Lin, X. (2006). Diaspora Entrepreneurs and Homeland Development in a Globalized World. Presentation at the United Nations – Academy of Management Joint Forum onBusiness as an Agent of World Benefit Forum, Oct., Cleveland, Ohio.

Lin, X., Guan, J., & Nicholson, M.J. (2008). Transnational Entrepreneurs as Agents of International Innovation Linkage. Presentation at the Asia Pacific Foundation – Ryerson University Research Workshop on Transnational Community as Innovation Linkage, Toronto.

McCormick, B., & Wahba, J. (2003). Return of international migration and geographical inequality: The case of Egypt. *Journal of African Economics*, 12(4): 500–532.

McDougall, P., Oviatt, B., & Shrader, R. (2003). A comparison of international and domestic new ventures. *Journal of International Entrepreneurship*, 1(1): 59–82.

Meyer, J.B. (2001). Network approach versus brain drain: Lessons from the diaspora. *International Migration*, 39(5): 91–108.

Niosi, J., & Reid, S.E. (2007). Biotechnology and nanotechnology: Science-based enabling technologies as windows of opportunities for LDCS? *World Development*, 35(3): 426–438.

Oviatt, B.M., & McDougall, P.P. (1994). Toward a theory of international new ventures. *Journal of International Business Studies*, 25(1): 45–64.

Oviatt, B.M., & McDougall, P.P. (2005). Defining international entrepreneurship and modeling the speed of internationalization. *Entrepreneurship Theory & Practice*, 29(5): 537–553.

Patterson, R. (2006).Transnationalism: Diaspora-homeland development. *Social Forces*, 84(4): 1891–1907.

Peng, M. (2001). How entrepreneurs create wealth in transition economies. *Academy of Management Executives*, 15(1): 95–110.

Phan, P.H., & Foo, M.D. (2004). Technological entrepreneurship in emerging regions. *Journal of Business Venturing*, 19: 1–5.

Rialp, A., Rialp, J., & Knight, C.A. (2005). The phenomenon of early industrializing firms: What do we know after a decade (1993–2003) of scientific inquiry? *International Business Review*, 14: 147–166.

Portes, A., & Landolt, P. (1996). The downside of social capital. *American Prospect*, 26: 18–24.

Portes, A., Guarnizo, L.E., & Haller, W.J. (2002). Transnational entrepreneurs: An alternative form of immigrant economic adaptation. *American Sociological Review*, 67: 278–298.

Radhakrishnan, R. (2003). Ethnicity in an age of diaspora. In J.E. Braziel & A. Mannur (Eds.), *Theorizing Diaspora*, 119–131. Malden: Blackwell.

Rauch, J.E. (2003). Diasporas and Development: Theory, Evidence, and Programmatic Implications. Unpublished manuscript, Department of Economics, University of California, San Diego.

Safran, W. (1991). Diasporas in modern societies: Myths of homeland and return. *Diaspora*, 1(1): 83–99.

Saxenian, A. (1999). *Silicon Valley's New Immigrant Entrepreneurs*. San Francisco: Public Policy Institute of California.

Saxenian, A. (2002). Transnational communities and the evolution of global production networks: The case of Taiwan, China and India. *Industry and Innovation*, 9(3): 183–202.

Shillingford, C.A. (2003). Growth Opportunities in Dominica: Role of the Diaspora. Speech delivered to the U.K. Symposium of Dominican Diasporas in the Development Process, Aug., London.

Skeldon, R. (2003). The Chinese diaspora or the migration of Chinese peoples?

In L.J.C. Ma & C. Cartier (Eds.), *The Chinese Diaspora: Space, Place, Mobility and Identity*, 51–66. Oxford: Rowan and Littlefield.

Tan, J. (2002). Culture, nation, and entrepreneurial strategic orientations: Implications for an emerging economy. *Entrepreneurship Theory & Practice*, Summer: 95–111.

Tan, J. (2005). Venturing in turbulent water: A historical perspective of economic reform and entrepreneurial transformation. *Journal of Business Venturing*, 20: 689–704.

Tan, J. (2006). Growth of industry clusters and innovation: Lessons from Beijing Zhongguancun Science Park. *Journal of Business Venturing*, 21: 827–850.

Tanzer, A. (1996). The Chinese way. *Forbes*, 150(7): 42–43.

Tung, R.L. (1993). Managing cross-national and intra-national diversity. *Human Resource Management Journal*, 23(4): 461–477.

Tung, R.L., & Lazarova, M. (2006). Brain drain versus brain gain: An exploratory study of ex-host country nationals in Central and Eastern Europe. *International Journal of Human Resource Management*, 17(11): 1853–1872.

Vanhanocker, W., Zweig, D., & Fung, C.S. (2006). Transnational or social capital? Returned scholars as private entrepreneurs. In A. Tsui, Y. Bian, & L. Cheng (Eds.), *China's Domestic Private Firms: Multidisciplinary Perspectives on Management and Performance*, 65–81. Armonk: M.E. Sharpe.

Wang, G. (1993). Greater China and the Chinese overseas. *China Quarterly*, 136: 926–948.

Wang, H. (2007). *Contemporary Chinese Returnees*. [in Chinese]. Beijing: China Development Press.

Wang, H., & Zweig, D. (2008). China's Diaspora and Returnees: Impact on China's Globalization Process. Presented at the Conference on China Goes Global, , 8–10 Oct., Harvard University, Cambridge.

Wright, M., Liu, X., Buck, T., & Filatotchev, I. (2008). Returnee entrepreneurs, science park location choice and performance. *Entrepreneurship Theory & Practice*, 32(1): 131–155.

Xia, Y. (2004). Preface. In Y. Xia (Ed.), *Overseas Returnees' Innovation in Zhongguancun*. [in Chinese]. Beijing: China Development Press.

Zaheer, S., & Mosakowski, E. (1997). The dynamics of the liability of foreignness: A global study of survival in financial services. *Strategic Management Journal*, 18(6): 439–463.

Zhou, M. (1992). *Chinatown: The Socioeconomic Potential of an Urban Enclave*. Philadelphia: Temple University Press.

3 Transnational Scientific Entrepreneurship: A Conceptual Framework

AMALYA L. OLIVER AND KATHLEEN MONTGOMERY

Research on transnational entrepreneurship (TE) has taken a conceptual shift in recent years (Portes, Guarnizo, & Haller, 2002). Instead of focusing on traditional concerns such as the origins of the immigrants and their adaptation in the receiving community, the emerging approach focuses on the continuing relations with the home country, or country of origin (CO), and on how the traffic back and forth builds complex social fields that straddle national borders. Scientific communities that span national borders and enhance internationally shared assets such as information, technologies, and contacts are issues of globalization (Portes, 1997). Saxenian (2002) suggests that transnational communities may become as important as states and multinational corporations (MNCs) in contributing to the growth of technology entrepreneurship. In addition, these communities can play an important role in the evolution of global production networks and can provide an important mechanism for diffusing knowledge internationally and upgrading local capabilities.

The sociological literature on transnational immigration has shifted in its scope from focusing initially on theories of assimilation to theorizing segmented assimilation. A recent perspective is on the active role such immigrants take in their country of origin while they become part of their new place (Levitt & Jaworsky, 2007). Migration occurs within four major domains of motivations: economic, political, social-family, and religion. Within the economic domain, Levitt and Jaworsky (2007) identify four major categories: (1) a transnational business class of highly mobile, skilled professional, managerial, and entrepreneurial elite; (2) unskilled and semi-skilled low-wage immigrants; (3) expensive specialists in art and culture; and (4) world tourists.

Knowledge entrepreneurs are classified in the first category. These immigrants are experienced in science-based entrepreneurship and are moving to another country in order to exploit the potential they find in their entrepreneurial scientific work. They could include academic scientists in areas such as biotechnology or computer sciences who move to a research position in another university in a different country, or they could be academic scientists who move to an industrial firm perceived to have the proper capabilities to move their inventions into the market.

Séguin et al. (2006) observed what they term a 'scientific diaspora,' arguing that highly skilled immigrating scientists and engineers constitute a 'brain drain' from their countries of origin. These authors note that there also is enormous potential in a scientific diaspora. Such diasporas have been defined as self-organized communities of expatriate scientists and engineers working to develop their country or region of origin, mainly in science, technology, and education (Barre et al., 2003). Yet, there is a concern that many of the diaspora networks depend on a few champions for sustainability, which can impair their continuity and effectiveness. To reap the benefits from scientific diasporas while avoiding the potential barriers, systematic research is needed on the transitions that scientific entrepreneurs undergo and their needs, constraints, and perceptions regarding their role as brokers of entrepreneurial science.

The Phenomenon of Transnational Scientific Entrepreneurship

Much of modern science takes place within complex social systems and intensive economies. These systems include various interacting factors associated with the scientists, industries, technology-transfer mechanisms, intellectual property rights regimes, and other institutions, suggesting the emergence of a new organizational field of transnational scientific entrepreneurship (TSE). This growing phenomenon remains theoretically underdeveloped in the literature. We aim in this chapter to provide a conceptual clarification of TSE.

As we explain below, transnational scientific entrepreneurship is a complex construct of three hybrids: (1) transnational entrepreneurship, in which entrepreneurial activities occur across national borders; (2) transnational science, in which a scientist and the scientist's own scientific knowledge (both 'know-how' and 'know-what') are moving transnationally; and (3) scientific entrepreneurship, entrepreneurship regarding scientific work, in which a scientist is aiming at bringing into the market various outputs (products, technologies, services) associated with the scientist's own basic and applied research and inventions.

Understanding the concept of transnational scientific entrepreneurship requires a careful integration of theoretical lenses that pertain to entrepreneurship, social networks, and institutional factors. First, the entrepreneurial literature lacks clarity regarding definitions and core characteristics or capabilities of entrepreneurship, in general, and more so for scientific entrepreneurship (Oliver, 2004; Portes, Guarnizo, & Haller, 2002). Second, social network theory is required to capture the role of social capital and scientific capital in scientific entrepreneurship in the transnational context. Third, institutional theory is needed to capture normative variations in the transnational environments in which scientific entrepreneurs act.

Transnational Entrepreneurship

Briefly, to have entrepreneurship, one must first have entrepreneurial opportunities. Shane and Venkatarman (2000) explain that entrepreneurial opportunities are those situations in which new goods, services, raw materials, and organizing methods can be introduced and sold at more than their cost of production. There are many forms of entrepreneurial opportunities, but in general an entrepreneurial discovery occurs when someone makes the conjecture that an existing set of resources is not put to its 'best use.'

Transnational entrepreneurship (TE) is an area of increased research interest (Portes, Guarnizo, & Haller, 2002; Saxenian, 2005), though greater attention has been devoted to ethnicity-based transnational entrepreneurship. A major feature of TE is its embeddedness in ethnic enclaves in the new country, which provide support and friendship networks as well as economic opportunities for entrepreneurial activities. Portes, Guarnizo, and Haller (2002) find that TE exists as distinct from more traditional forms of immigrant economic adaptation. They also find that transnational entrepreneurs (TEs) represent a large proportion of the self-employed in immigrant communities and that TEs are part of the elite in their respective communities in terms of the education and legal standing that leads to higher income.

Saxenian (2002) identifies another category of transnational entrepreneurs who are foreign-born, highly educated professionals in dynamic and technologically sophisticated industries, such as those working in

Silicon Valley. She estimated that Chinese and Indian engineers were running 29 per cent of Silicon Valley's technology businesses by 2000, and that these companies collectively accounted for more than U.S. $19.5 billion in sales and 72,839 jobs. An interesting finding of Saxenian's study is that, as the pace of immigrant entrepreneurship accelerated dramatically in the past decade, these individuals retained their ethnic ties to an even greater extent than their less-educated counterparts. As a result, they constitute social and professional networks with a global reach, connecting new immigrants with their counterparts in their countries of origin. Such transnational communities provide shared information, contacts, and trust, which allow local producers to participate in an increasingly global economy. Saxenian (2005) refers to this phenomenon as a shifting from 'brain drain' to 'brain circulation.'

Transnational Science

Scientific knowledge is based on ongoing learning processes that develop from initial knowledge, research, and integrative insights, coupled with exchanges and collaborations with other scientists. This complex knowledge construct is mainly internal to the scientist and is 'stored' in the form of 'tacit knowledge' (Nonaka, 1994; Nonaka & Takeuchi, 1995). As a result, such knowledge cannot be transferred fully and simply through formal channels of information or through other scientists, but only by the scientist directly. Tacit knowledge is different from explicit or formal knowledge (in the form of patents, books, publications, or known technology), which can move transnationally *without* the scientist. Such scientific products can be moved or transferred as 'entities' that are independent of the scientist, serving as the major form by which scientific knowledge is transferred to other scientists or scientific communities, regardless of geographical location.

In contrast, tacit scientific knowledge exists in the mind of the scientist and is hard to formulate and fully specify. Hence, tacit knowledge is transferred within networks of interested scientists, who possess overlapping knowledge and research experience capabilities, through research collaborations (Liebeskind et al., 1996) and other forms of exchanges. Transnational science is based on tacit scientific knowledge that represents the knowledge and capabilities of scientists that have not yet been formalized through publications of various types. Thus, transnational science encounters substantial difficulties associated with underdefined or primordial ideas and process insights. As a result, in order for tacit knowledge to have impact, the scientist must be mobile to participate in transferring the knowledge directly while collaborating with other scientists. Scientific networks in which the scientist is embedded are important components of the scientist's social capital (Nahapiet & Ghoshal, 1998) as it is through these networks that tacit knowledge is exchanged and transferred and can be transformed into explicit knowledge.

A primary complication involving transnational science is that it takes place across different institutional environments and organizational fields (Bourdieu, 2005; Powell et al., 2005). An organization field contains all actors (organizations) whose interactions 'constitute a recognized area of institutional life' (DiMaggio & Powell, 1983: 148). That is, a field is an activity domain in which organizations with similar activities operate and together constitute order. Since this order consists of many, and often contradictory, institutions at the same time, actors try to sort them out, delineating a field of relevance.

Transnational science takes place in a multifield arena, where similar organizational fields in different nations are loosely connected and are influenced by the institutional environment in which they operate. As a result, each field is exposed to different structural and institutional constraints and opportunities. This condition affects the nature of scientific entrepreneurship and scientists' effort to enhance the entrepreneurial processes.

Scientific Entrepreneurship

As academic scientific knowledge is transferred from the academic sphere to the market sphere, the following three elements need to be specified: (1) academic scientific knowledge is 'owned' by the scientist and the scientist's university; (2) scientific knowledge belongs to the scientist, but is also developed through its embeddedness in his or her scientific networks that constitute social capital; and (3) by its nature, scientific knowledge can be developed towards commercialization with the aid of various organizational resources, structures, facilities, and capabilities (such as investors, managers, technology transfer, and intellectual property experts, etc.). Unlike other forms of entrepreneurship that may exist outside of formal organizations, scientific entrepreneurship is generally conducted within firms and, more recently, also within universities (Oliver, 2008; Shane, 2004). These organizations provide the resources that facilitate the commercialization process (Oliver,

2008). The firms that facilitate the transfer of scientific knowledge into the market benefit not only from the potential of commercialization that results from the invention of the academic entrepreneur, but also from the added value of the explicit/formal and tacit knowledge that the entrepreneurial scientist brings into the organization as well as from his or her scientific social capital (Oliver, 1997).

Entrepreneurship includes new-venture creation as well as activities within organizations in the form of spin-offs for ideas generated within organizations (Guth & Ginsberg, 1990; Zahra & Dess, 2001). Scientific entrepreneurs are able to detect an entrepreneurial opportunity that is usually based on an invention made through their scientific research. The most distinct form in the life sciences refers to a PhD scientist with a research university background who is involved in founding an entrepreneurial firm (a 'start-up') to exploit the commercial potential in his or her invention derived from university-based research. The scientist usually continues working in collaboration with the research team while trying to move the invention into the marketplace. These collaborations are part of the scientist's social capital. The sociological definition of *social capital* is the totality of resources activated through an extended and mobilizable network of relations that procures a competitive advantage by providing higher returns of investments (Bourdieu, 2005: 194).

Challenges for Transnational Scientific Entrepreneurship

Given the complexities inherent in the three hybrid components of TSEs, it is not unexpected that special challenges will arise as this form of entrepreneurship becomes more prevalent. We elaborate here on four factors that are predicted to have an impact on the nature of TSEs – both in the country of origin (CO) where the scientist is based and in the country of exploitation (CE) where the entrepreneurial venture takes place – and which deserve greater attention: (1) scientific social capital and trust; (2) exploratory research capabilities; (3) exploitation and technological capabilities; and (4) entrepreneurial culture.

Scientific Social Capital and Trust

Trust in scientific collaborations is not easy to establish due to factors associated with the ownership of intellectual property (IP), competition over symbolic and material rewards, conflicting commitments, and scientists' tendency towards individualism. Liebeskind and Oliver (1998) argued that to establish trustworthiness in collaboration between academia and industry, where the parties have commercial interests, deeper and broader trust was needed than in a relationship based on pure academic research with no commercial intent. It is assumed that trust among professionals operating within the same occupational community can contribute to enhancing organizational efficiency, flexibility, legitimacy, and ability to learn, and at the same time, reducing organizational costs (Oliver & Montgomery, 2001). In a similar vein, cross-national scientific collaborations require a learning and adaptation process through which new social capital can be established.

Nahapiet and Ghoshal (1998) identify three dimensions of social capital: relational, structural, and cognitive, and argue that the attributes of these dimensions facilitate the exchange of resources within firms. They borrow the concepts of 'relational embeddedness' and 'structural embeddedness' from Granovetter (1992) to describe the kind of personal relationships people have developed with each other through a history of interactions such as respect and friendship that influence their behaviour. Through these personal relations, people achieve social capacities such as sociability, approval, and prestige. *Structural embeddedness* refers to the properties of the social system and of the network of relations; the term describes the configuration of linkages between people or units as paths for reaching other connected people. By *cognitive dimension* they refer to the network of resources that provide shared representations, interpretations, and systems of meaning among parties; this is a separate dimension because the authors perceive it as an asset that has not been discussed in the social capital literature but is highly related to strategy.

In a study of fifteen business units within a firm, Tsai and Ghoshal (1998) found that social interactions and trust were significantly related to interfirm resource exchanges and as a result to firm innovation. Liebeskind et al. (1996) found that the social capital of scientists in two leading biotechnology firms constituted a central aspect of the learning processes of the firms in which external knowledge was in-sourced.

In a different direction, the structure of networks that scientists have – in terms of occupying 'structural holes' positions (Burt, 2005) – is also important for understanding their future mobility. Gabby and Zuckerman (1998) investigated how scientists' positions in networks of work relations affect the probability that they expect future mobility. Their findings showed that, in general, actors with disconnected contacts gain a competitive advantage relative to others who do not enjoy the same degree of access to structural holes.

Another aspect of the structural dimension is physical proximity, as a dense proximity of scientists can be associated with their use of their social capital. And, indeed, the physical proximity of scientists has been found to be an important factor associated with collaborations of learning. Gittelman and Kogut (2003) found that regional collaborations are associated with commercialization and exploitation (as patents and co-citations) due to greater proximity of social capital, while distant collaborations have a greater association with exploration (as measured by paper-to-paper citations) within a large scientific epistemic community.

Exploratory Research Capabilities: Quality of Academic Research

The economic and scientific literature agree that national economic innovation and productivity performance are the result of public and private investments but also highly influenced by the learning collaborations between the industry and academic research (Debackere & Veugelers, 2005). Such university-industry collaborations allow for the translation of basic research into applied research. Basic research capabilities are also considered exploratory capabilities in which the scientific work focuses mainly on projects in which answers to unknown questions are explored; basic research is defined by the National Science Foundation as original investigation for the advancement of scientific knowledge that does not have immediate commercial objectives. Yet, it is known that strong academic research is not always associated with industrial innovation as additional capabilities are required in order to get to the market. Dosi, Llerena, and Labini (2006), for example, argue that although the scientific performance in the European Union is excellent in comparison with its competitors, the EU is weak in its ability to transform its research results into innovation and competitive advantage. It is thus plausible that countries do vary not only in their level of academic research capabilities but also in the degree to which academic innovative applied research can be transferred into the market.

Exploitation and Technological Capabilities: Industrial Advantage

In knowledge-based industries, academia provides the knowledge base of basic research, while industry provides the infrastructure for translating research into its applied features and further into products

(Liebeskind et al., 1996; Oliver, 2001; Powell, Koput, & Smith-Doerr, 1996). Therefore, in order to achieve national competitive advantage, both academia and industry should be able to develop advanced capabilities that are complementary. Once there are discrepancies between the academic basic and applied science capabilities and the industrial-technological capabilities, an entrepreneurial scientist can benefit while operating within the transnational arena. Such scientists can seek advantageous industrial opportunities in the country where they exist and facilitate the translation of their scientific inventions into applied technologies or products.

Entrepreneurial Culture

Culture is an underlying system of values relevant to specific groups or societies. As such, culture can shape the development of various personality traits and facilitate the involvement of individuals to engage in behaviours that may be unique to certain cultures. Research by Hofstede (1985) suggests that there are clear differences across countries and organizations in values, beliefs, and work roles, and related to the entrepreneurial features, Mueller, Thomas, and Jaeger (2001) found that some cultures are more conducive for entrepreneurship than others. In cultures characterized by individualistic traits, higher likelihoods for an internal locus of control and entrepreneurial aspirations and orientations were found. Thus, a scientist who comes from an entrepreneurial culture can take advantage of a less entrepreneurial culture by appropriating an entrepreneurial innovation in his or her country of origin after learning about it in the new country.

Examples of Balanced and Imbalanced Entrepreneurial Opportunities

In the effort to capture the potential of the nature of opportunities in balanced and imbalanced transnational conditions, we formulate a few examples. Table 3.1 provides examples of how the four contextual factors may operate in different ways across the scientific entrepreneur's country of origin (CO) and the host country (the country of exploitation, or CE).

For example, the relative capacities of the country of origin and the country of exploitation provide TSEs windows of opportunity to exploit the imbalances in ways that impact both the TSE collaboration and the countries on a broader scale. The proposed relationships in Table 3.1 constitute the foundation for testable hypotheses.

Beyond the cross-sectional availability of resources, technological and economic capabilities, social capital properties, and cultural aspects of TSE, there are additional factors that need to be accounted for in understanding TSE. In the next section we discuss individual factors and differences in intellectual property regimes.

Additional Factors Influencing Transnational Scientific Entrepreneurs

Individual Factors

In addition to the contextual, cultural, and institutional elements suggested above, a model of TSE should capture individual-level elements regarding the entrepreneurial scientist. We mention these only briefly since our primary focus has been on macro-structural elements. A key individual-level factor that may be relevant to consider is research specialty, as this is an important determinant that ties the scientist to the entrepreneurial arena. Some areas of basic research, such as in biotechnology or nanotechnology, are more closely associated with entrepreneurship opportunities than are others. Also, the scientific social capital of the scientists plays a significant role in their ability to attract entrepreneurial ventures and entrepreneurial associates. As scientific exchanges are based in networks (Liebeskind et al., 1996; Oliver, 2004), all informal scientific exchanges in which information and ideas are transferred become the supportive structures for entrepreneurial actions. Thus, the larger and more diverse the spectrum of the scientist's social capital, the greater will be the scientist's exposure to information regarding entrepreneurial opportunities and practices. In addition, scientists who invent unique technologies or master complex frontier technologies will be at higher 'risk' of entrepreneurial opportunities as they capture highly demanded scientific capabilities needed for entrepreneurial science. In many respects, these opportunities will 'search and attract' the scientist rather than the reverse.

Previous entrepreneurial experience is another individual-level factor associated with future entrepreneurship. Past experience is not only a signal for a self-selection process, but it also provides evidence for 'learning by doing' entrepreneurial insights. Finally, the scientist's positioning on the 'value chain' capabilities within scientific entrepre-

Table 3.1
Country Contextual Issues and Their Expressions in Balanced and Imbalanced Situations between the Country of Origin (CO) and the Country of Exploitation (CE) of a Transnational Scientific Entrepreneur (TSE)

Contextual Dimensions	Scientific Social Capital and Trust	Exploratory Capabilities of Academic Research	Exploitation Capabilities of Industry	Societal Support for Entrepreneurial Culture
Situation				
Balanced: Both CO and CE benefit	Dense scientific networks in both countries. TSE acts as a broker between two dense communities.	High in both countries	High in both countries	High in both countries
Unbalanced: Advantage to TSE's Country of Origin (CO)	Dense networks in CE. TSE acts as broker for CO colleagues.	Higher in CO. TSE establishes networks for exploitation in CE.	Higher in CO. TSE 'transfers' opportunities to exploit from CE to CO.	Higher in CO; encourages TSE to transport scientific opportunities from CE to CO.
Unbalanced: Advantage to Country of Exploitation (CE)	Dense networks in CO. TSE acts as a broker for new colleagues while connecting them to scientific networks in SE's CO.	Higher in CE. TSE moves in order to benefit.	Higher in CE. TSE 'transfers' opportunities to exploit from CO to CE.	Higher in CE; encourages TSE to transport scientific opportunities from CO to CE.

neurship is also associated with becoming a transnational scientific entrepreneur. Scientists who conduct applied research and who have developed capabilities and gained experience in bringing science closer to market are likely to have a higher probability of becoming transnational scientific entrepreneurs.

Norms and Intellectual Property Rights

Scientists and scientific networks are embedded in normative systems of information disclosure and protection, as well as cultural systems of exchanges. Evidence for the impact of cultural differences on intellectual property regimes and systems of knowledge sharing and exchanges is already established. For example, one cultural distinction is seen in the norms within collaborations of academic scientists and the norms within collaborations that involve academic scientists and industry for commercial interest.

Another extension of the conceptual framework proposed here that may be especially promising pertains to norms and intellectual property rights regimes. For example, norms of research integrity, especially with regard to rights for IP and conflict of interest, may vary substantially across national contexts, thus having important implications for the way TSEs function. Intellectual property rights regimes differ in the degree to which they offer protection to scientists over their IP while conducting collaborative research or seeking firms that will assist them in commercializing their inventions. These differences have also a related impact on differences in norms on scientists' social capital and trust relations within transnational collaborations, and this is another area of importance for future research. An intriguing question would be whether new norms, perhaps unique to the transnational collaboration, emerge among the entrepreneurs and the extent to which boundaries are erected within particular TSEs to define and distinguish them from other TSEs.

Norms can take different features, ranges, and importance in different cultures. This is true in general, but is even more reflective in cases where norms are established through formal mechanisms such as regulations and laws. Once a formal expectation has been set, the diffusion and clarity of these expectations can also vary between cultures. Understanding the intercultural differences is highly important, especially when the effort is to understand and explain transnational scientific entrepreneurship.

Conclusion

In this chapter we have identified the key conceptual building blocks associated with transnational scientific entrepreneurship. In addition, we established the grounds that will allow us to specify new research directions for further empirical research. Future studies can focus on each of the four factors detailed above to enrich our understanding and predictability of how TSEs are likely to function in both the country of origin and the country of exploitation or exploration. We offer some examples of how these factors combine into testable hypotheses in Table 3.1. We also suggest additional areas for future research that would focus on individual differences among TSEs, as well as differences in norms pertaining to intellectual property that may vary across countries and collaborations.

The conceptual framework developed in this chapter is designed to highlight areas where additional conceptual and empirical work is needed in a field that is rapidly growing but about which little is known to date.

ACKNOWLEDGMENTS

The authors gratefully acknowledge funding to support this research from the Israel Science Foundation (Oliver) and from the University of California Academic Senate (Montgomery).

REFERENCES

Barre, R., Hernandez, V., Meyer, J.B., & Vinck, D. (2003). *Scientific Diasporas: How Can Developing Countries Benefit from Their Expatriate Scientists and Engineers?* Paris: Institut de recherche pour le développement.

Bourdieu, P. (2005). *The Social Structures of the Economy.* Cambridge: Polity Press.

Burt, R.S. (2005). *Brokerage and Closure: An Introduction to Social Capital.* Oxford: Oxford University Press.

Debackere, K., & Veugelers, R. (2005). The role of academic technology transfer organizations in improving industry science links. *Research Policy*, 34: 321–342.

DiMaggio, P., & Powell, W.W. (1983). The iron cage revisited: Institutional isomorphism and collective rationality in organizational fields. *American Sociological Review*, 48: 147–160.

Dosi, G., Llerena, P., & Labini, M.S. (2006). The relationships between science, technologies and their industrial exploitation: An illustration through the myths and realities of the so-called 'European Paradox.' *Research Policy*, 35: 1450–1464.

Gabby, S., & Zuckerman, E. (1998). Social capital and opportunity in corporate R&D: The contingent effect of contact density. *Social Science Research*, 27: 189–217.

Gittelman, M., & Kogut, B. (2003). Does good science lead to valuable knowledge? Biotechnology firms and the evolutionary logic of citation patterns. *Management Science*, 49: 366–382.

Granovetter, M. (1992). Problems of explanation in economic sociology. In N. Nohria & R. Eccles (Eds.), *Networks and Organizations: Structure, Form, and Action*, 25–56. Boston: Harvard Business School.

Guth, W.D., & Ginsberg, A. (1990). Guest editors' introduction: Corporate entrepreneurship. *Strategic Management Journal*, 11: 5–15.

Hofstede, G. (1985). The interaction between national and organizational value systems. *Journal of Management Studies*, 22: 347–357.

Liebeskind, J., Oliver, A.L., Zucker, L., & Brewer, M. (1996). Social networks, learning, and flexibility: Sourcing scientific knowledge in new biotechnology firms. *Organization Science*, 7: 428–443.

Liebeskind, J., & Oliver, A.L. (1998). From handshake to contract: Trust, intellectual property and the social structure of academic research. In C. Lane & R. Bachmann (Eds.), *Within and between Organizations*, 118–145. Oxford: Oxford University Press.

Levitt, P., & Jaworsky, N. (2007). Transnational migration studies: Past developments and future trends. *Annual Review of Sociology*, 33: 129–156.

Mueller, S., Thomas, A.S., & Jaeger, A.M. (2001). Culture and entrepreneurial potential: A nine-country study of locus of control and innovativeness. *Journal of Business Venturing*, 16: 51–75.

Nahapiet, J., & Ghoshal, S. (1998). Social capital, intellectual capital, and the organizational advantage. *Academy of Management Review*, 23: 242–266.

Nonaka, I. (1994). A dynamic theory of organizational knowledge creation. *Organization Science*, 5: 14–37.

Nonaka, I., & Takeuchi, H. (1995). *The Knowledge-Creating Company*. New York: Oxford University Press.

Oliver, A.L. (1997). On the nexus of organizations and professions: Networking through trust. *Sociological Inquiry*, 67: 227–245.

Oliver A.L. (2001). Strategic alliances and the learning life-cycle of biotechnology firms. *Organization Studies*, 22: 467–489.

Oliver, A.L. (2004). Biotechnology entrepreneurial scientists and their collaborations. *Research Policy*, 33: 583–597.

Oliver, A.L. (2008). University-based biotechnology spin-offs. In H. Patzelt &

T. Brenner (Eds.), *International Handbook Series on Entrepreneurship: Handbook of Bioentrepreneurship*, 193–210. New York: Springer.

Oliver, A.L., & Montgomery, K. (2001). A system cybernetic approach to individual and organizational trust formation. *Human Relations*, 54: 1045–1065.

Portes, A. (1997). Immigration theory for a new century: Some problems and opportunities. *International Migration Review*, 31: 799–825.

Portes, A., Guarnizo, L.E., Haller, W.J. (2002). Transnational entrepreneurs: An alternative form of immigrant economic adaptation. *American Sociological Review*, 67: 278–298.

Powell, W.W., Koput, K.W., & Smith-Doerr, L. (1996). Interorganizational collaboration and the locus of innovation: Networks of learning in biotechnology. *Administrative Science Quarterly*, 41: 116–145.

Powell, W.W., White, D.R., Koput , K.W., & Owen-Smith, J. (2005). Network dynamics and field evolution: The growth of interorganizational collaboration in the life sciences. *American Journal of Sociology*, 110: 1132–1205.

Saxenian, A. (2002). Brain circulation: How high-skill immigration makes everyone better off. *Brookings Review*, 20: 28–31.

Saxenian, A. (2005). From brain drain to brain circulation: Transnational communities and regional upgrading in India and China. *Studies in Comparative International Development*, 40: 35–61.

Séguin, B., State, L., Singer, P.A., & Daar, A.S. (2006). Scientific diasporas as an option for brain drain: Re-circulating knowledge for development. *International Journal of Biotechnology*, 8: 78–90.

Shane, S. (2004). *Academic Entrepreneurship: University Spinoffs and Wealth Creation*. Cheltenham: Edward Elgar.

Shane, S., & Venkatarman, S. (2000). The promise of entrepreneurship as a field of research. *Academy of Management Review*, 25: 217–226.

Tsai, W., & Ghoshal, S. (1998). Social capital and value creation: The role of intrafirm networks. *Academy of Management Journal*, 41: 464–476.

Zahra, S., & Dess, G.G. (2001). Entrepreneurship as a field of research: Encouraging dialogue and debate. *Academy of Management Review*, 26: 8–10.

4 Building Effective Networks: Network Strategy and Emerging Virtual Organizations

INGRID WAKKEE, PETER GROENEWEGEN, AND PAULA
DANSKIN ENGLIS

Recent studies have broadened the perspective on different types of social, virtual, and organizational networks (Byrne, 1993; Lawrence, Morse, & Fowler, 2005). Yet, few models have been developed so far that explain the behaviour of emerging transnational organizations and how these can become 'liberated from geographic constraints by quantum leaps in communications, computing, and transportation technologies; unbound from traditional organizational structures by ongoing experimentation in management technology,' and necessitated by mounting pressures of global competition (Parkhe, Wasserman, & Ralston, 2006: 560). The purpose of this chapter, therefore, is to examine how transnational entrepreneurs (TEs) become immersed in their country of origin, their host country, and even the rest of the world, and what the causal relationships are between networking strategies employed by such ventures and their usage of virtual and social networks.

Building on the literature in the field of organization science, social network theory, and entrepreneurship, we develop a matrix consisting of two dimensions: network structure and network strategy. The cells in the matrix give rise to a series of propositions regarding effective network building and how this leads to more traditional versus more virtual modes of organization.

In this chapter, we focus on a micro-level perspective in terms of organizational development and relate this development to the entire network rather than the ego-network, thereby discerning between small-world and scale-free network structures (Watts, 1999). Thus when examining what networking strategies lead to virtual modes of organizing, we explore how transnational entrepreneurs position themselves within already existing networks in their home and host country and how they create either new clusters/cliques or how they alternatively seek to establish the large number of ties needed to survive in scale-free network structures.

The chapter is organized as follows. First, we discuss the concept of transnational entrepreneurship (TE) from both a sociological and international management perspective. Second, we discuss the issue of virtualness in organizations including a review of common organizational characteristics for more virtual versus more traditional organizations. Next, we discuss to what extent previous insights into the role of social networks in organizational emergence can be aligned with the notion of virtualness in order to develop a better understanding of the development of transnational ventures. In our view, the level of virtualness of the organization impacts the way network ties support TE processes. We develop a conceptual model that suggests logical ways in which emerging virtual organizations may build effective networks versus more traditional organizations. The chapter closes with a discussion and conclusions.

Transnational Entrepreneurship

Yeung (2002: 30) conceptualizes transnational entrepreneurs as 'businesspersons who take specific proactive action to overcome inherent problems and difficulties associated with international business activities.' He argues that the actions of TEs are strongly influenced by 'the social and business networks, in which these transnational entrepreneurs are embedded, political-economic structures and dominant organizational and cultural practices in the home and host countries' (ibid.).

In sociological studies the concept of transnational entrepreneurship has been used to describe the activities of foreign minorities or ethnic entrepreneurs (EEs) in advanced societies or, alternatively, the activities of Western-educated immigrant engineers who return to their home country mobilizing their cross-country social networks to launch businesses that span international borders (Portes, Guarnizo, & Haller, 2002; Saxenian, 2002). A number of studies have noted the potential significance for TEs to stimulate economic growth in both the receiving country and the country of origin (Zhao, 2005; Saxenian, 2002).

Within the strategic management domain, Bartlett and Ghoshal (1989) discuss transnational strategy in terms of attaining the benefits of global and multidomestic strategies: thinking globally, acting locally.

Part of localization is that decision-making and knowledge generation are distributed among the units or entities of a transnational organization, and part of globalization is that this information and knowledge is learned and shared across the firm. The global goal is to integrate components of the business into the overall corporate structure, where each component becomes a source of specialized innovation, while the local goal is to tailor products and services to local needs (Child & Yan, 2001).

This strategic management perspective of transnationality was originally developed to explain the behaviour of large and established multinational corporations (MNCs); yet, over the last two decades, two interdependent forces, digitalization and globalization, have led to a world that is characterized by a sort of 'hyperconnectivity' in which even start-ups are confronted from inception with a need to internationalize their own activities or deal with international competition at home (McDougall & Oviatt, 2005). This leads to a new type of transnational venture that, in more than one country, is simultaneously involved in three interrelated aspects of the entrepreneurial process: (1) the control of resources in different countries (e.g., capital, information, and knowledge); (2) strategic management in different countries (e.g., innovative and creative deployment of resources); and (3) the creation and exploitation of opportunities in different countries (Yeung, 2002).

In the context of emerging organizations we view transnational entrepreneurship as being represented by a range of cross-border activities. One end is anchored by (temporary) social migration aspects connecting the host country to the home country, as often studied in sociology (Poros, 2001; Kyle, 2000; Basch, Schiller, & Blanc-Szanton, 1994), while the other end consists of strategic management activities simultaneously capturing global-scale efficiency, responding to national markets, and cultivating a worldwide learning capability for driving continuous innovation across borders (Bartlett & Ghoshal, 1989). Both ends of this spectrum are important and are substantially different from what is the case with domestic entrepreneurship (Zhao, 2002), and at both ends the emerging ventures have to manage the dual challenge of globally and locally gaining legitimacy, securing resources, and pursuing opportunities in more than one cultural, social, and economic context. Indeed, McDougall and Oviatt (1996: 36) argue that the internationalization of new ventures 'does not appear to be a simple matter of applying established strategies and procedures developed for a domestic arena. Successful internationalization appears to be accompanied by changes in venture strategy.'

Virtualness

The term *virtual* is commonly used to focus attention on those aspects of organization that are not physical or that mainly consist of information and information infrastructures. Two main perspectives on virtual firms can be identified. The first views virtual organizations as temporary alignment networks of alliances between independent ventures or individuals linked (more or less spontaneously) by information technology to share skills, costs, and access to one another's markets using international and communication technology (Byrne, 1993; Chudoba, Wynn, Lu, & Watson-Manheim, 2005; Jäger & Steenbakkers, 1997). Such alignments are directed at combining capabilities of partners to specific services or products.

In the second perspective, the label *virtual organization* is extended into an internal principle of organization within the enterprise (Sandhoff, 1999). The information revolution that has taken place in recent decades has resulted in a situation where almost all, previously physical, elements of an organization can be converted to virtual (Czerniawska & Potter, 1998). Virtualness, then, is a component of organizing as it takes the form of information-supported interaction to such a degree that it can be considered ubiquitous. Virtual organizations are characterized by digitized social interaction and production processes within the organization and in relation to external network ties. We adopt this latter perspective as we seek to explain how TEs build networks and become immerged in multiple countries.

In the literature attention to virtualness started with an interest in the increasing importance of information and communications technologies. The virtual organization is mentioned as a relevant response to accelerating market changes. Fast changes in consumer preferences and demand make it more difficult for traditional companies to respond in timely ways. One solution is to increasingly rely on temporary manufacturing, research, and marketing alliances with others. The resulting networks are geared to exploit a specific opportunity (Byrne, 1993; Hedberg et al., 1997). Hedberg coined the concept of the imaginary organization to get away from 'the infotechnical overtones of the term, "virtual"' (Hedberg et al., 1997: 9). Increased virtualness translates to a different type of organization requiring different management practices.

More recent discussions of virtual enterprise organizations reinforce this view (Chudoba et al., 2005). The label *virtual enterprise* is applicable in the case of tapered and non-integration strategies and can be framed in terms of network organizational structures (Fitzpatrick & Burke, 2001). In this way, transnational entrepreneurs can gain competitive advantages by providing customers with better and faster service in both the home and host country and possibly even beyond. One example offered by these authors in a manufacturing setting concerns a virtual enterprise that is constructed by partners from different companies, who collaborate with each other to design and manufacture high-quality and customized products. A virtual enterprise is product-oriented, the style is team collaboration, and it features fast and flexible operations. Thus, being an entity constructed from a variety of elements in a loose assemblage that can be disconnected with much effort, a virtual enterprise is distinctively different from a traditional enterprise (Dowlatshahi & Cao, 2006).

Logically flowing from this view is the claim that virtual organizations are constantly in flux, existing but changing. Saabeel et al. (2002) combined the structural and the process views of virtualness in organizations to characterize virtual organizations in three different layers: a universe of modules, a dynamic web, and a dynamic organization. Each layer has its own structural and process characteristics. The notion of change denotes the interaction between the various layers; one layer is coupled to the next. The creation of a common purpose leads to the linking of several independent modules into a dynamic web. If subsequently market opportunities arise, the web may coalesce into a dynamic organization. When value is no longer generated from the opportunity, the organization falls apart into the original modules (Saabeel et al., 2002).

Regarding virtual as process creates the possibility to abandon the binary either/or logic implicitly adopted by many authors and to blur the boundary between traditional and virtual organizations. Indeed, 'firms become more virtual when a larger proportion of important production processes occur outside of traditional organization boundaries' (Kraut et al., 1999: 723–4).

More than two decades ago, Daft and Lengel (1984) argued that new organizing methods, such as virtualization, are likely to affect the extent to which organizational boundaries become increasingly blurred. Thus, traditional firms are likely to have more closed boundaries and virtual firms are likely to have permeable boundaries. Combining the insights from these previous studies, Table 4.1 shows the difference between traditional organizing and virtualizing organizations.

Table 4.1
Difference between Traditional and Virtual Organizations

Dimension	Traditional	Virtual
(Physical) Structure	Building	Platform
Boundary	Fixed entity	Permeable
Location	Place	Space
Governance	Command and control	Community and coalition
Existence	Finalization	Flux

Source: Derived from Schultze and Orlikowski (2001).

The five dimensions included in Table 4.1 will be used in the remainder of this chapter to determine the degree of virtualness in transnational entrepreneurship. Yet, to fully understand how TEs become embedded in existing networks operating in their home, host, or even global markets we first need to establish the interaction between virtual organizing and social relations. Following Fowler, Lawrence, and Morse (2004), we conclude that there are three main differences between socially and virtually embedded ties. First, while socially embedded ties are multiplex and characterized by high levels of reciprocity (Coleman, 1988), virtual ties are likely to be dedicated ties that are easily abandoned after completing a specific task. Second, due to the possibility to rely on electronic forms of communication rather than frequent face-to-face interaction, virtual ties are much less constrained geographically than social ties. Finally, while most socially embedded ties are based on dyadic relationships, virtual ties are typically based on clusters or coalitions in which multiple ties interact simultaneously with each other. Consequently, virtualness potentially breaches the gap between arm's-length and embedded social ties (Fowler, Lawrence, & Morse, 2004; Morse, Fowler, & Lawrence, 2007).

In the following section, we briefly describe how virtualness affects the emergence of new ventures operating in global markets. Then we examine what virtual network structures and strategies are associated with TE in increasingly global markets.

Transnational Entrepreneurship and Virtualness

The recognition of opportunities is at the heart of entrepreneurship, and it is the focus on this process that sets entrepreneurship studies apart from other management and strategy disciplines (Venkataraman, 1997). The process of recognizing opportunities has been widely studied in recent years (Ardichvili, Cardozo, & Ray, 2003; Baron, 2006; Krueger & Dickson, 1994), yet seldom within the context of the virtualization of transnational business. The widespread use of the Internet, however, has not led to the decline of real world opportunity recognition but, on the contrary, has led to additional possibilities for entrepreneurs to connect information that leads to the discovery of new ideas in several ways (Teece, 1998). First, the borderless nature of the Internet has led people to exchange new information with new people around the world that they would not have shared (at all) through other communication channels (Pantelli, 2002). This has allowed TEs to (re-)establish or maintain ties in their country of origin in a much more efficient and effective manner than they could have done even two decades ago. By bridging (previous) structural holes in this manner (Burt, 2004), entrepreneurs are able to connect pieces of information and possibly recognize opportunities to exploit in the real world. Second, well-known e-commerce examples have shown that not only the process of opportunity recognition can exist in the virtual world, but some opportunities exist only in virtual space leading to the rise of new industries (see, e.g., Shapiro & Varian, 1999).

To understand how transnational entrepreneurs actually create value from opportunities we need to take two additional processes into consideration: building a resource base and gaining legitimacy (Elfring & Hulsink, 2003). Building a resource base (Brush et al., 2001; Garnsey, 1998) is essential to develop ideas into opportunities and exploit these successfully across borders. It is highly unlikely that the required resources are available in adequate amounts within the newly formed organization. Moreover, in the early stages of new venture emergence, no revenues are generated to obtain these resources in the marketplace (Brito, 2001).

As argued by Morse, Fowler, and Lawrence (2007), the way transnational entrepreneurs can obtain access to resources, despite their lack of initial (financial) resources to buy others, has changed considerably in the virtual world. First, by becoming virtually embedded TEs can gain access to and acquire external skills, services, and systems that were not previously attainable in either the home or the host country alone. Also, in a virtual environment both the number of potential external network ties and the speed at which the relationships can be established has increased considerably. The establishment of expert and trade communities allows for checking the reputation of external parties and the exchange of information with collegial ventures at distant but similar markets. Consequently, it becomes easier to select exchange partners offering good quality goods at the lowest possible prices. Finally, access to funding has become more widespread and easier to locate in the virtual world (e.g., grants and scholarships are advertised online). Alternatively, potential investors can also become aware of the transnational entrepreneur's activities and can make an informed investment decision more easily once the TE has made his or her own presence known online (Morse, Fowler, & Lawrence, 2007).

Gaining legitimacy involves the process by which transnational entrepreneurs become established and accepted in the home and host market in a sustainable manner, overcoming their 'liability of newness' (Aldrich & Fiol, 1994; Stinchcombe, 1965). Organizational emergence is typified by significant levels of ambivalence (Gartner, Bird, & Starr, 1992) and uncertainty in relation to resources, routines, products, and the environment as the emerging venture seeks to do something it has never done before (Hite & Hesterly, 2001: 277). As argued previously, virtualness is grounded not only in the fact that these TEs are communicating online but also in the way they emerge, organize, and compete (Ehrler, Schögel, & Zimmermann, 1999; Teece, 1998). Clearly, this has a significant impact on the way that emerging virtual ventures build legitimacy (Fowler, Lawrence, & Morse, 2004). Specifically, online communication allows for the widespread dissemination of information regarding the TE's own reliability and helps TEs develop insight into the reliability of their potential trading partners regardless of their location. Further, as argued above, virtual TEs have more possibilities for gaining access to services, networks, and (financial) resources from their country of origin through online communication. By building a resource base more quickly, transnational entrepreneurs are able to reduce their liability of newness, gain market power in both the home and the host country, improve efficiency, and enhance learning (Butler & Croner, 1986), thereby becoming more legitimate partners for others in the industry regardless of their location.

Social Networking and Entrepreneurship

Network Structure

Many authors have indicated that a transnational entrepreneur's strategic advantages or ability to recognize and exploit opportunities flow from his or her position in the network. Entrepreneurs who are more central are more innovative and grow faster (Powell, Koput, & Smith-Doerr, 1996; Powell et al., 1999). Occupying a structural hole may endow the entrepreneur with information benefits that stimulate new approaches and innovation (Ahuja, 2000). To benefit fully from network positions TEs could benefit from awareness of the structure and the composition of the network. However, in reality, most TEs only have a limited overview of the networks surrounding them in their home and host countries and this is even more the case for the global networks (Shipilov, 2006). At the same time, we do expect that most TEs have a basic understanding of how their network is structured and will at least be able to differentiate between relevant connections, have an insight into the benefits of adding new ties, or 'sense' the advantages of structural holes. This would entail network navigation engaging in different strategies in order to improve their network position. The first of the elements of a strategy is obviously engaging in adding relations that enhance the network position. The second is playing on the cognitive reasons for which potential partners may become interested in engaging with the entrepreneur, for instance, by enhancing the salience of the entrepreneurial efforts (Fund et al., 2008).

Two recently introduced characterizations of networks – small world and scale free (Watts, 1999) – represent different social processes of the ordering of ties between actors that seem particularly important in the open information and collaboration environment shaped by virtualness. In this chapter we use these two types of network to extend the theories on social cohesion (Coleman, 1988) and brokerage positions between parties (Burt, 1992) to accommodate the influence of networks as more than the effects of bounded and sometimes local social structures. In a way the large-scale networks from which these characterizations are derived extend the relevant network environment for analysis of TE; although the theoretical explanation is still lacking, there is increasing evidence of the similarity in network topography of large (international) systems and TEs.

Small-world networks are characterized by dense cliques of actors connected by relationships that cut across cliques, acting as conduits for information and control (White, 1970). Small-world networks are known for their high degree of clustering and short path length. *Clustering* refers to the likelihood of two members of a network having a high chance of being acquainted if they have one or more acquaintances in common. *Path length* refers to the existence of short paths through network structures that link pairs (Watts & Strogatz, 1998). A large body of research supports the widespread presence of the small-world network structure (Adamic & Huberman, 2001; Davis, Yoo, & Baker, 2003; Newman, 2000; Powell et al., 2005; Uzzi & Spiro, 2005; Watts, 1999; Watts & Strogatz, 1998). Increased virtual connectedness through the actions by TEs induces possibilities to maintain more random ties and, because of the representation of activities and ideas of diverse groups, fosters the identification of potential gaps that can be breached between dense clusters. Thus, by knitting together various clusters with relatively little effort, a diverse set of capable global communities can be tapped into.

Scale-free network structures have a highly skewed degree of distribution of their network ties over the nodes in the network. Thus, a small number of members are connected with high numbers of others through a disproportionately large number of ties (Barabasi & Albert, 1999). With only a few steps, adding ties to well-connected others brings transnational entrepreneurs into contact with a huge number of other potential partners.

Both types of networks exhibit properties that are relevant to entrepreneurial action. The closely linked, dense network clusters characteristic of the small world may represent specialist communities with regard to knowledge; similar clusters may also be representative for niche markets. The clustering represents social groups that offer the possibility to become bridged, allowing for the exploitation of opportunities arising from demand or differentiation in expert knowledge. As Burt (2005) argues, while structural holes may offer rewards, they also may be logical places not to be bridged.

Scale-free networks are representative of a different type of social connection. When the network linkages represent demand for whatever the node can deliver, a node with a high number of linkages can be said to have a higher status (Podolny, 2005). For entrepreneurial action it might imply that maintaining high-status positions requires less time and effort. In addition, such nodes may introduce possibilities for quick interconnections. When seeking out others with high connectedness, the visibility in virtual space can be considered to be much higher.

Introducing the terminology from characterizations of large-scale networks allows for two steps in our model: it identifies dispersed but locally cohesive clusters that seem to be characteristic for the ordering of social and economic activities in the global economy, and it introduces the sort of hyperconnectivity that is part of large-scale networks in the networked world. While the first is related to the emergence and interconnections of specialist communities, the latter is a logical representation not only of a changed world but also of the increased communicative networking capabilities in virtual entrepreneurship.

Network Strategy

Except for some research on alliance strategies and the underlying processes of partner choice (Gulati & Gargiulo, 1999; Gulati & Singh, 1998), there is a surprising lack of network strategy analysis – how a firm chooses network partners. One exception is called the Scandinavian school of network strategy analysis (Gadde & Håkånsson, 2001; Håkånsson, 1989). Only recently has broader attention to network strategy been emerging (Baum & Rowley, 2008). Within this stream of literature, network cognition is seen as individual and dependent on the ability to convert available information on parties dependent on attention to the position of those other parties (van Liere, Koppius, & Vervest, 2008). The transnational entrepreneur is bound to use substantial knowledge of the network environment to inform alliance formation and network strategy. Do entrepreneurs manage their networks or do the networks manage the entrepreneurs? Who has control? Managing a network involves a complex sequence of moves and countermoves, adjustments and readjustments, actions and reactions, and even non-actions (McGuire, 2002). As argued by Baum, Shipilov, and Rowley (2003), small-world networks may arise from chance connections among firms in different cliques. In both scale-free and small-world networks we can often observe insurgent partnering by peripheral firms to improve their network position and controlled partnering by core firms to maintain their position.

These arguments suggest that we can distinguish between two types of network strategies: purposeful strategies that are characterized by a high level of strategic intent (Osland & Yaprak, 1995) or serendipitive strategies where TEs decide to 'go with the flow' and see where the network takes them (Andel, 1994). Purposeful strategies allow TEs to remain in control when seeking new strategies to compete effectively and survive, particularly in rapidly evolving industries and markets (Osland & Yaprak, 1995: 52), and to maintain their autonomy in other areas (Kosa & Lewin, 2000). Proactive engagement can also help TEs reduce the uncertainty that is inherent in doing business within and across borders (Osland & Yaprak, 1995). Indeed, networks offer a 'powerful means for adaptation in turbulent or uncertain environments' (Kosa & Lewin, 2000: 147), which may be essential for emerging transnational organizations.

Emerging transnational ventures pursuing purposeful network strategies can take a few approaches. When operating in a small-world network structure, they could try to establish connections with a large number of ties in different cliques across countries and thereby improve their own position in the network moving away from the periphery (Madhavan et al., 2008). Alternatively, when embedded in a scale-free network they could attempt to establish a connection to those network actors who have a disproportionate number of ties, as this would not only help them to gain access to resources but also to establish legitimacy relatively quickly and at low cost (Elfring & Hulsink, 2003).

At first glance, it seems that emerging transnational organizations that do not use proactive engagement to manage their networks but rather opt for the serendipitive approach are likely to be managed by the network. Yet, as pointed out by Baum, Shipilov, and Rowley (2003), chance connections are important in the formation of small-world networks. This suggests that a serendipitive strategy involving random rewiring from the perspective of the individual entrepreneur can make sense. Too much planning (or intent) may cause the TE to be less alert to the external environment or block out potentially relevant information that could possibly lead to the recognition of new opportunities (Gaglio & Katz, 2001; Kirzner, 1973, 1979, 1997). Further, planned behaviour is not always possible (Saxenian, 1994). Organizations may need to give up some autonomy and call on uncommon managerial skills (i.e., managing between organizations rather than within them). This is particularly difficult for emerging organizations and the TEs who lead them since they have few slack resources, and the TEs may have limited experience outside their own organization and little or undeveloped network management skills. This may be compounded when the TE is engaged in an industry area that is not clearly defined or is changing at an unstable pace. In these situations, a large number of random connections may be required (Stacey, 1995). In terms of network structure this would fit the so called scale-free phenomenon (Baum, Shipilov, & Rowley, 2003). By building random connections TEs can create linkages to communities and groups that have different backgrounds and perspectives, creating opportunities for new ventures.

The Model

Attempts to capitalize on new markets created by open access to organizing information on the Internet have altered the nature of entrepreneurial processes. However, the fundamental changes in the conditions under which TE processes take place due to virtual modes of organizing and networking and their effects on these TE processes have hitherto scarcely been assessed in entrepreneurial theory. We expect that transnational ventures that are more virtually organized will be positioned differently in their network and use different network strategies during their emergence than more traditional transnational ventures do. Virtualness eases the scanning for information regarding market opportunities and regarding potentially fruitful business models and partners to exploit these opportunities. When connectivity is used for monitoring, adjustment, and planning, it allows emerging TEs to operate without actually gaining ownership over the resources they need to exploit the recognized opportunity. Lastly, increased accessibility to information on other companies, their operations, and needs allows TEs to draw on a wide variety of examples and schemas and enables them to adjust their legitimization strategies accordingly (Ruef, 2002).

We expect that network structures and strategies change during each of the three processes. Although authors often present these processes of opportunity recognition, gaining legitimacy, and resource building as if they were constructed in a way that appears to be linear and sequential, in fact, the process is dynamic and iterative (Bygrave, Sexton, & Kasarda, 1992; Ropo & Hunt, 1995). As shown in Figure 4.1 as the processes unfold, changing circumstances may require actions to change or go back on certain decisions.

In the following section we develop a model in which we connect these two domains by suggesting plausible strategies for each of the three entrepreneurial processes (Van Der Veen & Wakkee, 2006).

The starting point for our model is a matrix consisting of structure and strategy as depicted in Figure 4.2. We argue that emerging organizations may utilize each of the four resulting quadrants in order to become immersed in their market of choice. In the following paragraphs we argue how virtual and traditional TEs move through the different quadrants during their processes of opportunity recognition, gaining legitimacy, and building a resource base dependent on their level of virtualness.

Opportunity Recognition

A classic insight from social network theory, that is, brokerage and closure (Burt, 2005), is when a known multitude of loosely unconnected or

Figure 4.1: A model of organizational emergence

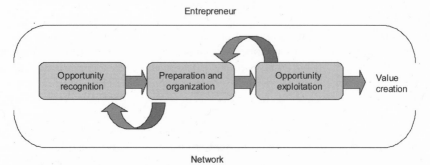

Source: Van Der Veen and Wakkee (2006).

Figure 4.2: The impact of network strategy and structure on emerging virtual organizations

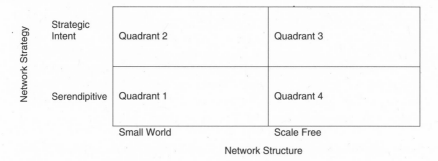

sparsely connected regions exists using strategic intent to occupy and maintain structural holes as active bridged groups. Brokerage allows emerging ventures to benefit from clearly articulated needs or insights in coherent communities or market niches. Increased networking capability will lead to the ability to organize linkages to a larger variety of groups. A large number of random connections in a network is more likely to increase creativity and, perhaps, opportunity recognition. While recognition of differences is essential, it is not clear from the outset that advantages may be obtained. Although brokerage is an articulate act, it would be extraordinary for the connection of clusters providing new ideas that only the TE would benefit with a clear vision of the over-all structure. Thus, by undertaking more random or serendipitive connections in a network, a TE is more likely to develop a highly flexible response to external environmental opportunities. Therefore, the strategy of non-proactive network engagement or even 'muddling through' (Lindblom, 1959) may be more appropriate for acquiring new ideas in highly competitive, emerging technological arenas (Quinn, 1980).

We argue that transnational organizations that are more virtually organized will be better able to follow these desired patterns of interaction than traditional transnational firms. The low marginal costs of adding additional contacts and the ability to connect to individuals and organizations around the globe facilitates occupying positions of brokerage as well as random rewiring, allowing entrepreneurs to bridge structural holes and connect pieces of information that lead to the recognition of opportunities (Burt, 1992). Further, in the virtual world, the exchange of information does not only take place on a dyadic level between individuals and organizations but rather in so-called communities of problem solving that can be characterized as small-world networks. The existence of communities of problem solving implies that online structural holes do not exist between individuals but rather between communities. This means that if TEs are searching for opportunities they should become aware of the capabilities of multiple communities. If they engage in interaction with these communities, they either can forge linkages from within the community or between communities. While Burt's (2004) structural-hole argument is based on both information differentiation and networking efficiency, in terms of the energy spent on contacts, the shift to virtual ties enables a broader range of strategies. More time implies a potentially closer alliance with relevant communities across borders, even perhaps embeddedness in more than one community, as well as the ability to occupy more gaps between clusters in different countries. The main benefit of doing so is that entrepreneurs are not only able to obtain access to information from various sources, but to use information that has been validated within and by the communities where it originates (Fowler, Lawrence, & Morse, 2004). These different forms of network engagement or strategy are more likely to produce a changing variety of emergent patterns of interaction to match external change. The underlying combination of virtualness and small network characteristics leads to a higher number of small network linkages.

Proposition 1: During opportunity recognition, transnational entrepreneurs with emerging virtual organizations are more likely to encounter more un-

intentional contact with a variety of clusters to recognize opportunities than transnational entrepreneurs with emerging traditional organizations (thus they will operate in Quadrant 1).

Building a Resource Base

To develop ideas into opportunities and exploit these successfully, emerging ventures must build a resource base (Brush et al., 2001). Limited size and age make it unlikely that the resource base is available within the boundary of the firm or that it can be obtained by economic transactions in the marketplace. Social networking has often been seen as the main way to compensate for this lack (e.g., Birley, 1985; Elfring & Hulsink, 2003). It has been argued that particularly strong ties (Elfring & Hulsink, 2003; Granovetter, 1973) should be used for this purpose as they might be willing to provide resources below market price. In a traditional world only a limited number of strong ties can be maintained (Granovetter, 1973; White & Houseman, 2003). This suggests that purposeful establishment of linkages to so-called super nodes or hubs in scale-free networks is a fruitful strategy for building a resource base. By being connected to a much larger than average share of contacts in the network, these super nodes provide the network with searchability from a global perspective (Barabasi & Albert, 1999). As such connections are available to competitors, these network contacts will mainly function to routinize connections to resources such as capital that are accessed on a regular basis.

Proposition 2a: Transnational entrepreneurs with emerging traditional organizations are more likely to engage in purposefully establishing connection to super nodes in scale-free networks to develop a resource base than transnational entrepreneurs with emerging virtual organizations (thus they will operate in Quadrant 4).

It has been suggested that the more virtual a venture is, the more likely it uses resources that are external to the company while more traditional ventures seek to gain access to resources by obtaining ownership of these or by creating them internally (Kraut et al., 1999). This approach leads to a focus on establishing partnerships for exploiting their opportunity (Dowlatshahi & Cao, 2006; Fitzpatrick & Burke, 2001). As argued previously, these (information-based) capabilities are developed not through dyadic interactions, but in different clusters and coalitions.

In a virtual world, the limited marginal costs associated with adding (virtual) connections enable TEs operating in small-world networks to easily and rapidly access a vast range of individuals, organizations, and communities with specialized information, skills, and experience. In such networks, the actors are not as much motivated by reciprocal services and the need to build long-term socially embedded relationships as by expected return in reputation effects stemming from the visible exchange of information and other resources within the coalition (Fowler, Lawrence, & Morse, 2004; Morse, Fowler, & Lawrence 2007). To benefit from this, TEs operating in small-world networks will engage in purposefully establishing connections to various functionally differentiated clusters. Their ability to organize their resources in this way may be based on elements that are traditionally regarded as internal to such production capacity or external with suppliers or in cooperation with customers. Constraints on working together in this fashion are eased by the ability to apply a variety of tools provided by interconnectedness and digital content of primary processes. Therefore, with regard to emerging small-world networks, we expect strategies to be stable in Quadrant 2. Thus, the following proposition is offered:

Proposition 2b: Transnational entrepreneurs with emerging virtual organizations are more likely to purposefully establish contacts with a variety of clusters in small-world networks to build their resource base than transnational entrepreneurs with emerging traditional organizations (thus they will operate in Quadrant 2).

Gaining Legitimacy

To establish a market position and overcome their 'liability of newness' (Aldrich & Fiol, 1994; Stinchcombe, 1965), all emerging ventures need to gain legitimacy. It is well known in classic network theory that ventures that are connected to a common partner can obtain reliable information about each other from that partner (Baker, 1990; Burt & Knez, 1995; Elfring & Hulsink, 2003).

As argued by Stuart, Hoang, and Hybels (1999), particularly new ventures that are based on radical innovations or business models need endorsements from some of the prominent players in the industry, as their information is often considered more valuable than that of less prominent players. Because prominent players are also expected to have a higher than average connectivity, being associated with such 'super nodes' also increases the visibility of the new venture (Barabasi & Albert, 1999). Thus, it seems that establishing connections to super nodes in scale-free networks would seem to be a favourable strategy in this situation. Such strategies are also common in building relations by high-tech ventures, for instance, associating with large companies to establish credibility. We argue that TEs who operate in a virtual mode can more easily identify organizations with characteristics relevant for them. Thus, we propose:

Proposition 3a: Transnational entrepreneurs with emerging traditional organizations are more likely to engage in purposefully establishing connection to super nodes in scale-free networks to build legitimacy than transnational entrepreneurs with emerging virtual organizations (thus they will operate in Quadrant 4).

In the context of virtual networks, however, the high level of connectedness of small-world networks will lead information to spread and be validated rapidly within the cluster (Fowler, Lawrence, & Morse, 2004; Morse, Fowler, & Lawrence, 2007). Emerging TEs can thus build reputation by contributing small pieces of information to the discussions in the cluster even without being connected directly to a prominent partner with above average connectivity. In small-world networks, new ventures thus benefit from the fleeting character and randomness of virtual contacts across geographically dispersed clusters to spread reputation, thus fostering the development of legitimacy beyond their local network. Thus the final proposition offered is:

Proposition 3b: During legitimization, transnational entrepreneurs with emerging virtual organizations will be more likely to use unintentional contacts with small-world networks to build legitimacy than transnational entrepreneurs with emerging traditional organizations.

Discussion and Conclusion

The purpose of this chapter has been to examine how emerging organizations become immersed in the markets in which they operate and what the causal relationships are between network strategies that are enabled by a switch from social to more virtual networks. We argued that it is important to consider how emerging ventures position themselves within an existing network, how they are enabled by new tools to create linkages with a variety of clusters/cliques, and how they are able to establish a large number of ties, leading to a discussion of options open in a small-world or scale-free network. In particular we focused on the differences between virtual and traditional emerging organizations in relation to their network strategies and structures during the processes of opportunity recognition, resource-building, and gaining legitimacy and formulated propositions associated with these differences. Clearly, future research is required to elaborate these propositions and test them in an empirical setting. Yet, with this conceptual chapter, we contribute to several theoretical debates within entrepreneurship and networking.

The main contribution is a theoretical framework that starts to specify two developments that characterize organizing in the Internet age. First, we are drawing attention to the potential application of recent discussions on social network theory. The propositions address the challenges to develop theory that makes use of these new tools (Uzzi & Spiro, 2005). Both small-world and scale-free networks suggest strategy formation in a way that may be based on enabling and limiting embedded action because of the added abilities of virtualization. Also our approach promises continuity with core elements of the research body on brokerage and closure on the role of structure. The main new opening concerns the extension of virtualization.

Our work also contributes to the theory of transnational entrepreneurship. Despite the fact that many scholars have pointed to the importance of the Internet in explaining the emergence of international and transnational new ventures, until now a theoretical conceptualization regarding virtualization of both networks and business models was absent from the debate within the TE field. Following Kleinberg (2000), we showed that network structure is important not only locally (i.e., because an entrepreneur's neighbourhood provides access to the information and resources to recognize and exploit opportunities) but also globally, as it enables the entrepreneur to navigate when searching for information and resources outside his or her neighbourhood (Watts, 2004). This might explain how transnational new ventures have been able to become involved in activities around the world from a very early stage in their existence.

ACKNOWLEDGMENTS

The authors thank the anonymous reviewers of the Academy of Management Conference 2007, as well as the organizers and participants of the NeXt (Centre for Nascent Entrepreneurship and the Exploitation of Technology) Conference, 28 April 2008, at Wilfrid Laurier University.

REFERENCES

Adamic, L.A., & Huberman, B.A. (2001). The Web's hidden order. *Communications of the ACM*, 44(9): 55–60.

Ahuja. (2000). The duality of collaboration: Inducements and opportunities in the formation of interfirm linkages. *Strategic Management Journal*, 21: 317–343.

Aldrich, H.E., & Fiol, C.M. (1994). Fools rush in? The institutional context of industry creation. *Academy of Management Review*, 19(4): 645–670.

Andel, P. (1994). Anatomy of the unsought finding serendipity: Origin, history, domains, traditions, appearances, patterns and programmability. *British Journal for the Philosophy of Science*, 45(2): 631–648.

Ardichvili, A., Cardozo, R., & Ray, S. (2003). A theory of entrepreneurial opportunity identification and development. *Journal of Business Venturing*, 18(1): 105–123.

Baker, W.E. (1990). Market networks and corporate behavior. *American Journal of Sociology*, 96: 589–625.

Barabasi, A.L., & Albert, R. (1999). Emergence of scaling in random networks. *Science*, 286: 509–551.

Baron, R.A. (2006). Opportunity recognition as pattern recognition: How entrepreneurs 'connect the dots' to identify new business opportunities. *Academy of Management Perspectives*, 20(1): 104–119.

Bartlett, C.A., & Ghoshal, S. (1989). *Managing across Borders: The Transnational Solution*. Boston: Harvard Business School Press.

Basch, L., Glick Schiller, N., & Szanton Blanc, C. (1994). *Nations Unbound: Transnational Projects, Postcolonial Predicaments, and Deterritorialized Nation States*. Amsterdam: Gordon and Breach.

Baum, J.A., & Rowley, T.J. (2008). Evolving webs in network economies. In J.A. Baum and T.J. Rowley (Eds.), *Advances in Strategic Management*, vol. 25, xiii–xxxiii. Oxford: Emerald.

Baum, J.A., Shipilov, A.V., & Rowley, T.J. (2003). Where do small worlds come from? *Industrial & Corporate Change*, 12(4): 697–725.

Birley, S. (1985). The role of networks in the entrepreneurial process. *Journal of Business Venturing*, 1: 107–117.

Brito, C.M. (2001). Towards an institutional theory of the dynamics of industrial networks. *Journal of Business & Industrial Marketing* 16(3): 150–166.

Brush, C.G., Greene, P.G., Hart, M.M., & Haller, H.S. (2001). From initial idea to unique advantage: The entrepreneurial challenge of constructing a resource base. *Academy of Management Executive,* 15(1): 64–78.

Burt, R.S. (1992). *Structural Holes: The Social Structure of Competition.* Cambridge: Harvard University Press.

Burt, R.S. (2004). Structural holes and good ideas. *American Journal of Sociology,* 110: 349–399.

Burt, R.S. (2005). *Brokerage and Closure: An Introduction to Social Capital.* Oxford: Oxford University Press.

Burt, R.S., & Knez, M. (1995). Kinds of third-party effects on trust. *Rationality and Society,* 7: 225–292.

Butler, R., & Croner, M. (1986). Strategy and strategic choice: The case of telecommunications. *Strategic Management Journal,* 7: 161–177.

Bygrave, W., Sexton, D., & Kasarda, J. (1992). *The State of the Art of Entrepreneurship.* Boston: PWS-Kent.

Byrne, J.A. (1993). The virtual corporation. *Business Week,* 8: 98–103.

Child, J., & Yan, Y. (2001). National and transnational effects in international business. *Management International Review,* 41(1): 53–75.

Chudoba, K.M., Wynn, E., Lu, M., & Watson-Manheim, M.B. (2005). How virtual are we? Measuring virtuality and understanding its impact in a global organization. *Information Systems Journal,* 15(4): 279–306.

Coleman, J.S. (1988). Social capital in the creation of human-capital. *American Journal of Sociology,* 94: 95–120.

Czerniawska, F., & Potter, G. (1998). *Business in a Virtual World: Exploiting Information for Competitive Advantage.* Houndmills: Macmillan.

Daft, R.L., & Lengel, R.H. (1984). Information richness: A new approach to managerial information processing and organizational design. *Research in Organizational Behavior,* 6: 191–234.

Davis, G.F., Yoo, M., & Baker, W.E. (2003). The small world of the American corporate elite, 1982–2001. *Strategic Organization,* 1(3): 301–326.

Dowlatshahi, S., & Cao, O. (2006). The relationships among virtual enterprise, information technology, and business performance in agile manufacturing: An industry perspective. *European Journal of Operational Research,* 174(2): 835–860.

Ehrler, B., Schögel, M., & Zimmermann, H.D. (1999). The virtualization of value creation. *Journal of Organizational Virtualness,* 1(1): 262–264.

Elfring, T., & Hulsink, W. (2003). Networks in entrepreneurship: The case of high-technology firms. *Small Business Economics,* 21(4): 409–422.

Fitzpatrick, W.M., & Burke, D.R. (2001). Virtual venturing and entry barriers: Redefining the strategic landscape. *SAM Advanced Management Journal,* 66(4): 22–30.

Fowler, S.W., Lawrence, T.B., & Morse, E.A. (2004). Virtually embedded ties. *Journal of Management,* 30(5): 647–666.

Fund, B.R., Pollock, T.G., Baker, T., & Wowak, A.J, (2008). Who's the new kid? The process of developing centrality in venture capitalist deal networks. *Network Strategy,* 25: 563–593.

Gadde, L.E., & Håkånsson, H. (2001). *Supply Network Strategies.* Chichester: Wiley.

Gaglio, C.M., & Katz, J. (2001). The psychological basis of opportunity identification: Entrepreneurial alertness. *Small Business Economics,* 16: 95–111.

Garnsey, E. (1998). A theory of the early growth of the firm. *Industrial and Corporate Change,* 7(3): 523–556.

Gartner, W.B., Bird, B.J., & Starr, J.A. (1992). Acting as if: Differentiating entrepreneurial from organizational behavior. *Entrepreneurship Theory & Practice,* 16(3): 13–31.

Granovetter, M. (1973). The strength of weak ties. *American Journal of Sociology,* 78(6): 1360–1380.

Gulati, R., & Gargiulo, M. (1999). Where do interorganizational networks come from? *American Journal of Sociology,* 104(5): 1439–1493.

Gulati, R., & Singh, H. (1998). The architecture of cooperation: Managing coordination costs and appropriation concerns in strategic alliances. *Administrative Science Quarterly,* 43: 781–814.

Håkånsson, H. (1989). *Corporate Technological Behaviour, Co-operation and Networks.* London: Routledge.

Hedberg, B., Dahlgren, G., Hansson, J., & Olve, N.G. (1997). *Virtual Organizations and Beyond: Discover Imaginary Systems.* Baffins Lane: Wiley.

Hite, J.M., & Hesterly, W.S. (2001). The evolution of firm networks: From emergence to early growth of the firm. *Strategic Management Journal,* 22: 275–286.

Jäger, H.W.J., & Steenbakkers, S. (1997). Characteristics of virtual organizations. *Electronic Journal of Organizational Virtualness,* 1: 65–76.

Kirzner, I. (1973). *Competition and Entrepreneurship.* Chicago: University of Chicago Press.

Kirzner, I. (1979). *Perception, Opportunity and Profit: Studies in the Theories of Entrepreneurship.* Chicago: University of Chicago Press.

Kirzner, I. (1997). Entrepreneurial discovery and the competitive market process: An Austrian approach. *Journal of Economic Literature,* 35: 60–85.

Kleinberg, J. (2000). Navigation in a small world. *Nature,* 406(6798): 845.

Kosa, M., & Lewin, A. (2000). Managing partnerships and strategic alliances: Raising the odds of success. *European Journal of Management,* 18(2): 146–151.

Kraut, R.C., Steinfield, A.P., Butler, B., Chan, A.P., & Hoag, A. (1999). Coordination and virtualization: The role of electronic networks and personal relationships. *Organization Science*, 10(6): 722–740.

Krueger, N., & Dickson, P.R. (1994). How believing in ourselves increases risk taking: Perceived self-efficacy and opportunity recognition. *Decision Sciences*, 25(3): 385–400.

Kyle, D. (2000). *Transnational Peasants: Migrations, Networks, and Ethnicity in Andean Ecuador*. Baltimore: Johns Hopkins University Press.

Lawrence, T.B., Morse, E.A., & Fowler, S.W. (2005). Managing your portfolio of connections. *MIT Sloan Management Review*, 46(2): 59–62.

Lindblom, C.E. (1959). The science of 'muddling through.' *Public Administration Review*, 19: 79–88.

Madhavan, R., Caner, T., Prescott, J., & Koka, B. (2008). *Networking as an Antecedent to Network Structure*. Bingly, UK: JAI/Emerald.

McDougall, P.P., & Oviatt, B.M. (1996). New venture internationalization, strategy, change, and performance: A follow-up study. *Journal of Business Venturing*, 11(1): 23–40.

McGuire, M. (2002). Managing networks: Propositions on what managers do and why they do it. *Public Administration Review*, 62(5): 599–609.

Morse, E., Fowler, S., & Lawrence, T. (2007). The impact of virtual embeddedness on new venture survival: Overcoming the liabilities of newness. *Entrepreneurship Theory & Practice*, 31(2): 139–159.

Newman, M.E.J. (2000). Models of the small world. *Journal of Statistical Physics*, 101(3): 819–841.

Osland, G.E., &Yaprak, A. (1995). Learning through strategic alliances. *European Journal of Marketing*, 29(3): 52–66.

Oviatt, B.M., & McDougall, P.P. (2005). Defining international entrepreneurship and modeling the speed of internationalization. *Entrepreneurship Theory & Practice*, 29: 537–554.

Pantelli, N. (2002). Richness, power cues, and Email text. *Information & Management*, 40: 75–78.

Parkhe, A., Wasserman, S., & Ralston, D. (2006). New frontiers in network theory development. *Academy of Management Review*, 31: 560–568.

Podolny, J.M. (2005). *Status Signals: A Sociological Study of Market Competition*. Princeton: Princeton University Press.

Poros, M.V. (2001). The role of migrant networks in linking local labour markets: The case of Asian Indian migration to New York and London. *Global Networks: A Journal of Transnational Affairs*, 1: 243–260.

Portes, A., Guamizo, L.M., & Haller, W.J. (2002). Transnational entrepreneurs: An alternative form of immigrant economic adaptation. *American Sociological Review*, 67: 278–298.

Powell, W.W., Koput, K.W., & Smith-Doerr, L. (1996). Interorganizational collaboration and the locus of innovation: Networks of learning in biotechnology. *Administrative Science Quarterly*, 41: 116–145.

Powell, W.W., Koput, K.W., Smith-Doerr, L., & Owen-Smith, J. (1999). *Network Position and Firm Performance: Organizational Returns to Collaboration in the Biotechnology Industry*. Stanford: JAI Press.

Powell, W.W., White, D.R., Koput, K.W., & Owen-Smith, J. (2005). Network dynamics and field evolution: The growth of interorganizational collaboration in the life sciences. *American Journal of Sociology*, 110(4): 1132–1205.

Quinn, J.B. (1980). *Strategies for Change: Logical Incrementalism*. Homewood: Richard D. Irwin.

Ropo, A., & Hunt, J.G. (1995). Entrepreneurial processes as virtuous and vicious spirals in a changing opportunity structure: A paradoxical perspective. *Entrepreneurship Theory & Practice*, 19(3): 91–111.

Ruef, M. (2002). Strong ties, weak ties and islands: Structural and cultural predictors of organizational innovation. *Industrial & Corporate Change*, 11(3): 427–449.

Saabeel, W., Verduijn, T.M., Hagdorn, L., & Kumar, K. (2002). A model of virtual organisation: A structure and process perspective. *Electronic Journal of Organizational Virtualness*, 4(4): 1–16.

Sandhoff, G. (1999). Virtual organizations as power-asymmetrical networks. *Electronic Journal of Organizational Virtualness*, 1(1): 103–119.

Saxenian, A. (1994). *Regional Advantage: Culture and Competition in Silicon Valley and Route 128*. Cambridge: Harvard University Press.

Saxenian, A. (2002). Silicon Valley's new immigrant high-growth entrepreneurs. *Economic Development Quarterly*, 16: 20.

Schultze, J., & Orlikowski, W.J. (2001). Metaphors of virtuality: Shaping an emergent reality. *Information & Organization*, 11: 45–77.

Shapiro, C., & Varian, H.R. (1999). *Information Rules: A Strategic Guide to the Network Economy*. Cambridge: Harvard Business School Press.

Shipilov, A.V. (2006). Network strategies and performance of Canadian investment banks. *Academy of Management Journal*, 49(3): 590–604.

Stacey, R.D. (1995). The science of complexity: An alternative perspective for strategic change processes. *Strategic Organization*, 16: 477–495.

Stinchcombe, A.L. (1965). Social structure and organizations. In J.G. March (Ed.), *Handbook of Organizations*, 142–193. Chicago: Rand McNally.

Stuart, T.E., Hoang, H., & Hybels, C. (1999). Interorganizational endorsements and the performances of entrepreneurial ventures. *Administrative Science Quarterly*, 44: 215–249.

Teece, D. (1998). Capturing value from knowledge assets: The new economy,

markets for know-how, and intangible assets. *California Management Review,*
40(3): 55–79.

Uzzi, B., & Spiro, J. (2005). Collaboration and creativity: The small world problem. *American Journal of Sociology,* 111(2): 447–504.

Van Der Veen, M., & Wakkee, I. (2006). Understanding the entrepreneurial process. In P. Davidsson (Ed.), *New Firm Startups.* Cheltenham: Edward Elgar.

van Liere, D.W., Koppius, O.R., & Vervest, P.H. (2008). Network horizon: An information-based view on the dynamics of bridging positions. In J.A. Baum and T.J. Rowley (Eds.), *Advances in Strategic Management,* vol. 25, 595–639. Oxford: Emerald.

Venkataraman, S. (1997). The distinctive domain of entrepreneurship research: An editor's perspective. In *Advances in Entrepreneurship, Firm Emergence and Growth,* 119–138. Greenwich: JAI Press.

Watts, D.J. (1999). *Small Worlds: The Dynamics of Networks between Order and Randomness.* Princeton: Princeton University Press.

Watts, D.J. (2004). The 'new' science of networks. *Annual Review of Sociology,* 30: 243–270.

Watts, D.J., & Strogatz, S.H. (1998). Collective dynamics of 'small-world' networks. *Nature,* 393(6684): 409–410.

White, D.R., & Houseman, M. (2003). The navigability of strong ties: Small worlds, tie strength, and network topology self-organization in strong-tie small worlds. *Complexity,* 8(1): 72–81.

White, H.C. (1970). Search parameters for the small world problem. *Social Forces,* 49: 259–264.

Yeung, H. (2002). Entrepreneurship in international business: An institutional perspective. *Asia Pacific Journal of Management,* 19(1): 29–61.

Zhao, H. (2002). Exploring the synergy between entrepreneurship and innovation. *International Journal of Entrepreneurial Behavior and Research,* 11(1): 35–42.

5 One World or Worlds Apart? Dual Institutional Focus to Enhance Venture Performance

PANKAJ C. PATEL AND BETTY CONKLIN

Due to a number of factors including reduced transportation and communication costs of globalization, the ability of entrepreneurs to conduct new venture activities across different institutional settings is unprecedented. However, the entrepreneurship literature typically considers opportunity exploitation within a single setting. It is often assumed that entrepreneurs identify and exploit a given opportunity under a single set of economic, social, and political regimes. However, transnational entrepreneurs (TEs) could enjoy increased gains from exploiting institutional differences in two different institutional settings. By focusing on comparative advantages due to differences in social, economic, and political conditions across different institutional settings, TEs may be able to identify and exploit opportunities that are unfeasible within single institutional settings. Scholars such as Drori, Honig, and Ginsberg (2006) and Portes, Guarnizo, and Haller (2002) have explored transnational phenomena and found that the transnational entrepreneurship (TE) process has important implications not only for individuals, but also for markets and economies.

Because of the significant global impact of TE, recent research has sought to uncover underlying structures (Basch, Schiller, & Blanc, 1994; Rouse, 1992) and processes (Evans, 2000; Guarnizo, Sanchez, & Roach, 1999; Kastoryano & Programme, 1998) involved in TE activities. Additionally, to explain factors leading to the choice to engage in TE activities, sociological factors such as the degree of assimilation and individual factors such as human capital have been explored (Portes, Guarnizo, & Landolt, 1999). A framework that has been usefully applied to TE activities is Bourdieu's theory of practice, which requires bifocality (focus in two countries / institutional settings) for the mobilization of capital in two different institutional settings (Drori, Honig, & Ginsberg, 2006). Extending organizational learning and innovation research to transnational settings suggests that the ability of TEs to focus their search and exploitation activities in both environments may lead to increased ability to leverage resources and capabilities, thus creating comparative advantage and enhancing the TEs' chances of success (Ethiraj & Levinthal, 2004; March, 1991). Although existing literature theoretically acknowledges the importance of bifocality in the mobilization of capital (Drori, Honig, & Ginsberg, 2006), to our knowledge empirical tests examining the effects of even distribution of focus in dual environments and their impact on TE activities have not been undertaken. Therefore, we pose the following research question: Does increased balance in focus across two environments enhance transnational entrepreneurial activities? Given the central role of bifocality in developing comparative advantage, its empirical relevance is central to furthering our understanding of the TE phenomenon.

To effectively address this gap, we draw on Bourdieu's theory of practice, extending this framework in the transnational context, drawing on Guarnizo (1997) and Rouse (1992). First, we begin by presenting Bourdieu's theory of practice and demonstrating its relevance to transnational entrepreneurship. Second, we explore the concept of comparative advantage where TEs must combine capital in host and home environments to create unique combinations of capital from both. The process of searching for such combinations is central for increased comparative advantage. Drawing on Kauffman's (1993) NK search model in transnational landscapes (i.e., home and host environment), we formally explain why a balanced focus in two environments leads to a greater number of successful combinations, which in turn lead to greater levels of TE activity. We test the importance of bifocality using a simulation to examine the role of balancing in dual environments, and an empirical test of our TE model.

Exploring bifocality, we make at least three contributions. First, in applying Kauffman's NK learning model, we extend organizational learning to the context of transnational entrepreneurship. This NK learning model demonstrates the effects of balanced focus in searching across two fields to maximize comparative advantage. Second, balanced focus helps TEs better allocate their efforts and scarce resources more effectively among various environments in which they operate. Third, recent research has focused on the choice to engage in transnational entrepreneurship (Portes, Guarnizo, & Haller, 2002) or the processes of transnational entrepreneurship (Guarnizo, Sanchez, & Roach, 1999). However, our focus on the proximal outcomes provides a better understanding of the roles of antecedent factors and the importance of transnational processes to firm-level outcomes, thus contributing to the strategic management literature.

Transnational Entrepreneurship and Theory of Practice

Transnationalism is described by Basch, Schiller, and Blanc (1994: 22) as 'a process by which migrants, through their daily activities and social, economic, and political relations, create social fields that cross national boundaries.' Thus, transnational entrepreneurs are individuals engaging in transnationalism for business-related purposes (Portes, Guarnizo, & Landolt, 1999). In contrast to traditional entrepreneurship operating within a single country, transnational entrepreneurship encompasses economic adaptation through the mobilization of social, economic, and political capital across two or more institutional settings (Drori, Honig, & Ginsberg, 2006). Such economic adaptation results in effective development and deployment of resources and capabilities to exploit comparative advantage through mechanisms described in Bourdieu's theory of practice.

Bourdieu's theory of practice encompasses three dimensions – social field, capital, and habitus – that result in the actions (practice) of individuals in society. Whereas a habitus encompasses an individual's set of assumptions and modes of behaviour, the social field encompasses intersubjective rules. Thus, although an individual may occupy a given position within a habitus, the individual's actions in the social field may be limited without sufficient capital. *Capital* is the power of an agent that helps to improve one's position within the social field (Bourdieu, 1977). For a detailed glossary of terms in theory of practice, please refer to Appendix 1. Overall, for an individual to enact a practice, one must leverage one's accessible capital with one's habitus in the context of a given social field. More formally:

$$[(habitus)(capital)] + social\ field = practice \qquad (1)$$

Theory of Practice in Transnational Settings

To explain the TE phenomenon, Bourdieu's framework must be expanded in order to accommodate dual institutional settings. TEs cannot simply combine capital across social fields in home and host countries because the capital might not be valued in a similar way in two separate fields. Similarly, capital may have different value in different institutional settings. For example, professional experience (i.e., human capital) from the country of origin may not transfer to the host country, as when an immigrant who was a physician in the home country cannot work as a physician in the host country. The disposition to leverage such capital is contingent on the entrepreneur's transnational habitus, the dual disposition of an entrepreneur to act in two distinct social fields (Guarnizo, 1997; Drori, Honig, & Ginsberg, 2006). Guarnizo (1997: 311) describes transnational habitus as 'a particular set of dualistic dispositions that inclines migrants to subconsciously act and react to ... generat[e] transnational practices adjusted to specific situations.'

'Bifocality' is the a dual frame of reference through which entrepreneurs constantly compare their situation in their host society with their situation in the home society abroad to enact TE activities (Golbert, 2001; Guarnizo, 1997; Mountz & Wright, 1996; Rouse, 1992; Vertovec, 2004). Whereas a habitus constitutes a single disposition, bifocality is the ability to focus on two different social fields. Bifocality is crucial to TE success because it hinges on entrepreneurs' ability to apply their capital to generate rents greater than those possible when operating in one setting alone.

Bifocality allows TEs to identify diverse capital available in both fields to develop unique and potentially valuable combinations. Economic, social, and cultural types of capital are crucial to facilitating transnational entrepreneurship activities. Economic capital constitutes the assets and financial worth of an individual that are 'immediately and directly convertible into money and may be institutionalized in the form of property rights' (Bourdieu, 1977: 243). Cultural capital, such as accents, comportment, and race, or objectified cultural capital, like dress, music, or art, refers to 'long-lasting dispositions of the mind and body' (ibid.). Social capital helps in mobilizing resources through networks and connections. By drawing on resources in each social field, TE creates unique combinations of capital that result in rent-generating transnational business activities.

Comparative Advantage and Bifocality

To develop comparative advantage, a TE must have a bifocal approach to accessible capital in different institutional settings (Mahler, 1992).

Bifocality is the ability of individuals in transnational settings to adjust to two different environments (Rouse, 1992). The ability of TEs to manage their social position and context facilitates their economic adaptation (Guarnizo, 1997). Bifocality enhances TEs' abilities to scan and analyse different resource environments, allowing them to appropriate capital, develop favourable positions to exploit opportunities, and acquire novel resources and capabilities through stakeholders in diverse environments. Overall, TEs combine capital from two social fields to acquire resources, establish boundaries, and develop exchanges, thus establishing the firm (Katz & Gartner, 1988).

Although prior work has defined bifocality as a focus on two social fields, there is limited information on the extent of bifocal *distribution* across two social fields. In other words, should TEs focus evenly in the two social fields, that is, a balanced perspective, or should they have different degrees of focus? More importantly, what degree of balance in the two social fields is most advantageous to TEs? Different levels of focus may be necessary, depending on the degree of assimilation in the host environment.

Kauffman's (1993) NK model explains search and learning processes, replication, and imitation (Rivkin & Siggelkow, 2003), modularity and innovation (Ethiraj & Levinthal, 2004), and learning under uncertainty (Sommer & Loch, 2004), among other phenomena. The search for new varieties by creating combinations from two different social fields is similar to what is described in the search and learning research. Organizations search for innovations by combining different knowledge attributes. Creating comparative advantage by operating in dual environments could be quite similar. Not all combinations of cultural, social, or economic capital can lead to successful TE activities. Only a limited set of activities should increase the fitness of a transnational venture; thus the search for comparative advantage by combining capital from two different social fields is somewhat analogous to exploring technological landscapes.

A balanced approach to search in organizational landscapes applied to transnational entrepreneurship (e.g., Ethiraj & Levinthal, 2004; March, 1991) is intuitively appealing. Consider that a TE has a choice of whether to focus only on the host or the home environment. However, focusing exclusively on either field should result in limited identification of variations that can be created for eventual selection and retention. As the focus becomes increasingly balanced, more and more possible combinations become available. The greater the number of combinations, the higher the probability becomes of finding more appropriate combinations of capital. Further, it is advantageous to develop complex combinations by focusing on two social fields because complexity increases causal ambiguity for potential imitators. In addition, greater balance means greater incidence of variation due to increased diversity in available capital, and hence a better pool of combinations from which to select. Finally, two social fields may provide a more modular search setting for complex combinations, making the search process more efficient (Ethiraj & Levinthal, 2004). However, complexity increases the ruggedness of the landscape, and decreases the probability of finding an appropriate combination. This creates a paradox since, over time, more complex combinations appear necessary in order to sustain comparative advantage. Thus, to demonstrate this result, we present the following simulation model: (1) when TEs create different combinations, they may incorporate attributes from prior combinations to different extents, and (2) they may also vary the proportion of attributes from the two social fields. The purpose of these steps is to increase fitness in transnational landscapes while creating comparative advantage. Our simulation results indicate that increased balance of focus is necessary as complexity increases. Furthermore, an increasingly even focus on both environments increases fitness. Thus, greater levels of balance in TE activities (practice) reflect the firm's level of fitness. Overall, transnational entrepreneurs with greater levels of bifocality in their transnational habitus will experience greater balance in TE activities.

Methodology

To ensure robustness, we test this bifocality hypothesis in two steps. First, we conduct an agent-based simulation to model the effects of TEs searching two landscapes. Second, we conduct an empirical test to directly establish the relationship between TEs' balanced focus between two countries and transnational activities. Both analyses are described below.

Simulation Analysis

Kauffman's (1993) NK model has been widely employed in the learning and organizational search literature (e.g., Ethiraj & Levinthal, 2004). Using a variant of the NK model for transnational entrepreneurship, we specify that a possible comparative advantage combination results from combining different types of capital. Such capital is assumed to be present and accessible to an entrepreneur in two different social fields (host country and home country). The fitness landscape – transnational habitus – created by the NK model maps the set of attributes onto fitness values. The fitness values of each of the N attributes are determined by random draws from a uniform distribution over the unit interval. The fitness of the organizational form is the average of the values assigned to each of its N attributes. A TE can combine N attributes (i.e., capital) from the host and home environments. Each unit of capital is assumed to take two states – used in combination or not – thus, there are 2^N possible combinations.

Capital in the two fields can be more or less interdependent, in that the value of each of the N individual attributes is affected by both the state of that attribute itself and the states of K other attributes. For example, individuals with poor social capital may also have lesser economic capital or vice versa. If $K = 0$, there are no interdependencies among the attributes of a combination. As K increases, more and more attributes become interdependent. When $K = N - 1$, all attributes of a combination are interdependent. The number of interdependencies given by K determines the surface of the fitness landscape. With $K = 0$, the fitness surface is smooth. As K increases, the fitness surface becomes more rugged. Higher K leads to a loss of order in the correspondence between combinations of capital from different fields and fitness values, that is, whether a combination increases a venture's performance by operating with transnational habitus. With higher values of K, there are larger fitness differences among close combinations of capital (a neighbour differs only on a single attribute), and there are more local peaks (combinations whose neighbours all have lesser values). As K increases, there are fewer paths leading to the configuration with greater fitness through small changes in combinations. By focusing on small incremental capital combinations, TEs become victims of their randomly assigned initial configurations. Thus, TEs can only escape being trapped in inferior combinations in the fitness landscape if they risk changing more attributes at a given time. When $K = N - 1$, even distant search, where all N attributes are changed at a time, can be advantageous.

Our results are based on an average of 100 TEs searching on each of a 100 distinct landscapes, for a simulation of 100,000 possible transnational combination efforts. Each of these landscapes has the same structure in terms of K, the degree of interdependence among attributes in contributing to performance, but represents a distinct realization of random draws. We set $N = 10$, and to facilitate a comparison of the results across values of K, we normalized the maximum performance level on each surface so that average performance equals 0.5 and maximum performance equals 1. The proposed model is as follows: (1) when TEs create different combinations they may use attributes to different extents from prior combinations, and (2) they also have a choice to vary the proportion of attributes from two social fields. The goal of steps (1) and (2) is to increase fitness in transnational landscapes while creating comparative advantage.

Focusing on Host or Home Social Fields

In any time step, a TE changes each of the N attributes by combining capital with probability, P_i. For each simulation, the probability P_i does not change. The expected number of attributes to be changed in a time step is $P_i N$. All N attributes are changed if $P_i = 1$, and no attributes are changed if $P_i = 0$. For intermediate values of P_i ($0 < P_i < 1$), on average $P_i N$ attributes are changed. For example, if $P_i = 0.5$ and $N = 10$, the organization *on average* changes five attributes. Thus, focusing on just one social field (say, social field$_1$) has the probability P_i, and focusing on the other social field (say, social field$_2$) is the probability $1 - P_i$. The higher P_i is, the greater the diversity of combinations and the fewer the local searches. Lower P_i means greater emphasis on using prior combinations.

   We set $P_i = \{0, 0.1, 0.2 \ldots 1.0\}$, examining the effect of changing one (P_i N) attribute *on average*, whereas the local search is constrained to literally changing a single attribute in *each time step*. Although P_i explains changes in existing combinations of capital, differing degrees of focus on two social fields may lead to novel combinations. The degree of focus is at the heart of bifocality to create new combinations.

Bifocality

Having explained the changes in attributes, that is, combinations of capital from different social fields, the degree of focus in either field is equally important to enhance learning. TEs must avoid the danger of being prematurely trapped in inferior combinations of capital in the fitness landscape, a danger exacerbated by high levels of similar P_i over time. Thus, although a TE may vary the proportion of capital from different social fields, P_i, it does not mean the learning efforts are evenly distributed. Changes in P_i over time would mean inertia because no new combinations would have come to light; only the degree of combinations varies. This analogy is similar to the exploration/exploitation argument. Different levels of P_i indicate periods of exploitation, but constantly adopting and learning new capital forms may limit the ability to exploit full comparative advantage. Yet, TEs must also avoid spending too much time 'in transit' on inferior peaks while searching for the global peak.

We define a weight, W_i, determining the extent to which a TE relies on a given social field to create comparative advantage combinations. We examine whether TEs focus on just one field ($W_i = 1$) or completely on the other field ($W_i = 0$) and combinations in between ($W_i = 0, 0.05, 0.10...1.0$). To assess the degree of balance, we use the weight that an organization puts on imitation (as opposed to relying on its own experience) in changing each of the N attributes:

$$P_{(t,\,i)} = (1 - W_i)\,P_i + W_i\,F_{(t-1,\,i)}$$

where $P(t, i)$ is the probability of updating attribute i in time-step t, P_i is a hard-coded propensity to innovate ($1 - P_i$ is inertia), W_i is the weight that a TE puts on lower exploration of two fields, and $F_{(t-1,\,i)}$ is the population average of the attributes that were actually changed during the previous period. To sustain comparative advantage, TEs must monitor the extent to which attributes are combined by other TEs. By shifting weights, W_i, from using comparative advantage combinations others are using, that is, $F_{(t-1,\,i)}$, firms can create a better comparative advantage. Initial conditions are defined by setting $F(0, i) = P_i$.

Simulation Results

Figure 5.1a shows the results from the simulation. The results suggest that extreme focus in either field is counterproductive. Continually changing attributes in a given combination without changing the types of combinations over time is counterproductive as well. Irrespective of the level of complexity, TEs that apply some mixture of social fields have higher fitness than organizations characterized by focusing on one field. TEs that put a relatively higher weight on one field (> 0.5) generally have higher fitness.

As complexity (i.e., more combination of capital) increases, it be-

Figure 5.1: Simulation results

(a) Effect of focus in two fields with increasing complexity

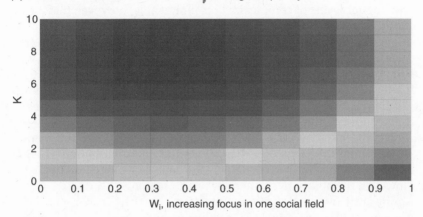

W$_i$, increasing focus in one social field

(b) Effect of degree of focus in two transnational fields

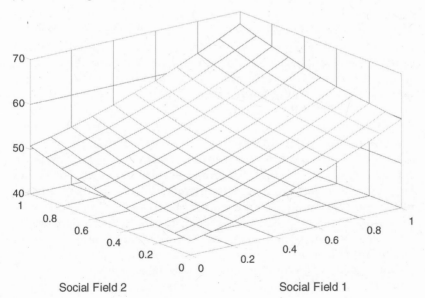

Social Field 2   Social Field 1

comes more difficult to balance the risk of being trapped on inferior peaks with the risk of spending too much time 'in transit' while searching for better combinations. Consequently, fitness generally decreases with higher levels of complexity. It is remarkable, however, that an appropriate mixture of social fields will only lead to a very slight decrease in maximum fitness even when all attributes are interdependent ($K = 9$). Even with the highest level of complexity ($K = 9$), organizations with balanced social fields and distribution of focus between 0.4 and 0.6 are highly successful. The realistic intermediate mixtures of social fields are much more viable. As more weight is put on one field, fitness converges to the population average.

Overall, one may infer that focusing on either field is detrimental. However, as the focus, W_i, changes and as the distribution of effort becomes even in the two fields, greater levels of fitness are obtained. However, the ability to create novel combinations, P_i, increases fitness significantly over that of competitors ($F_{(t-1,i)}$). Thus, increased balance of focus in two separate social fields appears crucial for comparative advantage of TEs. Figure 5.1b shows the respective graphs from the simulation.

Empirical Analysis

DATA

The Comparative Immigrant Enterprise Project (CIEP) is a collaborative study conducted jointly in 1998 by universities on the east and west coasts (Johns Hopkins University, Brown University, and the University of California at Davis) to examine the prevalence of transnational entrepreneurship in immigrant populations (detailed data description is available on the CIEP website, http://cmd.princeton.edu/ciep.shtml). In 1998 the project's headquarters was moved to the Center for Migration and Development at Princeton University. We highlight key characteristics of the data here; however, for a detailed description of the survey, please refer to Portes, Guarnizo, and Haller (2002). The survey targeted newer Latin American immigrants in their primary areas of residential concentration in the United States, and included questions concerning the characteristics and regularity of their interactions among ties they maintain in their countries of origin. Colombian, Dominican, and Salvadoran immigrants were the target nationalities because they are all sizeable immigrant groups, comprising three-quarters of a million persons each in 1996 (U.S. Bureau of the Census, 1999). Also, their contexts of exit and reception are sufficiently diverse to provide a basis for comparing different types of economic adaptation. Finally, their ethnic diversity is representative of distinct institutional environments in which these entrepreneurs operate.

The survey resulted in 1,202 unweighted sample units for all sites, while the weights project the unweighted sample to the population sizes of each immigrant group within its respective U.S. community. Following Portes, Guarnizo, and Haller (2002), we identified transnational entrepreneurs using two screening statements: (1) The success of my firm depends on regular contact with foreign countries. (2) The success of my firm depends on regular contact with (Colombia / Dominican Republic / El Salvador, according to respondent's country of origin). Based on the screening statements for transnational entrepreneurs, we selected 452 transnational firms weighting them to ensure proper representativeness for analysis (ibid.).

Dependent Variable: Balance of TE Activities

While numerous measures such as firm profit, years of survival, or sales may be used as outcome indicators, these measures may be of limited relevance in testing the effectiveness of an entrepreneur operating in a transnational habitus. As shown in the simulation, the effectiveness of TE efforts is reflected in how entrepreneurs balance business-related activities in two separate environments. The ability to balance TE activities is an indirect indicator of the combination of capital from two different social fields. Considering only firm-level outcomes may confound transnational effectiveness with other firm-level outcomes that may also play a role in overall firm performance. However, focusing on the degree to which business activities are carried out in two different environments is a more proximal reflector of transnational effectiveness. This measure is in line with work by Drori, Honig, and Ginsberg (2006), who argue that the fundamental aspect of TE is the ability to mobilize social networks in dual institutional settings. A relevant indicator of such mobilization is the distribution of TE activities in dual habitus.

To operationalize the degree of balance in TE activities, we calculate the deviance in densities of activities in host and home environments. The list of activities is shown in the latter part of Table 5.1. The activities are on a 3-point interval scale with values 'never,' 'once in a while,' or 'regularly.' The deviance index, that is, the balance of TE activities shown below, measures the degree to which transnational business activities are carried out in two separate environments. Imbalance in either direction may indicate that there is room for improvement in enhancing venture performance. We use an entropy index to measure the concentration of activities in a given environment:

Balance of transnational activities

$$= \left[\left(-\sum_{n=1}^{N} \sum_{i=0}^{I} \pi_{in}^{home} \ln(\pi_{in}) \right) - \left(-\sum_{n=1}^{N} \sum_{i=0}^{I} \pi_{in}^{host} \ln(\pi_{in}) \right) \right]^2$$

where π indicates the proportion of a given activity; never, once in a while, or regularly for a given activity, i, over a total number of activities, n. The above operationalization may be viewed as a matrix, where the rows are the list of activities and the columns are the degree of partaking in the activities coded as: 2 (regularly), 1 (once in a while), and 0 (never). The joint consideration of the number of activities and the extent of participation helps us to understand the distribution of activities. Thus, the best distribution will be regular participation in all the activities, and the worst will be no participation in any activity. When a transnational entrepreneur does not engage in an activity in either home or host country, the entropy index for a given environment will be zero, and the highest concentration possible is $\log(n*i)$ (Theil, 1969). Other operationalizations of balance follow similar logic. Also note, the greater the deviance score, the greater the imbalance. However, for ease of interpretation of the relationship among the variables, all the items have been reverse coded so that the hypothesis that greater balance leads to better performance is tested conveniently.

Independent Variable: Bifocality

As explained previously, duality is the degree of disposition an entrepreneur has in operating in dual habitus, and thus two different environments. We operationalize home habitus using a set of activities in the home country (Table 5.1), and the host habitus as degree of assimilation (Table 5.1). To make the balance numbers comparable, we standardize scores on home habitus and host habitus. Differing disposition levels may mean that the entrepreneur is more effective in one habitus than in the other. According to Portes, Guarnizo, and Haller (2002), and Vertovec (2002), the degree of embeddedness in TE environments is re-

Table 5.1
Empirical Results

(a) Correlation Table

	1	2	3	4	5	6	7	8	9
1. Balance of TE Activities	1								
2. Sex	.05*	1							
3. Age	.06*	−.04*	1						
4. Marital Status	.04*	−.04*	.11	1					
5. Years of Education	.07*	.16*	−.19*	.00	1				
6. Work Experience	.04*	.16*	−.11	.00	−.17*	1			
7. No. of Children	.04*	−.06*	.7*	.03*	−.18*	.2*	1		
8. Group	−.02	−.09*	.15	.12*	−.21*	−.05	.01*	1	
9. Bifocality	.05*	.13*	.13*	−.03*	.32*	.06	−.04	.09	1

(b) OLS Regression

	Model 1: Controls	Model 2: Main Effects
Constant	16.735	13.432
Sex	.05**	.07**
Age	.06**	.14**
Marital Status	.03	.05
Years of Education	.12*	.11*
Work Experience	.07	.11
No. of Children	−.03	-.02
Nationality: Colombian	.05*	.05*
Nationality: Salvadoran	.04*	.03*
Main Effects		
Bifocality		.18*
Model F-Statistic	88.50 (8)**	74.03 (9)**
Adjusted-R^2	.06	.12
Δ Adjusted-R^2	–	0.06
Δ F-statistic	–	14.47 (1)**
N	452	452

$*p < .05; **p < .01; N = 452$

flected through 'ties with home country' and 'degree of assimilation in the host country.' Studies on migrants in Europe (Crul & Vermeulen, 2003; Kastoryano & Programme, 1998) and the United States (Levitt, 2001; Portes, Guarnizo, & Haller, 2002) have shown that greater levels of assimilation lead to greater levels of embeddedness in the host environment, which in turn result in greater levels of entrepreneurial effort (Bertaux & Thompson, 1997).

Indicators for both types of embeddedness are listed in Table 5.1. The scales for each measure ranged from 'never,' 'once in a while,' to 'regularly.' Given that bifocality requires one to measure the degree of duality in two separate environments, we use the deviance index, but with respective concentration ratios of home country and host country embeddedness:

Bifocality

$$= \left[\left(-\sum_{n=1}^{N}\sum_{i=0}^{I} \pi_{in}^{assimliation} \ln(\pi_{in}) \right) - \left(-\sum_{n=1}^{N}\sum_{i=0}^{I} \pi_{in}^{ties\ with\ home\ country} \ln(\pi_{in}) \right) \right]^2 \quad (2)$$

where π indicates the proportion of a given assimilation or ties with home country for a given indicator in Table 5.1, i, over a total number of indicators in the two environments, n. The entropy index for a given environment will be zero when an entrepreneur is not embedded in a given environment, and the highest concentration, $\log(n^*i)$, when an entrepreneur is highly engaged in both environments. The deviance index is reflective of the bifocality. Greater deviance indicates that an entrepreneur is embedded in one of the two environments to a greater extent than in the other, representing a lower bifocality.

CONTROLS

We control for sex, age, marital status, years of education, years of work experience, number of children, and ethnic group (reference category, Dominicans).

OLS Regression

For intuitive appeal we reverse coded the dependent and independent measures to reflect that a greater degree of balance may lead to greater transnational success. Table 5.1(a) shows the correlations among the variables and the results from regression. Correlations show that not only do control variables lead to choice of transnational entrepreneurship, but they may also affect the firm's eventual success. We also see that bifocality is significantly correlated with the balance of transnational activity.

Recall that Hypothesis (1) proposed that greater bifocality would assist transnational entrepreneurs to positively balance their TE activities.

Model 2 in Table 5.1(b), shows that bifocality is positively related to the dependent variable ($\beta = 0.18$; $p < .05$), and explains 6 per cent of additional variance – significantly different from Model 1 (ΔAdjusted-R^2 = 0.06; ΔF-statistic = 14.47 (1), $p < 0.01$). Overall, increased level of bifocality helps enhance transnational activities.

Discussion and Implications

Our focus in this chapter has been on the TE's ability to balance focus in dual institutional settings to enhance venture activities. We find that a key factor in enhancing transnational activities is balance – relative focus in two different habitus. To our knowledge, this is the first study assessing the degree to which the ability to operate in dual environments matters, and how transnational entrepreneurs can enhance this duality. As such, our study offers important implications for theory and practice.

We extend Drori, Honig, and Ginsberg's (2006) application of Bourdieu's theory of practice framework by exploring the distribution of focus in two different institutional environments. The ability to combine capital across institutional settings allows TEs to effectively search for and develop unique combinations, which is important because some variations lead to competitive advantage. By achieving more balanced focus, TEs increase their odds of developing effective combinations. Second, Portes, Guarnizo, and Haller (2002) found that the choice to be a transnational entrepreneur is contingent on individual human capital, and the size and reach of the TE's social networks. They further demonstrate the significant importance of contextual factors and national origin on human capital and network size. This chapter extends the findings of Portes, Guarnizo, and Haller (2002). Not only are network size and human capital crucial in the choice of whether to engage in transnational entrepreneurship; these factors also affect the degree of success as a transnational entrepreneur in terms of transnational activities.

Third, these findings extend the notion of social embeddedness from a specific social environment to dual environments. In contrast to Granovetter's (1985) concept of embeddedness within a given environment, the implications of an entrepreneur embedded in two different environments may be very different. The results show that embeddedness in two environments is not mutually exclusive, and that dual focus actually helps enhance venture performance. Therefore, these relations may not only change in nature and degree of social capital effectiveness, but also how they are managed in dual environments. This is in stark contrast to traditional notions of strong and weak ties in a given environment. Embeddedness in two environments may require a different set of abilities than those necessary in managing embeddedness in one environment. The mutual dependencies across two different networks may mean degrees of compensatory ties in one network for those lacking in the other. Such abilities to manage dual environments may result in requisite bridges for resources, technologies, and human capital across national borders.

Finally, in contrast to the roles of power in typical business exchanges, in transnational habitus power takes meaning beyond the resource dependence perspective (Pfeffer & Salancik, 2003). Power in transnational habitus may accrue from material or symbolic artefacts. More importantly, resource dependence may be less important as resource providers in different settings may be less able to collude to enhance their resource rents. Due to their unique positioning, transnational entrepreneurs reduce dependence significantly. The ability to balance focus further increases available resource combinations that could further facilitate advantageous resource exchanges. Thus, these findings reflect important implications for theoretical and practical sides of transnational entrepreneurship.

Limitations and Future Research Directions

This study is not without limitations. First, our analysis does not examine the internal venture processes of TEs, particularly relational and cognitive social capital, although these may be equally important in affecting outcomes (Nahapiet & Ghoshal, 1998). Future research efforts may focus on a finer analysis of the roles of different types of social capital. Second, while the study accounts for key habitus-related factors that affect transnational outcomes, balance in cognitive frameworks could also be necessary. For TEs to operate effectively in different environments, variations in cognitive outlook, personality traits, motivation, and other cognitive factors could be important. Third, whereas the study focused on existing transnational *firms*, transnational *entrepreneurs* could experience different requirements for balancing dual environments. At various stages of venture commercialization, different types and degrees of ability to manage in dual environments might be necessary. Finally, we cannot rule out the limited generalizability of our findings. Different immigrant groups living in other host countries could have profoundly different effects on the TE process.

Future research could focus on contingent factors that may affect bifocality. We did not consider contingent effects of factors such as degree of assimilation, effects of the host environment, and other factors. It may be that such factors could at times lead to detrimental effects from excessive balance. Bifocality may be important only as conditions of adequate proficiency in each institutional environment. Thus, contingent effects of such factors may provide better insights into the role of bifocality. Second, while the study focuses on proximal outcome – transnational activities – economic outcomes such as profit may also provide a reliable indicator of the effectiveness of combinations. Third, bifocality may be extended to different forms of capital such as social, cultural, and economic. Finer analysis of the interplay among the different types of capital may help us better understand the effectiveness of capital in varying contexts.

Conclusion

The study focused on the role of bifocality – the degree to which a TE focuses on two different institutional settings – in enhancing TE activities. We found that entrepreneurs with greater levels of balance in bifocality engage in greater levels of transnational entrepreneurial activities. Deriving equal balance could be crucial along all dimensions. Expanding the logic of Bourdieu's framework on performance to dual habitus, entrepreneurs must first be able to operate in dual habitus and develop social networks, and then derive power in a transnational field to engage in enhanced TE activities. Policy-makers could focus on similar sequences of logic in order to encourage transnational entrepreneurship among present and future immigrants.

REFERENCES

Basch, L.G., Schiller, N.G., & Blanc, C.S. (1994). *Nations Unbound: Transnational Projects, Postcolonial Predicaments, and Deterritorialized Nation-States*. Amsterdam: Gordon and Breach.

Bertaux, D., & Thompson, P. (1997). *Pathways to Social Class: A Qualitative Approach to Social Mobility*. London: Clarendon Press.

Bourdieu, P. (1977). *Outline of a Theory of Practice*. Cambridge: Cambridge University Press.

Bourdieu, P., & Wacquant, L. (1992). *An Invitation to Reflexive Sociology*. Chicago: University of Chicago Press.

Crul, M., & Vermeulen, H. (2003). The second generation in Europe. *International Migration Review*, 37(4): 965–986.

Drori, I., Honig, B., & Ginsberg, A. (2006). Transnational Entrepreneurship: Toward a Unifying Theoretical Framework. Presented at the Academy of Management Conference, Aug., Atlanta, Georgia.

Ethiraj, S.K., & Levinthal, D. (2004). Bounded rationality and the search for organizational architecture: An evolutionary perspective on the design of organizations and their evolvability. *Administrative Science Quarterly*, 49: 404–437.

Evans, P. (2000). Fighting marginalization with transnational networks: Counter-hegemonic globalization. *Contemporary Sociology*, 29(1): 230–241.

Golbert, R. (2001). Transnational orientations from home: Constructions of Israel and transnational space among Ukrainian Jewish youth. *Journal of Ethnic and Migration Studies*, 27(4): 713–731.

Granovetter, M. (1985). Economic sociology and social structure: The problem with embeddedness. *American Journal of Sociology*, 91(3): 481–510.

Guarnizo, L.E. (1997). The emergence of a transnational social formation and the mirage of return migration among Dominican transmigrants. *Identities*, 4(2): 281–322.

Guarnizo, L.E., Sanchez, A.I., & Roach, E.M. (1999). Mistrust, fragmented solidarity, and transnational migration: Colombians in New York City and Los Angeles. *Ethnic and Racial Studies*, 22(2): 367–396.

Kastoryano, R., & Programme, T.C. (1998). *Transnational Participation and Citizenship: Immigrants inside the European Union*. Oxford: Oxford University, Transnational Communities Programme.

Katz, J., & Gartner, W.B. (1988). Properties of emerging organizations. *Academy of Management Review*, 13(3): 429–441.

Kauffman, S.A. (1993). *The Origins of Order*. Oxford: Oxford University Press.

Levitt, P. (2001). Transnational migration: Taking stock and future directions. *Global Networks*, 1(3): 195–216.

Mahler, S.J. (1998). Theoretical and empirical contributions toward a research agenda for transnationalism. In M.P. Smith & L.E. Guarnizo (Eds.), *Transnationalism from Below*, 64–102. London: Transaction Publishers.

March, J.G. (1991). Exploration and exploitation in organizational learning. *Organization Science*, 2(1): 71–87.

Mountz, A., & Wright, R.A. (1996). Daily life in the transnational migrant community of San Agustin, Oaxaca, and Poughkeepsie, New York. *Diaspora*, 5: 403–428.

Nahapiet, J., & Ghoshal, S. (1998). Social capital and the organizational advantage. *Academy of Management Review*, 23(2): 242–266.

Pfeffer, J., & Salancik, G.R. (2003). *The External Control of Organizations: A Resource Dependence Perspective*. Palo Alto: Stanford University Press.

Portes, A., Guarnizo, L.E., & Haller, W.J. (2002). Transnational entrepreneurs: An alternative form of immigrant economic adaptation. *American Sociological Review, 67*(2): 278–298.

Portes, A., Guarnizo, L.E., & Landolt, P. (1999). The study of transnationalism: Pitfalls and promise of an emergent research field. *Ethnic and Racial Studies, 22*(2): 217–237.

Rivkin, J.W., & Siggelkow, N. (2003). Balancing search and stability: Interdependencies among elements of organizational design. *Management Science, 49*(3): 290–311.

Rouse, R. (1992). Making sense of settlement: Class transformation, cultural struggle, and transnationalism among Mexican migrants in the United States. *Annals of the New York Academy of Sciences, 645*(1): 25–52.

Saxenian, A.L. (1994). *Regional Advantage: Culture and Competition in Silicon Valley and Route 128*. Cambridge: Harvard University Press.

Sommer, S.C., & Loch, C.H. (2004). Selectionism and learning in projects with complexity and unforeseeable uncertainty. *Management Science, 50*(10): 1334.

Theil, H. (1969). The desired political entropy. *American Political Science Review, 63*(2): 521–525.

Vertovec, S. (2002). *Transnational Networks and Skilled Labour Migration*. Oxford: Oxford University, Transnational Communities Programme.

Vertovec, S. (2004). Migrant transnationalism and modes of transformation 1. *International Migration Review, 38*(3): 970–1001.

Appendix 1: Glossary

Bourdieu's Theory of Practice

Term	Explanation
Habitus	'A system of acquired dispositions functioning on the practical level as categories of perception and assessment ... as well as being the organizing principles of action.' In other words, habitus is an individual's everyday habitual practices and assumptions in the context of a particular social environment.
Capital	Social resources, power, or energy that is managed by the agents' *habitus* that are embodied in them. Specifically, economic, human, cultural, social, and symbolic capital; Bourdieu considers these forms of capital to be interchangeable.
Field	A *field* or a market may be seen as a structural space of positions in which the positions and their interrelations are determined by the distribution of different kinds of resources or 'capital' that agents possess and that can be exchanged. While habitus determines the subject's goal and internal constraints, the social field focuses on the objective goal and external conditions (Bourdieu, 1977: 78–9; Bourdieu & Wacquant, 1992: 97).
Practice	Practice is a result of interaction between individual habitus and individual capital in a given field. It is a shifting, relational system of disposition and of the state of feeling, while internally structured (by individuals) and externally developed (through objective social themes).
Theory of practice	[(habitus)(capital)] + (field) = practice
TE activity	An activity related to a venture conducted in a transnational space – two social fields, host and home – where an entrepreneur has comparative advantage by combining capital from two different social fields; in other words, activities that help TEs leverage capital in two social fields so that the combination is greater than the sum of its parts.
Transnational habitus	'A particular set of dualistic dispositions that inclines migrants subconsciously to act and react to ... generat[e] transnational practices adjusted to specific situations' (Guarnizo, 1997: 311).
Bifocality	Bifocality is a dual frame of reference through which entrepreneurs constantly compare their situation in their 'home' society to their situation in the 'host' society abroad to enact TE Activities (Guarnizo, 1997; Rouse, 1992; Mountz & Wright, 1996; Golbert, 2001; Vertovec, 2004). Such a frame of reference is necessary to enact TE activities by leveraging capital in two social fields.

Appendix 2: Measures and Indicators of Bifocality

Measures	Indicators
Transnational entrepreneurial activities	My clients live abroad.
	I import from home country.
	I export to home country.
	I invest in firms in home country.
	I have business communications with home country.
	My clients live here.
	I receive investments from home country.
	My business partners live abroad.
	My business partners live here.
	I have employees in home country.
	I trade in home country.
	I trade from home country.
	I invest money in business in home country.
	I invest money in real estate in home country.
	I transport money or goods between this and home country.
	I arrange trips, immigration papers for money.
Bifocality: Ties with home country	I participate in home town associations.
	I provide money for projects in home town.
	I visit home town/celebrations.
	I contribute money for politics in home country.
	I organize politicals campaign in home country.
	I participate in sports clubs with links to home country.
	I contribute to charity organizations in home country.
	I own properties in home country.
Bifocality: Assimilation	Year of arrival in U.S.
	Occupation equals education & aptitudes in respondent's opinion
	Has been discriminated against
	Is a U.S. citizen
	Personal monthly income

6 The Progression of International Students into Transnational Entrepreneurs: A Conceptual Framework

GERRY KERR AND FRANCINE K. SCHLOSSER

This chapter clarifies the process of creating an important category of transnational entrepreneurs (TEs). Theoretical understanding is developed through a focus on integral transforming institutions, universities, and on a central group, international students. This latter group is uniquely prepared to link countries through venture creation. We present a framework that begins by discussing the entrepreneurial attitude inherent or developed in many international students. We describe the types of human and social investments that may aid in developing a bicultural mindset, as students are forced to adapt to national differences in personal and business expectations and routines. We consider how the ability to function within each distinct culture – and yet conceptualize the whole – facilitates the recognition of opportunities and the development of creative transnational business propositions. Subsequently, we outline how resources, opportunity sets, individual market conditions, and human and social capital development connect within a bicultural mindset to create fertile conditions for nascent transnational entrepreneurs. We begin by reviewing the limited, but growing literature related to the transnational entrepreneur and connecting it to the international student experience.

The Transnational Entrepreneur

Transnational entrepreneurs are defined as individuals who migrate from one country to another and found businesses, simultaneously maintaining regular, critical organizational linkages with both countries (Portes, Guarnizo, & Haller, 2002). Transnational entrepreneurs represent a large percentage (often the majority) of immigrants (to the

United States) who are self-employed (ibid.). However, the low overall percentage of the self-employed among immigrants has spawned debates over the importance and recent emergence (as opposed to a long-standing existence) of transnational entrepreneurship (TE), and it has caused some researchers to overlook a key point.

Small percentages can belie large economic and social effects. For instance, in the United States, immigrants have been shown to exert significant economic power through monetary remittances (e.g., Cervantes-Rodriguez, 2006; Saxenian, 2002a), as well as through the cross-flow of 'social remittances,' cultural artefacts like ideas and music (Levitt, 1998; Itzigsohn et al., 1999). The ties of immigrants to their home countries have also been linked with notable economic effects, besides those associated with remittances: 'For every 1 percent increase in the number of first-generation immigrants from a given country, for example, California's exports to that country go up nearly 0.5 percent' (Saxenian, 2002b: 30). Furthermore, the admixture of national origin, education and skills, and industry segment has led to significant outcomes. In information and communication technologies, for example, Chinese and Indian nationals with engineering and science backgrounds have had pronounced influence in Silicon Valley (Saxenian, 2002a).

The effects are arguably even more prevalent in Canada. Under the country's multiculturalism policies, many new immigrants are encouraged to see themselves as 'bi-national' (Szonyi, 2003), and many times they are entrepreneurs who conduct international trade primarily with their country of origin. The impact is potentially very large, with about 20 per cent of Canada's population being foreign-born (Statistics Canada, 2008). Moreover, in recent years, between 55 and 60 per cent of Canada's annual intake of newcomers are economic immigrants (Hawthorne, 2006), far exceeding the numbers associated with the family (25%–30%) and refugee categories (10%–15%) (Citizenship and Immigration Canada, 2009). Again, the effects are sizeable: Canadian immigrants with higher levels of human and social investments have been found to engage in entrepreneurship and to generate higher household incomes at significantly higher levels than other comparable immigrants (Kerr & Schlosser, 2007).

Addressing the Gaps in Transnational Entrepreneurship Research

Given the evidence, we accept the phenomenon of the transnational entrepreneur as a fact, discernible from the other (domestic) mode of entrepreneurship available to immigrants, in both focus and complexity. We also recognize that research on the transnational entrepreneur stands at the crossroads of entrepreneurship and strategic management research (Ireland, Hitt, & Sirmon, 2003) and entrepreneurship and international business research (Yeung, 2002). An appreciable literature focused on the transnational entrepreneur is currently developing; however, the research also exhibits a number of prominent gaps. One of these concerns the level of understanding of the mechanisms by which transnational entrepreneurship can come into being – at the level of the entrepreneur.

As stated, the existing literature has mainly centred on establishing the phenomena of transnationalism and the transnational entrepreneur (e.g., Portes, Guarnizo, & Haller, 2002) and with mapping their effects, often in specific locations and industries (i.e., Saxenian, 2002a). The preoccupation with the first issue (establishing the phenomena) is at least partly attributable to the overwhelmingly case-based studies that have been undertaken on the subject, causing some to call into question the validity of the knowledge being accumulated (Waldinger, 1998; Lopez, 2001). The second thrust in the literature (mapping the effects of the TE) is intent on tracing out and better understanding transnational entrepreneurship by focusing on a specific location, for example, Silicon Valley, California (Saxenian, 2002a, 2002b), or Oaxaca, Mexico (Grieshop, 2006), and specific industries (high-tech manufacturing and services, and family-scale package services, respectively). However, methodological limitations present in the first stream are also apparent in the second stream. As a result, questions can be raised about the extent to which the research conclusions can be generalized to other contexts. Moreover, a case-based approach may not be well suited for developing a theoretical basis for grasping the phenomena that can be applied in multiple settings.

The International Student

A demonstrable need exists, therefore, for a research focus that produces and explicates a decision model of transnational entrepreneurship (Yeung, 2002). In response, insights from the fragmented literatures on international students (in North America) and on immigrant/ethnic entrepreneurship (and its supporting theories) were assembled into a framework that incorporates temporal change and learning. Simultaneously, the work had to be open to the vagaries of opportunity context as well as to the aspirations and market conditions perceived to be facing the nascent entrepreneur (Lee & Venkataraman, 2006).

Fortunately, the international student provides a ready means for better understanding the creation of transnational entrepreneurs. Many international students exhibit the common profile of those who become self-employed immigrants in North America (Toussaint-Comeau, 2005): they possess higher levels of education, English-language proficiency, acceptability for professional or managerial occupations, and a proximity to a concentrated group of their ethnic community. Furthermore, international students also enjoy inclusion in the 'educational enclaves' that surround their colleges and universities, allowing access to a variety of resources (Li, 2007).

The numbers of students are large in many jurisdictions. For instance, international students in Canada constitute a potent force, with just over 178,000 in Canada in 2008 (Citizenship and Immigration Canada, 2008a). This group represented one-fourth of all temporary residents coming to the country between 1996 and 2005 (Citizenship and Immigration Canada, 2007, 2008b). As a result, the mobility of international students is a topic of great interest, embraced by large project-based researchers, such as Atlas (www.atlas.iienetwork.org) and Metropolis (www.international.metropolis.net). One major research topic, among many, is the difficulty of immigrants in receiving recognition of their credentials by North Americans, spurring some to study in Western countries, including Canada, in order to increase their acceptability (Adams, 2007).

Moreover, international student mobility has been connected to the creation of transnational entrepreneurs. For example, Silicon Valley is a prominent area which was transformed by thousands of (mainly) engineering students who completed their degrees and stayed to work and start businesses. These activities, however, were merely the first step in the transformation. For many of the immigrant entrepreneurs, the decision to remain in North America was followed in later years by the development of active business ties with their home countries (Saxenian, 2005). International students are exposed to anticipatory and new entrepreneur socialization (Starr & Fondas, 1992) by virtue of their risk-taking in embracing educational opportunities outside their home countries, and by the experiences of motivating factors, socializing agents, and structural elements indigenous to their adopted countries. In essence, the act of becoming an international student also creates fertile conditions for later transnational entrepreneurship.

The Experience of the International Student: A Force in Creating Transnational Entrepreneurs

A number of positions in theory are used to aid in understanding the process of TE development in international students, from latency to full-blown development. For example, two perspectives, human and social capital theories and the concept of bisociation, are combined to describe how ongoing investments in education, language acquisition, and enculturation lead international students to generate business opportunities and options and to a heightened creativity. The third and fourth perspectives outline the movement from opportunities to entrepreneurial outcomes. Here, prospect theory, especially as examined by Lee and Venkataraman (2006), and the literature of international entrepreneurship (IE) are employed. However, an exhaustive review of the relevant literatures is not provided, given the exigencies of a short chapter. Instead, the theoretical perspectives are fitted together as a means for illuminating an important social and economic process and outcome.

The framework initially examines the individual level (the international student as potential transnational entrepreneur) in order to move to the organizational level (the creation of a transnational venture). Time and learning are specifically integrated into the discussion. The international student experience is an unusually intense period of enculturation and learning, often forcing the exploration and synthesis of markedly different locations, ways of life, and opportunities (Currie, 2007). The interplay of investment, capitalization, opportunity creation, analysis, and realization is described, which plays out, again, across time.

Consequently, the creation of one category of transnational entrepreneurs is illustrated as occurring within a rich decision-making context. The major mechanisms guiding the outcome are also included, with the emergence of transnational entrepreneurs represented as a product of the relationship among individual contextual variables (personal investment, entrepreneurial opportunity, perceived value in the market, and resource stocks). But, transnational entrepreneurship is not presented as an inevitable outcome of the student experience. Rather, transnational entrepreneurs emerge as one prominent possibility, after encountering the rigours of education and market forces. The four perspectives will now be briefly explained, with particular use made of the example of Canada, a country with a large immigrant and international student population.

The Experience of the International Student: Investments Comprising an Entrepreneurial Mindset

In part, the creation of transnational entrepreneurs is captured in investments that contribute to developing an entrepreneurial mindset. Three major types of investments (tangible, human, and social) are an endemic part of being an international student. The combination of the investment and a growing entrepreneurial mindset leads, in some cases, to a latent transnationality.

Tangible Investments

The student experience is rife with financial investments. These begin, of course, with tuition charges, but they extend to the financial burdens of lodging, food, clothing, and sundry other costs. For example, the 600,000 or so international students in the United States have been found to contribute a massive $13 billion to the U.S. economy – as a result of their yearly tuition payments, living expenses, and other related costs (Baruch, Budhwar, & Khatri, 2007: 100). Even small numbers of international students can have sizeable effects. A recent study of 232 international students in Bendigo, Australia, found they injected over $3 million into the local economy in a single year (Yao & Bai, 2008).

Yet, while the economic effects are large, others are even larger: students are learning the unique constellation of routines, activities, and institutional agents that guide national culture and the economic system in their host country. The ongoing investments, therefore, provide understanding of a new culture. Furthermore, the transactions attune students to the key socioeconomic differences between their home and host countries. A process of enrolment is under way (Yeung, 2002) whose end effects are a significant accumulation of cultural knowledge, achieved through indirect means, accruing entirely to the student. As well, an advantage is supplied to international students over their domestically trained counterparts, with the value of that advantage determined by the range of options that are subsequently made available to the individual student and the context in which they appear.

Human Investments

Two distinct combinations of human and social investments, described in 'push' and 'pull' scenarios, have been associated with the general creation of immigrant entrepreneurs. In the 'push' or barrier-based scenario, a group of forces blocks outside employment in organizations. These can typically include high unemployment levels in the general economy (van Tubergen, 2005), difficulties related to government policies (Tsui-Auch, 2005), and challenges in labour markets, including discrimination (Mata & Pendakur, 1999; Mora & Davila, 2005). Immigrants are, therefore, 'pushed' into self-employment because of their constrained choices for employment within organizations. By comparison, immigrants may also undertake high levels of human and social investments whose value realization is not impeded. The investments, in turn, may become capital, measurable in a wide array of opportunities that entice or 'pull' an immigrant into self-employment. For example, investments in English-language abilities and a useful second language are associated with self-employment in immigrants (Toussaint-Comeau, 2005). Also, small immigrant communities which have been long established in the host country are linked with heightened reserves of social capital and are anticipated to lead to greater self-employment (van Tubergen, 2005).

Both the 'push' and 'pull' scenarios seem to have relevance in understanding the emergence of transnational entrepreneurs from the ranks of international students, with the latter scenario appearing to offer greater currency. For example, previous researchers have concluded that when students make significant human investments in education and international experiences, they are likely to have higher incomes and to seek out entrepreneurial opportunities. Research has shown that those who leave a country are likely to experience greater earnings upon their return (Finnie, 2007). Approximately 5 per cent of American and 21 per cent of Canadian doctoral degree recipients indicate that they intend to leave North America after graduation, with about one-quarter of these being foreign students (Bordt & Bernier, 2005). These expatriates can expect to move more quickly through the executive ranks in their country of origin (Klie, 2006). Additionally, Canadian, U.S., and British studies have indicated that formal schooling and qualifications are associated with higher employment income (Clark & Drinkwater, 1998; Kerr & Schlosser, 2007), higher self-employment rates (Brown, Farrel, & Sessions, 2006), and greater job creation and returns for the self-employed (Henley, 2005).

Moving in a virtuous circle, knowledge of the positive investment-payout relationship can further spur education and language acquisition. Many immigrants choose to stay, if possible, in their host countries, attracted by a better quality of life and more opportunities. A portion, of course, become entrepreneurs, clearly reflecting the 'pull' scenario anticipated among some international students.

However, as noted, some international students may also be 'pushed' into self-employment, specifically as transnational entrepreneurs. A portion of the students may not possess the requisite language skills, for example, to be able to realize an opportunity in their host country or may be blocked because of regulatory barriers and/or a closing window of opportunity. A possible response is a new business based in their home country, but based in part on the knowledge, techniques, and/or contacts acquired during the time studying abroad. Or, as in a process described by Saxenian (2005), domestic businesses in their home countries could be established first by the international students. After successful establishment, and sometimes after considerable time, a transnational strategy can be pursued once the requisite resources are finally amassed.

Social Investments

The 'pull' scenario also appears to be especially prevalent in the case of social investments. International students make the conscious decision to develop their expertise in another country and, in so doing, they invest time, money, and energy in developing a new social network. This network can become a conduit through which entrepreneurs gain key supports, in a variety of forms (Adler & Kwon, 2002; Seibert, Kraimer, & Liden, 2001). Both the type and content of a social network can provide a source of capital (Burt, 1997). However, the value of social networks is often determined by more than simply their size, which is important, but also by the access to complementary resources they provide, both economic and cultural, and by the speed at which they can be marshalled (Neergaard, Shaw, & Carter, 2005).

In the course of their studies, international students have opportunities to meet other students, both international and from the host country. The exposure increases the size of the social networks and the likelihood that international students will be able to establish friendships. Previous research suggests that these friendships facilitate the formation of a management team, and they can contribute significantly to the performance of new ventures (Francis & Sandberg, 2000). Of special interest, international students are often well positioned while studying to develop a network of friends who are also from their home country, creating the strong potential for transnational partnerships (Neri & Ville, 2008). Furthermore, as with ethnic entrepreneurs (e.g., Tsui-Auch, 2005), access to ethnic networks in both countries may allow international students to have a more ready source of key resources that include money, but could also expand to possible key personnel or advisers. International students may also be able to strengthen often critical familial ties (Bagwell, 2008), in both their host country, if applicable, and to those at home, and graft them onto the networks developed through their education experiences. The speed by which the resources may be accessed could also be aided by cultural dimensions like shared languages and social mores and/or by familial relationships (e.g., Allen, 2000; Carroll & Mosakowski, 1987).

The Entrepreneurial Mindset

At the individual level, the broad investments and experiences of international students that were just described are likely to trigger a greater openness to entrepreneurialism. Entrepreneurial cognitions are 'the knowledge structures that people use to make assessments, judgments, or decisions involving opportunity evaluation, venture creation, and growth' (Mitchell et al., 2002: 93). Researchers in entrepreneurial cognition indicate that entrepreneurial individuals view risks more positively than non-entrepreneurs do, seeing opportunities where others do not (Palich & Bagby, 1995).

The entrepreneurial mindset is also better able to deal with uncertainty, which has been defined as 'a perceptual phenomenon derived from an inability to assign probabilities to future events largely because of a lack of information about cause/effect relationships' (Ireland, Hitt, & Sirmon, 2003: 968). In fact, the act of migration itself has been positively correlated with new-business formation (Levie, 2007). Furthermore, in small- and medium-sized firms – those entities most closely identified with, and subject to, their founders' proclivities – intensive knowledge renewal and a greater risk-taking propensity are both linked with internationalization (De Clercq, Sapienza, & Crijns, 2005).

Understanding the concept of *bisociation* (Koestler, 1964) is also helpful. It 'occurs when a person combines two or more previously unrelated matrices of skills or information' (Ireland, Hitt, & Sirmon, 2003: 981). In effect, international students are forced through their experiences to combine information about two previously unrelated cultures and manners of doing business. Through synthesis, opportunities are often identified and creativity fostered (Smith & Di Gregorio, 2002).

Moreover, geography appears to affect the synthesis. For instance, significant differences have been found across Western industrialized countries in both their institutional profiles and in their general influence on entrepreneurship (Busenitz, Gomez, & Spencer, 2000). Positive entrepreneurial influence and related activity rates have been high for a sustained period in North America (Timmons & Spinelli, 2007), our geographical focus.

Consequently, we suggest that international students are more likely to exhibit an entrepreneurial attitude, in comparison with those lacking the equivalent experiences. Again, although only some will proceed to found their own businesses, international students represent a high-potential group that might be nurtured into entrepreneurship. Robinson et al. (1991) developed an attitudinal scale based on an individual's achievement, innovation, locus of control, and self-esteem in business. Despite the fact that no work has been done directly linking the four attitudes and entrepreneurialism in international students, we suggest that in the act of pursuing their studies, students may come to display the four attitudes. For example, a significant relationship has been found between higher education and nascent entrepreneurship (Rotefoss & Kolvereid, 2005). As well, a significant correlation has been established between the level of education and the planning for a new venture, with start-up six times more likely for entrepreneurs with a business plan (Liao & Gartner, 2007). Finally, a natural relationship may exist between entrepreneurship and university education because about 20 per cent of international university students in Canada, for example, study business, management, and marketing (Canadian Bureau for International Education, 2005).

Capitalizing Investments Inherent in the Entrepreneurial Mindset

International students appear to become naturally primed for transnationalism through their sustained travel experiences. Resource stocks are built up through time which figures directly in the creation of options for employment. As well, a true binational entrepreneurial mindset comes into being for some students. For these latent transnationals, the field of opportunities is opened markedly.

Resource Stocks and Options

International students can come to accumulate a stock of resources because of their activities. But, regulatory conditions at the national level vary, and the ability to find gainful employment is often restricted, limiting the growth of tangible assets. Furthermore, as mentioned, international students may be blocked by unwelcoming regulatory hurdles and discrimination of a variety of types (Tsui-Auch, 2005; Mata & Pendakur, 1999; Mora & Davila, 2005).

However, notwithstanding the restrictions for employment, the most critical resource stocks – as with every type of nascent entrepreneur – are those related to human and social capital (Davidsson & Honig, 2003). Human and social capital is defined here as strictly the value derived from human and social investments, respectively. The creation of value is posited to be a direct function of a growing binational entrepreneurial mindset that is leading towards start-up in a more focused manner.

The Bicultural Entrepreneurial Mindset

McGrath and MacMillan (2000) describe concrete steps towards the identification and realization of entrepreneurial goals. In our framework, we consider the international student's personal investments in school and international experiences and how these investments come to grow in value (become capital) and shape the student's ability to delineate strategic knowledge and skills. By investing across national boundaries, international students expose themselves to business opportunities in their host country that might complement their experiences in their home country. When combined with the explicit business skills many learn in university, the ability to understand such international opportunities may inform a bicultural entrepreneurial mindset.

Successful intelligence involves a balance of analytical (IQ-based), creative, and practical intelligences, and is important to the entrepreneurial actions involved in innovating, and then eventually capitalizing and selling those ideas (Sternberg, 1997). Sternberg also notes that entrepreneurs will shape their own environments and convince others to share their view of the world (ibid.). Entrepreneurs must employ successful intelligence to balance how they adapt to, select, and shape their environments.

Similarly, many international students develop tacit knowledge as they experience new cultures. International students extend their analytical and creative bases of knowledge through formal schooling and develop practical intelligence through work and social experiences in the culture of the host country. Indeed, once the initial shock of introduction to a new culture subsides, international business students exhibit significant sociocultural adaptation (Townsend & Wan, 2007). Additionally, students may be more likely to develop cultural intelligence, whereby they are successful across varied cultures. Recently, Sternberg and Grigorenko (2006) extended the theory of successful intelligence to consider differences in the way intelligence is perceived, valued, and operationalized across cultures. Students who take advantage of international academic opportunities may have the ability to contextualize their intelligence and develop tacit knowledge bases in both the country of origin and the host country. In support, a recent study of undergraduate business scholars found that international students were significantly higher in the four dimensions of cross-cultural adaptability: emotional resilience, flexibility/openness, perceptual acuity, and personal autonomy (Elmuti, Tuck, & Kemper, 2008). Moreover, the development of a bicultural orientation has been linked with lower levels of psychological stress in international students (Cemalcilar & Falbo, 2008).

International students therefore have the high potential to amass many valuable resources that may induce them to pursue transnational entrepreneurship at some point in time. Moreover, both the 'push' and 'pull' scenarios again appear to be relevant. The average international student emerges after graduation with above-average-to-high levels of human investment, not all of which can be readily turned into the requisite capital. For example, in some students, insufficient English-language abilities may still preclude the pursuit of some types of opportunities in the country in which the studies took place. Instead, opportunities could be realized in students' home countries, while relying on the human and social investments made during the international student experience. But, the more common scenario is expected to be the 'pull' entrepreneur, mirroring the findings related to immigrant entrepreneurs in Canada with high human and social investments (Kerr & Schlosser, 2007). Furthermore, the confluence of high levels of human investment, social investment, and the binational orientation that is often present in the international student is expected to generate attractive opportunities, as well as the appropriate mindset and resource-acquiring abilities to realize them. Our focus now turns to delineating the emergence of transnational entrepreneurs from international students who often face a broad array of opportunities, some of which are frequently neither transnational nor entrepreneurial.

Opportunity Selection: Towards Transnational Enterprises

Potentially, the available business opportunities take a number of different forms. The options include employment with organizations, the establishment of businesses in the home or host country, and true transnational entrepreneurship. The most influential factors guiding a student's decision to stay in a host country are the perception of the labour market in that country, the student's adjustment process, the nature of the presence of his or her family in the home country, and the support (if any) of family in the host country (Baruch, Budhwar, & Khatri, 2007). We argue, with general support from Lee and Venkataraman (2006), that the selection of which opportunity to pursue is a calculation involving an international student's personal aspirations, the perceived market offerings connected to an option, and the resource position associated with each. Furthermore, the decision to stay abroad after study is typically treated as an 'either-or' proposition in the literature, while transnational entrepreneurship may actually present a viable synthesis for graduates.

Aspirations and Perceived Market Offerings

The decision to pursue entrepreneurial opportunities instead of non-entrepreneurial opportunities elicits a discussion of choices under conditions of uncertainty (e.g., Kahneman & Tversky, 1979). As pointed out by Lee and Venkataraman (2006), entrepreneurial options are uncertain by their nature, and, therefore, they are based on a subjective assessment. First, a decision-maker's employment goals, called 'the aspiration vector' by Lee and Venkataraman (2006), are weighed. Aspirations are 'composed of the combination of economic, social, and psychological benefits that an individual would like to have or that she believes she has the means and motivations to achieve for herself' (ibid.: 114). The second element under investigation is what the labour market offers to the individual at the time the decision is being made, what Lee and Venkataraman call the 'market offering vector.' This construction is defined as 'the combination of economic, social, and psychological dimensions that are implicitly or explicitly available to the individual from the labor market at a given point in time' (ibid.).

A comparison is made between aspirations and the benefits offered in the market. The mismatch of aspirations and labour market offerings gives rise to entrepreneurship. Specifically, entrepreneurship is likely when an individual's aspirations exceed the value of the labour market's offerings. Furthermore, the conditions are more likely when an individual's human and intellectual capital cannot be easily verified (conditions of information asymmetry), when an individual has developed rich social capital, and/or when the individual has characteristics that are dynamic, highly situational, and not easily measured (Lee & Venkataraman, 2006).

Indeed, many of these conditions can apply to the average immigrant, generally, and to international students, in particular. The decision-making by international students is again expected to be directly influenced by barrier- and opportunity-based scenarios (related to 'push' and 'pull' entrepreneurs). For instance, immigrants to Canada may encounter delays in having their full credentials recognized by authorities of various types (Adams, 2007). Moreover, the international student experience is marked by a wide number of barriers or challenges related to language abilities, immigrant status, cultural distance, and the lack of access to networks, among other issues (Li, 2007). On balance, the aforementioned could heavily skew the market offering vector and 'push' international students into entrepreneurship.

However, international students are again strongly expected to be 'pulled' into entrepreneurship as well. Education and social contacts facilitate the identification and realization of opportunities, as well as rewarding the risks being shouldered. A similar opportunity-oriented or 'pull' perspective on immigrant entrepreneurship is based upon enablers secured from the country of origin (Tsui-Auch, 2005). Recent research involving Duke University, the Kauffman Foundation, and the University of California, Berkeley, concluded that highly educated immigrants, for example, are likely to found new high-tech ventures in locations that already have a technology-based cluster (Wadhwa et al., 2007). Often, immigrants arrive as graduate students in North America and create their ventures upon completing their degrees. The international student can typically expect to find internship opportunities, mentoring, networking inroads, a variety of educational aids, and online help at universities that are entrepreneurially advanced (Li, 2007). The 'pull' of entrepreneurship, therefore, potentially emanates from a number of sources.

The Transnational Outcome

Two final, critical points must be made about the emergence of transnational entrepreneurs from international students. The first occurs at the individual level and focuses on the manner in which strategic, entrepreneurial decision-making unfolds. The second issue transpires at the level of the organization and market, and involves the combination of opportunity characteristics that must be present for a transnational venture to be created. The heavy demands of transnationalism help to explain the fact that ripe conditions in international students for transnationalism may not necessarily lead to that outcome.

Entrepreneurial Cognition, Resource Fit, Opportunity Scope, and Entrepreneurial Outcome

The answers to many basic entrepreneurial questions ('Why do only certain people become entrepreneurs? Why do only certain people recognize particular opportunities? Why are certain entrepreneurs more successful than others?') appear to reside, in part, in the cognition of individual aspiring entrepreneurs (Baron, 2004: 221–2). At the individual level, therefore, transnational entrepreneurs operating sustainable businesses are anticipated to possess the required, highly developed structured knowledge (or 'scripts') in three key areas (Mitchell et al., 2000: 977–8): arrangements scripts ('the contacts, relationships, resources, and assets necessary to form a new venture'), willingness scripts ('commitment to venturing and receptivity to the idea of starting a venture'), and ability scripts ('the knowledge structures or scripts that individuals have about the capabilities, skills, knowledge, norms, and attitudes required to create a venture').

Arrangements and ability scripts are both at least partially attributable to the experiences and connected knowledge base of the individual. Indeed, the international student appears well suited to construct the required scripts. These are contained perhaps most visibly in the human and social capital developed through international study, as well as in the cultural and opportunity-oriented learning that has been cultivated. However, the vagaries of individual volition, contained in the willingness scripts, offer a source of uncertainties connected to the emergence of transnational entrepreneurs.

Similar uncertainties exist at the level of the organization, in terms of strategy and markets. As stated, transnational entrepreneurship exists at the confluence of entrepreneurship, strategic management, and international business. Thus, the emergence of a successful transnational entrepreneur is contained in the ability to overcome the sometimes severe challenges related to opportunity recognition, resource accumulation, and risk-acceptance (entrepreneurship); competitive positioning, organizational fit, and sustained performance (strategic management); and all the exigencies emerging from doing business in different countries (international business). The businesses best poised for 'breakout' will likely be innovative, led by young managers who are better educated and can construct and exploit diverse networks (Bagwell, 2008; Davidsson & Honig, 2003). By necessity, therefore, understanding the emergence of the transnational entrepreneur entails multilevel analysis.

In order to launch transnationally, the accumulated resources of the international student must be scaled to meet the needs of the venture. At the same time, the perceived geographical scope of the opportunity must be international. Moreover, an overlap must exist between the geographical centres of the international student's expertise and the market scope of the opportunity. Deviations from the aforementioned parameters can result in domestic start-up or in failed launch. Transnational entrepreneurs will eventually emerge through the unique mixed embeddedness (Kloosterman, van der Leun, & Rath, 1999; Rath, 2002) of select international students: the specific conditions of the relevant social, political, and economic processes will combine to advance or hinder the transnational option.

International students can be uniquely placed to manage the forces that many times play out over a protracted period of time. The multiple requirements along the lines of entrepreneur, strategy, and market help to explain why transnational businesses can take years to develop and unfold. For instance, many transnational entrepreneurs have emerged in Taiwan, building on education acquired in North America in prior years (Saxenian, 2002a, 2005). As well, despite limited supporting research, there is evidence to suggest that the vast majority (98%) of international students (in the United States from India and China) do not plan transnational businesses at the outset (Li, 2007). Thus, the complexity, positive economic effects, and seemingly long latency period often exhibited in international students as they make the transition to transnational entrepreneurs exemplify a rich research topic now only in its infancy. Much remains to be learned about the steps, incentives, and barriers to transnational entrepreneurship.

The Relationship between the International Student and the Transnational Entrepreneur

Our research offers a three-part contribution. First, we provide a comprehensive discussion of the transformation of international students into transnational entrepreneurs. We describe developmental issues for barrier- and opportunity-based ('push' and 'pull') transnational entrepreneurship, including the dimensions and temporal nature of the choice sets available to international students. The basic elements of the discussion and their temporal dimensions should be tested empirically. The insights hold promising value for researchers and policy makers and for a nascent category of transnational entrepreneurs, the international student.

Practical Implications

International students represent a mobile demographic complete with a bicultural mindset and a broad spectrum of entrepreneurial options. Yet, historically, a number of rules have made it difficult for international exchange students to start their own businesses. Again, the situation in Canada is instructive. For example, until recently, if students wished to start a business, the Canadian government required that students commit several hundred thousand dollars to the venture. By comparison, countries such as India and China entice expatriates to return home using special policies and incentives (Klie, 2006). But, a new system instituted by the government of Canada, the 'Canadian Experience Class,' allows up to 25,000 people to achieve permanent residency status through their work experience in the country (Godbout, 2008). However, while work in entrepreneurial firms counts towards the points requirements for permanent residency, self-employment does not (Citizen and Immigration Canada, 2009).

Adding to the barriers in all relevant localities, international students may not have the funds to start a business simultaneously in two countries. Initial financial capital is an important determinant of survival and growth (Cooper & Gimeno-Gascon, 1994), yet it is often difficult for immigrants to obtain financing without a multiyear domestic credit history.

Consequently, a number of ways exist to aid the creation of transnational business ventures. Policy-makers fostering economic development could begin by noting the strong potential connections between the international student experience and a valuable economic outcome (transnational entrepreneurship) and then tailor their offerings to support that development. For example, free mentoring programs that match seasoned business students, in particular, with established entrepreneurs and lawyers in the host country may help the students to navigate the legal and regulatory hurdles in starting their own businesses. In fact, recent research has demonstrated the significant influence of mentoring, in general, and the large effect of academic mentoring, in particular (Eby et al., 2008). Furthermore, mentoring has been demonstrated to be a powerful force in improving opportunity recognition, providing key information, and sharpening cognitive processes (Ozgen & Baron, 2007). Colleges and universities could encourage students to take advantage of international exchanges in a third country, as this action will expand scholars' cultural intelligence and open the door to transnational opportunities. Recent research (Stuart & Ding, 2006) has pointed to the significant influence of human and social capital, as well as reputational effects in guiding U.S. university scientists to become entrepreneurs. Similarly, if the student cohort at a college or university is active in starting businesses and the school's reputation and networks offer valuable resources, start-up rates and eventual transnationalism among international students could reasonably be expected to grow. Finally, providing ready sources of seed funding will help the students to manage the expenses of operating businesses in two or more countries. Thus, a few key policy initiatives appear to hold attractive possibilities for transforming international students into successful transnational entrepreneurs, benefiting many with a global reach.

ACKNOWLEDGMENTS

This research was funded, in part, by a Research and Teaching Innovation Fund Grant (RTIF) awarded by the Odette School of Business at the University of Windsor.

REFERENCES

Adams, T.L. (2007). Professional regulation in Canada: Past and present. *Canadian Issues*, Spring, 14–16.
Adler, P.S., & Kwon, S. (2002). Social capital: Prospects for a new concept. *Academy of Management Review*, 27: 17–41.
Allen, W.D. (2000). Social networks and self-employment. *Journal of Socio-Economics*, 29: 487–501.
Bagwell, S. (2008). Transnational family networks and ethnic minority business development. *International Journal of Entrepreneurial Behavior and Research*, 14: 377–394.

Baron, R.A. (2004). The cognitive perspective: A valuable tool for answering entrepreneurship's basic 'why' questions. *Journal of Business Venturing*, 19: 221–239.

Baruch, Y., Budhwar, P., & Khatri, N. (2007). Brain drain: Inclination to stay abroad after studies. *Journal of World Business*, 42: 99–112.

Bordt, M., & Bernier, S. (2005). Survey of earned doctorates: A profile of doctoral degree recipients. *Innovation Analysis Bulletin*, 7. Accessed 17 Jan. 2008 at http://www.statcan.gc.ca/pub/88-003-x/88-003-x2005003-eng.pdf.

Brown, S., Farrel, L., & Sessions, J.G. (2006). Self-employment matching: An analysis of dual earner couples and working households. *Small Business Economics*, 26: 155–172.

Burt, R. (1997). The contingent value of social capital. *Administrative Science Quarterly*, 42: 339–365.

Busenitz, L.W., Gomez, C., & Spencer, J.W. (2000). Country institutional profiles: Unlocking entrepreneurial phenomena. *Academy of Management Journal*, 43: 994–1003.

Canadian Bureau for International Education. (2005). *The National Report on International Students in Canada 2002*. Ottawa: CBIE. Accessed 3 Dec. 2008 at http://www.cbie.ca.

Carroll, G.R., & Mosakowski, E. (1987). The career dynamics of self-employment. *Administrative Science Quarterly*, 32: 570–589.

Cemalcilar, Z., & Falbo, T. (2008). A longitudinal study of the adaptation of international students in the United States. *Journal of Cross-Cultural Psychology*, 39: 799–804.

Cervantes-Rodriguez, A.M. (2006). Nicaraguans in Miami-Dade County: Immigration, incorporation, and transnational entrepreneurship. *Latino Studies*, 4: 232–257.

Citizenship and Immigration Canada. (2007). Third Quarter Data 2006. *The Monitor*. Accessed 17 Jan. 2008 at www.cic.gc.ca/english/resources/statistics/monitor/index.asp.

Citizenship and Immigration Canada. (2008a). *Facts and Figures 2008. Immigration Overview: Permanent and Temporary Residents, Canada. December 1 Stock of Foreign Students by Province or Territory and Urban Area, 2004–2008*. Accessed 29 July 2009 at http://www.cic.gc.ca/English/resources/statistics/facts2008/temporary/04.asp.

Citizenship and Immigration Canada. (2008b). *Facts and Figures 2008. Immigration Overview: Permanent and Temporary Residents, Canada. Total Entries by Province or Territory and Urban Area, 2004–2008*. Accessed 29 July 2009 at http://www.cic.gc.ca/English/resources/statistics/facts2008/temporary/03.asp.

Citizenship and Immigration Canada. (2009). *Application for Permanent Residence: Canadian Experience Class (IMM 5609)*. Accessed 28 Aug. 2009 at http://www.cic.gc.ca/English/information/applications/guides/5609E2.asp.

Clark, K., & Drinkwater, S. (1998). Ethnicity and self-employment in Britain. *Oxford Bulletin of Economics and Statistics*, 60(3): 383–407.

Cooper, A.C., & Gimeno-Gascon, F.J. (1994). Initial human and financial capital as predictors of new venture performance. *Journal of Business Venturing*, 9: 371–395.

Currie, G. (2007). Beyond our imagination: The voice of international students on the MBA. *Management Learning*, 38(5): 539–556.

Davidsson, P., & Honig, B. (2003). The role of social and human capital among nascent entrepreneurs. *Journal of Business Venturing*, 18: 301–331.

De Clercq, D., Sapienza, H.J., & Crijns, H. (2005). The internationalization of small and medium-sized firms. *Small Business Economics*, 24: 409–419.

Eby, L.T., Allen, T.D., Evans, S.C., Ng, T., & DuBois, D.L. (2008). Does mentoring matter? A multidisciplinary meta-analysis comparing mentoring and non-mentored individuals. *Journal of Vocational Behavior*, 72: 254–267.

Elmuti, D., Tuck, B., & Kemper, F. (2008). Analyzing cross-cultural adaptability among business students: An empirical investigation. *International Journal of Management*, 25: 551–568.

Finnie, R. (2007). *International Mobility: A Longitudinal Analysis of the Effects on Individuals' Earnings*. No. 11F0019MIE. Ottawa: Statistics Canada.

Francis, D.H., & Sandberg, W.R. (2000). Friendship within entrepreneurial teams and its association with team and venture performance. *Entrepreneurship Theory and Practice*, 25(2): 5–25.

Godbout, A. (2008). Ottawa puts out welcome mat for foreign students, skilled workers. *Canwest News Service*, wirefeed 12 Aug. 2008.

Grieshop, J.I. (2006). The envios of San Pablo Huixtepec, Oaxaca: Food, home, and transnationalism. *Human Organization*, 65: 400–406.

Hawthorne, L. (2006). Labour market outcomes for migrant professionals: Canada and Australia compared. Citizenship and Immigration Canada. Accessed 6 Dec. 2008 at http://www.cic.gc.ca/ENGLISH/resources/research/2006-canada-australia.asp.

Henley, A. (2005). Job creation by the self-employed: The roles of entrepreneurial and financial capital. *Small Business Economics*, 25: 175–196.

Ireland, R.D., Hitt, M.A., & Sirmon, D.G. (2003). A model of strategic entrepreneurship: The construct and its dimensions. *Journal of Management*, 29(6): 963–989.

Itzigsohn, J., Dore, C., Hernandez, E., & Vazquez, O. (1999). Mapping Dominican transnationalism. *Ethnic and Racial Studies*, 22: 316–339.

Kahneman, D., & Tversky, A. (1979). Prospect theory: An analysis of decision under risk. *Econometrica*, 47: 263–291.

Kerr, G., & Schlosser, F.K. (2007). Start-up and success in ethnic new ventures. *Frontiers of Entrepreneurship Research*, 27: 166–181.

Klie, S. (2006). India, China call expats home. *Canadian HR Reporter*, 19(3): 1, 9.

Kloosterman, R., van der Leun, J., & Rath, J. (1999). Mixed embeddedness: (In)formal economic activities and immigrant business in the Netherlands. *International Journal of Urban and Regional Research*, 23: 252–266.

Koestler, A. (1964). *The Act of Creation*. New York: Dell.

Lee, J.-H., & Venkataraman, S. (2006). Aspirations, market offerings, and the pursuit of entrepreneurial opportunities. *Journal of Business Venturing*, 21: 107–123.

Levie, J. (2007). Immigration, in-migration, ethnicity and entrepreneurship in the United Kingdom. *Small Business Economics*, 28: 143–169.

Levitt, P. (1998). Social remittances: Migration driven local-level forms of cultural diffusion. *International Migration Review*, 32(4): 926–948.

Li, W. (2007). Ethnic entrepreneurship: Studying Chinese and Indian students in the United States. *Journal of Developmental Entrepreneurship*, 12(4): 449–466.

Liao, J., & Gartner, W.B. (2007). The influence of pre-venture planning on new venture creation. *Journal of Small Business Strategy*, 18(2): 1–21.

Lopez, D. (2001). Los Angeles: Transnational City or Mélange of Transnational Communities? Paper presented at the annual meeting of the American Sociological Association, 18–21 Aug., Anaheim, California.

Mata, R., & Pendakur, R. (1999). Immigration, labor force integration, and the pursuit of self-employment. *International Migration Review*, 33(2): 378–402.

McGrath, R.G., & MacMillan, I. (2000). *The Entrepreneurial Mindset: Strategies for Continuously Creating Opportunity in an Age of Uncertainty*. Boston: Harvard Business School Press.

Mitchell, R.K., Smith, B., Seawright, K.W., & Morse, E.A. (2000). Cross-cultural cognitions and the venture creation decision. *Academy of Management Journal*, 43(5): 974–993.

Mitchell, R.K., Busenitz, L.W., Lant, T., McDougall, P.P., Morse, E.A., & Smith, J.B. (2002). Toward a theory of entrepreneurial cognition: Rethinking the people side of entrepreneurship research. *Entrepreneurship Theory & Practice*, 27(2): 93–104.

Mora, M.T., & Davila, A. (2005). Ethnic group size, linguistic isolation, and immigrant entrepreneurship in the USA. *Entrepreneurship and Regional Development*, 17: 389–404.

Neergaard, H., Shaw, E., & Carter, S. (2005). The impact of gender, social capital and networks on business ownership: A research agenda. *International Journal of Entrepreneurial Behaviour & Research*, 11(5): 338–357.

Neri, F., & Ville, S. (2008). Social capital renewal and the academic performance of international students in Australia. *Journal of Socio-Economics*, 37: 1515–1538.

Ozgen, E., & Baron, R.A. (2007). Social sources of information in opportunity recognition: Effects of mentors, industry networks, and professional forums. *Journal of Business Venturing*, 22: 174–192.

Palich, L.E., & Bagby, D.R. (1995). Using cognitive theory to explain entrepreneurial risk-taking: Challenging conventional wisdom. *Journal of Business Venturing*, 10: 425–438.

Portes, A., Guarnizo, L.E., & Haller, W.J. (2002). Transnational entrepreneurs: An alternative form of immigrant economic adaptation. *American Sociological Review*, 67: 278–298.

Rath, J. (2002). A quintessential immigrant niche? The non-case of immigrants in the Dutch construction industry. *Entrepreneurial and Regional Development*, 14: 355–372.

Robinson, P.B., Stimpson, D.V., Huefner, J.C., & Hunt, H.K. (1991). An attitude approach to the prediction of entrepreneurship. *Entrepreneurship Theory and Practice*, 29: 13–27.

Rotefoss, B., & Kolvereid, L. (2005). Aspiring, nascent and fledgling entrepreneurs: An investigation of the business start-up process. *Entrepreneurship and Regional Development*, 17: 109–127.

Saxenian, A. (2002a). Transnational communities and the evolution of global production networks: The cases of Taiwan, China and India. *Industry and Innovation*, 9(3): 183–202.

Saxenian, A. (2002b). Brain circulation: How high-skill immigration makes everyone better off. *Brooking Review*, 20: 28–31.

Saxenian, A. (2005). From brain drain to brain circulation: Transnational communities and regional upgrading in India and China. *Studies in Comparative International Development*, 40(2): 35–61.

Seibert, S.E., Kraimer, M.L., & Liden, R.C. (2001). A social capital theory of career success. *Academy of Management Journal*, 44: 219–238.

Smith, K.G., & Di Gregorio, D. (2002). Bisociation, discovery, and the role of entrepreneurial action. In M.A. Hitt, R.D. Ireland, S.M. Camp, & D.L. Sexton (Eds.), *Strategic Entrepreneurship: Creating a New Mindset*, 129–150. Oxford: Blackwell.

Starr, J., & Fondas, N. (1992). A model of entrepreneurial socialization and organizational formation. *Entrepreneurship Theory & Practice*, 17: 67–76.

Statistics Canada. (2008). *Census Snapshot. Immigration in Canada: A Portrait of*

the Foreign-Born Population, 2006 Census. Accessed 4 Dec. 2008 http://www
.statcan.gc.ca/pub/11-008-x/2008001/article/10556-eng.htm.

Sternberg, R.J. (1997). *Successful Intelligence.* New York: Plume.

Sternberg, R.J., & Grigorenko, E.L. (2006). Cultural intelligence and successful intelligence. *Group & Organization Management,* 31(1): 27–39.

Stuart, T., & Ding, W. (2006). When do scientists become entrepreneurs? The social structural antecedents of commercial activity in the academic life sciences. *American Journal of Sociology,* 112: 97–144.

Szonyi, M. (2003). *Asian-Canadians and Canada's International Relations.* Foreign Policy Dialogue Series 2003-7. Vancouver: Asia Pacific Foundation.

Timmons, J.A., & Spinelli, S. (2007). *New Venture Creation.* (7th ed.). New York: McGraw-Hill/Irwin.

Toussaint-Comeau, M. (2005). *Chicago Fed Letter: Self-employed Immigrants: An Analysis of Recent Data.* Chicago: Federal Reserve Bank of Chicago.

Townsend, P., & Wan, C. (2007). The impact of multicultural experience in the development of socio-cultural adaptation for international business students. *International Journal of Educational Management,* 21: 194–212.

Tsui-Auch, L.S. (2005). Unpacking regional ethnicity and the strength of ties in shaping ethnic entrepreneurship. *Organization Studies,* 26(8): 1189–1216.

van Tubergen, F. (2005). Self-employment of immigrants: A cross-national study of 17 Western societies. *Social Forces,* 84(2): 709–732.

Wadhwa, V., Rissing, B., Saxenian, A., & Gereffi, G. (2007). *Education, Entrepreneurship and Immigration: America's New Immigrant Entrepreneurs, Part II.* SSRN.

Waldinger, R. (1998). Comment. Presented at the International Conference on Nationalism, Transnationalism, and the Crises of Citizenship, April, University of California, Davis.

Yao, L.J., & Bai, Y. (2008). The sustainability of economic and cultural impacts of international students to regional Australia. *Humqnonics,* 24: 250–262.

Yeung, H.W. (2002). Entrepreneurship in international business: An institutional perspective. *Asia Pacific Journal of Management,* 19(1): 29–61.

7 The Trade and Immigration Nexus in the India-Canada Context

MARGARET WALTON-ROBERTS

In this chapter I address the broader context of trade and immigration literature and, using fieldwork on India-Canada relations, assess what this particular case can tell us about seemingly underdeveloped levels of transnational entrepreneurship (TE). In place of economic models and measures, I use qualitative material gathered from immigrant traders and government officials in Vancouver, Canada, and Delhi and Mumbai, India, to explore not only how trade and immigration might be linked but also how structural and cultural dimensions inform this relationship. This chapter offers an empirical response to the demand that 'transnational entrepreneurship needs to focus more on the micro-level processes of social construction that occur through daily practice' (Drori, Honig, & Ginsberg, this volume).

Using the idea of practice as derived from Bourdieu, Drori, Honig, & Ginsberg (this volume) advocate that any focus on transnational entrepreneurs must take into account both the macro-structural dimensions of the economic frameworks they operate within and the transnational cultural milieu they are embedded in, both of which shape their decision-making processes. Such a practice-based reading is shaped by a number of contexts and processes, and research that can adequately interpret them will provide valuable comparative data allowing us to understand the emergence, or absence, of transnational entrepreneurship in different contexts. This structuration-inspired research focus is already well developed in work by economic geographers. Economists have arguably (re)discovered geography at the same time that economic geographers have embraced culture. Since the publication of Krugman's *Geography and Trade* in 1991 we have seen the emergence of a 'new economic geography' (Schmutzler, 1999), which encourages economists to develop a geographical sensibility. For example, a basic geography of trade suggests that tariffs and freight are the major explanatory variables in assessing trade costs (Hummels, 1999), but increasing trade in services and new transmission technologies are transforming circuits of exchange, thereby demanding more complex spatial thinking (Morley & Robins, 1995). These economic changes create important space for alternative forms of transnational networks to emerge (Coe & Bunnell, 2003). Responding to this transformation in economic space and social practice, economic geographers have become more aware of the importance of culture and local context (Amin & Thrift, 1995; Barnes, 1996; Castells, 1996; Sayer, 1997; Schoeberger, 1996; Scott, 2004). But how do we examine culture and local context in terms of the immigration/ trade nexus? Explicit attention to the recursive relationship between institutional norms and individual cultural practice has been usefully explored, using a discourse and cultural capital approach (Kothari, 2006; Stampnitzky, 2006), and this has been particularly useful for examining the socio-spatial identity construction of the ethnic entrepreneur (EE) (Plüss, 2005; Raghuram & Strange, 2001). In the case of India-Canada trade, I explore how the relatively weak trading relationship is assessed vis-à-vis the presence of a large, Indian immigrant population.

Setting the Scene: Research on Trade and Immigration

In the pre-9/11 world, the spectre of an economy where goods, ideas, and people would freely flow across political borders was widely debated and anticipated. Kenichi Ohmae's bestseller *The Borderless World* (1999) spoke to an era of economic growth where states would increasingly become irrelevant. Though Ohmae's work was widely critiqued, especially by geographers, some of us may nostalgically reflect on the ability to even consider the retreat of the border. Today, borders are back on the agenda, and their thickening and intrusion into trade and human mobility is clearly evident from the false starts of the Doha Round to safe third country agreements. During the 1990s a small number of scholars explored the connection between people who crossed borders and goods and money that did likewise. Research on remittances is clearly one dimension of this connection (Nayyar, 1994; Russell & Teitlbaum, 1992; Prakash, 1998; Page & Plaza, 2006), and an explicit link between goods and people moving, or trade and immigration, has also become more prominent. This is especially evident in the rising interest paid to the transnational immigrant entrepreneur (Zahra & George, 2002).

Historically there are examples of ancient cities along important trading routes that exhibited culturally diverse cosmopolitan relations (Briggs, 2004), and anecdotally many have argued that a contemporary link does exist between immigration and increased trade. Until recently, however, explicit interest in this modern-day connection has been surprisingly sparse. This has lately been rectified by social scientists interested in transnational entrepreneurs, and by economists who are intrigued by the link between trade and immigration, yet struggle to model and quantify it.

In Canada Globerman (1995) concluded that there is no relationship between trade and immigration, yet Baker and Benjamin (1996) and Wagner, Head, and Ries (2002) argue that a positive link exists. Globerman (1995) discusses two aspects of the trade immigration relationship. The first is factor price equalization, where free trade should eventually eradicate economic disequilibria, and hence international migration. Of course, this neoclassical view assumes that all immigration is economically motivated – ignoring political, cultural, or social causes – and also that trade is framed purely by economic rationales rather than political connections (such as colonial linkages and strategic geopolitical motivations). The second aspect Globerman considers is that immigration potentially enables reduced transaction costs. Transaction cost reductions, unlike factor price equalization, would support the view that increased immigration can lead to increased trade. Looking at the data for Canada, Globerman concludes that there is no relationship between trade (aggregated imports and exports) and immigration and that the two policies should not be considered together. Baker and Benjamin tackle the same question, yet take a different view. They suggest that a strong link exists between trade and immigration in relation to Asia Pacific countries (excluding India) and conclude by saying: 'We are left with a reasonably robust conclusion that immigration is correlated with trade, with the correlation with imports being slightly higher than with exports' (1996: 338). Head, Ries, and Wagner (1998), following Head and Ries (1998), test three variants within a gravity model framework to consider the effect of immigration on trade. Each of these models is subjected to 'fixed country effects,' which control for various connections that could mistakenly be credited to immigration, such as commonwealth country links. The first model Head, Ries, and Wagner use assumes constant elasticity between trade and immigration levels, the second posits that immigrants possess a greater propensity for trade than non-immigrants do, and the third allows for the immigrant effect to decrease as the number of immigrants in a province rises. They conclude that only the first model provides statistically significant results when subjected to 'fixed country effects,' suggesting that total annual trade associated with immigration ranges from U.S. $91 billion to U.S. $105 billion for exports and from U.S. $60 billion to U.S. $138 billion for imports. The failure of the other more theoretically sophisticated models to produce any statistically significant results forces Head, Ries, and Wagner to conclude: 'Determining how immigration and trade are linked has proved elusive. Yet, there continues to be strong evidence that the link is there' (1998: 33).

In the United States, Light, Zhou, and Kim (2002) are far more definitive in their analysis of the link between immigration and trade, arguing that immigrant entrepreneurship, English fluency, and middleman minority status expand American foreign trade. Their results support and extend Gould's (1994) original findings that immigrant entrepreneurs expand exports but not imports, which is contrary to findings for Switzerland (Kohli, 2002), Canada (Baker & Benjamin, 1996; Wagner, Head, & Ries 2002), and the United Kingdom (Girma & Yu, 2002). Dunlevy's (2006) analysis of the immigrant trade effect on U.S. states found the pro-trade impact of immigrants is strengthened when higher levels of corruption exist in the source country and also enhanced by language dissimilarity between the sending and receiving country. Light, Zhou, and Kim (2002) argue that since the U.S. import market is saturated, immigrant traders can have little impact on imports but do have an impact on exports because they counteract the cultural and linguistic insularity of the United States. This later attention to national context highlights one reason for the difference in findings between various countries. Overall, it is fair to say that conclusive evidence of a positive link between immigration and trade has been frustratingly difficult to come by, but in general, evidence for the link is there. Part of the problem in building definitive models for this connection is the complexity and diversity of the processes and geographies involved, and this, I argue, illustrates the necessity of conducting geographically contextualized empirical research on the matter. Such attention contributes to understanding the complex arena that shapes the practice of TE.

Assessing Trade and Immigration Links: Problems with Economic Measurements and Models

While researchers struggle to quantify the relationship between trade and immigration, a number of critical issues must be addressed with regard to this approach in general. DeVoretz (1996) has argued that the metropolitan scale is more appropriate to this research topic because immigration is disproportionately directed towards urban centres. This is particularly evident in Canada, where Montreal, Toronto, and Vancouver receive over 75 per cent of the immigrants to this country. Most national data collection regimes, however, only measure at the national or provincial scale, and even at the Canadian provincial scale, the researcher's only tool is merchandise import/export data based on the province in which the goods clear customs, not where they are consumed. Moreover, state-compiled data fail to comprehensively capture international service exports and intrafirm flows (Assanie & Woo, 2004), thereby posing important concerns when such data are used as a basis for modelling such complex interactions as those between trade and immigration. In general, when measuring links between immigration and trade, the quality of the trade data collected by government bodies and their consistency over time pose problems for economists searching for explanatory or predictive laws.

Another shortcoming with immigration-trade models is the assumption that the potential for increased trade will be seen primarily in relation to the immigrant's country of origin, spatially essentializing, in effect, the position and potential contribution of immigrants to international trade. This is particularly relevant for the millions of Indians overseas who are known for their ability to trade across a wide geographical range (Kotkin, 1992; White, 1994). This interpretation promotes a static bond between the immigrant trader and his or her nation of origin and settlement, despite the fact that immigrant businesses, even small and medium-sized ones, increasingly operate across more than one country (Crick, Chaudhry, & Batstone, 2001). Capturing this global dimension of enhanced trade through immigration is likely to be difficult to conclusively demonstrate in aggregate econometric models.

Other concerns emerge when we consider the language used to represent relations between these complex processes. The classic statement made by Gunnar Olsson in his examination of gravity models – 'that what I say may reveal as much about the language I am talking in as it does about the phenomena I am talking about' (1975: 452) – is particularly relevant when thinking through how economists illustrate complex sociospatial processes, such as the links between trade and immigration. Olsson argues that regression analysis and causal explanation do not capture recursive processes: for example, that individuals' behaviour might begin to adapt to the opportunity sets they are forced to make their decisions within. In the context of trade and immigration, for instance, immigrants' role as traders might not necessarily be due to their greater propensity for trade but rather to their lack of access to other forms of employment – the classic blocked mobility thesis (Light & Bonacich, 1988). Olsson argues that gravity model regression may sometimes conceal, rather than reveal, important social processes shaping the phenomena under discussion. But Olsson's consideration of the limitations that space places upon human interaction – the utility of interaction balanced by the disutility of travel – also needs to be critically viewed in light of increased transnational immigrant practices. In an era of technological transformation, spatial distance is being reshaped, and together with social context, that is, the type of networks and resources one is linked to, the basic geometry of distance and the disutility of travel are being transformed. This suggests that we have to continue to examine how much these new geographies really do change the social and economic processes of exchange and associated power relations, and therefore calls for greater attention to the geographical context of such exchanges.

Economists themselves have recognized that in attempts to understand the links between trade and immigration, trade theory itself needs to be altered. Stanton and Lee (1996) argue that only trade theories based on imperfect market competition could capture the dynamic nature of trade and immigration links. Helliwell (1997) has also argued that international trade theory needs to work with the assumption of imperfect competition in order to effectively explain international trade. He highlights the relative failure of international trade theory to account for 'border effects' that reduce trade even when controlled for distance. According to Helliwell, institutions, ranging from the family to firms to national institutions, play an important role in facilitating trade and thereby overcoming border effects. This view resonates with the transnational immigrant entrepreneur literature.

Transnational Immigrant Entrepreneurs

While economists struggle to prove there is a link between trade and immigration, other social scientists have recently focused more attention on understanding how immigrant entrepreneurs actually conduct international trade (Kyle, 1999; Maas, 2005; Saxenian, 2002, 2006; Lever-Tracy, Ip, & Tracy, 1996; Portes & Guarnizo, 1991; Portes, Guarnizo, & Haller, 2002; Zahra & George, 2002). Though much research on immigrant enterprise highlights the links between economic activity and the sociocultural capital that immigrant trading networks are built around (Granovetter, 1995; Portes, 1995; Walton-Roberts & Hiebert, 1997), relatively less attention has been paid to the explicit connection between increased trade and immigration (but see Saxenian, 1999, 2006; Lever-Tracy, Ip, & Tracy, 1996; Portes & Guarnizo, 1991). The key point in these arguments has been that networks (especially but not exclusively family-based) serve as conduits for information, capital, labour, and goods exchange, and are imbued with cultural as well as economic significance. Immigrant entrepreneurs thereby act as trade facilitators, linking distant markets through their unique position as knowledgeable transnational actors.

The cultural competencies that transnational entrepreneurs possess are of central importance because under conditions of globalization networks of communication and possibilities for trade have expanded and small- and large-scale operators alike are positioned in important ways to benefit from, and contribute to, efficient, flexible, and often highly trust-based trading networks (Castells, 1996; Wong, 2004; Wong & Ng, 2002; van Apeldoorn, 2004; Hsing, 2003; Coe & Bunnell, 2003). Certain immigrant groups exhibit higher rates of self-employment (Light & Bonancich, 1988; Fawcett & Gardner, 1995; Kim & Hurh, 1985), and research on immigrant enterprise highlights the sociocultural capital that immigrant trading networks are built upon (Granovetter, 1995; Portes, 1995; Walton-Roberts & Hiebert, 1997). This interest now includes a focus on increased international trade and immigration explicitly in reference to transnational practices (Kyle, 1999; Maas, 2005; Saxenian, 2002, 2006; Lever-Tracy, Ip, & Tracy, 1996; Portes & Guarnizo, 1991; Portes, Gaurnizo, & Haller, 2002; Zahra & George, 2002). As communication networks and trade have globalized, small- and large-scale operators alike become positioned to create and benefit from flexible trust-based trading networks (Castells, 1996; Coe & Bunnell, 2003). Immigrant traders can facilitate and anchor such trust-based trade networks (Wong, 2004; Wong & Ng, 2002; van Apeldoorn, 2004; Hsing, 2003).

Despite the growing recognition of the linkage between trade and immigration, these two policy agendas often operate in opposition to each other (Keely, 2003; Peberdy, 2000; Peberdy & Crush, 2001; Gallegos, 2004; Mosk, 2005). For example, Wong (2004) highlights how Canadian residency requirements for citizenship suppress the success of transnational entrepreneurs. Furthermore, research on transnational immigrant entrepreneurs has assessed how policy contexts can constrain opportunity structures for immigrants (Crick, Chaudhry, & Batstone, 2001; Stanton & Lee, 1996; Collins, 2003; Rath & Kloosterman, 2000; Kloosterman, 2003; Teixeira, Lo, & Truelove, 2007). In the case of Canada, ineffective immigrant labour market policies can create the context for 'blocked mobility' (Light & Bonancich, 1988), leaving immigrants little option but the entrepreneurial route. We see this in the non-recognition of foreign credentials and in immigrant earnings discrepancies (Bauder, 2003), which create a cohort of recent immigrants where transnational behaviour is born of necessity, not necessarily of desire (Wong, 2004; Ley, 2003, 2005, 2006; Waters, 2002; Hiebert, 2002). Assessing the link between immigration and trade, therefore, also necessitates identifying the ruptures that forge such a link in the first place.

Much of the recent literature examining transnational entrepreneurs has focused on immigrants from 'new' Asia, especially Hong Kong and Taiwan. In comparison, TEs of Indian origin are a relatively underexplored group, especially if we look beyond the fashion and design industries (Bhachu, 2004; Dwyer, 2004; Dwyer & Jackson, 2003; Dwyer & Crang, 2002; Raghuram, 2004; Walton-Roberts & Pratt, 2005; Hardill & Raghuram, 1998). This study aims to address this gap by assessing the role of Indian immigrant entrepreneurs in Canada who are active in developing trade between India and Canada.

Methodology

In this chapter I attempt to work through this trade-immigration complexity and relate it to the apparent lack of substantial transnational entrepreneurship in the case of India-Canada, drawing upon interviews with government trade officials as well as immigrant business professionals and traders involved in trade with India. To explore these complex intersections, I draw from semi-structured in-depth interviews conducted in 1999–2000 with eight Canadian trade officers in Vancouver, Delhi, Mumbai, and Chandigarh, and nine immigrant entrepreneurs/corporate employees in Vancouver who were actively involved in trade with India at that time. The sample is small but very specific, and I supplement and further contextualize these data with more recent secondary data from government and media publications relating to trade with India. This subsequent data, as well as ongoing research into the trade-immigration nexus, strongly suggest that the issues highlighted by these respondents in 1999–2000 are still relevant today. Insights from the qualitative data shed light on the prevailing context of

India-Canada trade, since there continues to be a general agreement that this trade relationship is still drastically underdeveloped (Dobson, 2006). This general assessment has not radically changed despite the rapid economic growth of 'shining' India. The data from qualitative interviews offer some important insights into the social construction of the trade and immigration connection, or lack thereof, in the case of India-Canada. After first introducing a general context for India-Canada relations, I explore the qualitative data with reference to three sets of agents who inform the trade-immigration nexus: immigrant traders, the mainstream Canadian business community and economy, and the non-entrepreneurial immigrants and trade creation.

Trade and Immigration: The India-Canada Case

Indian immigrants comprise just over 1 per cent of the total population in Canada. In terms of Indian immigrant categories, the largest component in Canada has typically been the family class, and migration has historically been network migration between specific regions, primarily Punjab in northwest India and both the Greater Vancouver Regional District and the Greater Toronto Area in Canada (Walton-Roberts, 2003). In 2000 the number of economic class immigrants from India slightly exceeded family class for the first time – 48 per cent were economic class versus 46 per cent family class (CIC, 2005). This shift reflected modifications in immigrant processing priorities and slight changes in the regional origin of Indian immigrant applications, as determined by the native language of Indian immigrants to Canada (Walton-Roberts, 2009). While Canada may have a large Indian-origin community (over 400,000 in 2006), it has a less than stellar trade relationship with India relative to other nations. This fact seems to challenge the assumption about the positive links between trade and immigration.

Canada has an uncertain strategy regarding relations with India (Gupta, 2006). Tension over terrorism linked to Sikh separatists in the past and Sri Lankan groups in the present has undeniably contributed to undermining diplomatic and trade relations (Delvoie, 1998; Rubinoff, 2002; Bolan, 2005; Hyndman, 2003; MacQueen & Geddes, 2007; Swamy, 2007). Canada's relations with India were especially strained during the 1970s and 1990s over India's testing of nuclear devices (Wood, 1999), and Canada's nuclear sanctions remained in place during the 1990s despite U.S. and European efforts at easing relations in order to pursue enhanced trade and investment opportunities. Canada's minister of foreign affairs at the time, Lloyd Axworthy, maintained a strong – some would argue moralistic – stance on nuclear sanctions, and this restrained Indo-Canadian relations. Sanctions were reversed by Axworthy's successor, John Manley, who argued that India was an important market that Canada could not afford to distance itself from: 'When the U.S. and other trading countries have re-engaged, it makes little sense for Canada to be on the outside looking in' (Trickey, 2001).

In 1998 Delvoie was optimistic that the increasing connections emerging from India's economic growth would be the most likely way to overcome the relative indifference between Canada and India, but in 2002 Rubinoff saw that 'Indo-Canadian relations remain virtually stillborn' (2002: 854). In the mid-to-late 2000s, Canadian export trade with India was an eighth the size of that of the United States, and less than a quarter the size of Australia's (which offers a far more realistic comparison based on population size and economic strengths). From 2000 through 2007, even though Canadian trade with India increased, relative to other nations Canada lost ground, dropping from twenty-third to thirty-first position in total exports to India over this period. Indeed, in 2007 Canada only just moved above the Netherlands in terms of exports to India (see Table 7.1). The recent explosive growth of India's economy (between 6% and 9% GDP growth annually over the past five years) has a number of business commentators concerned that Canada is not taking the region seriously and is failing to capitalize on opportunities to the same degree other nations are (Olive, 2007; Dobson, 2006), despite the fact that both countries have so many commonalities: 'Why should Canada be interested in an FTA with India? The obvious answer lies in the opportunities for deeper integration with one of the world's increasingly dynamic large economies with which we have ties through common language and institutions and the large Indian diaspora. Each of these factors suggests the two-way economic flows should be larger than they are' (Dobson, 2006: 20).

Despite the relatively weak trading position Canada holds with India, increased interest in trade with India (indeed, with Asia as a whole) over the last few years has led to several trade visits organized by a consortium of government ministries and business leaders. These trips act as networking exercises and generate political support to initiate and close deals, both in India and Canada. Table 7.2 highlights some of the key meetings over the past twenty years or so. One important thing to note about these trade missions is the role Indo-Canadian ministers,

Table 7.1
India's Imports from Major Trade Partners (in U.S. $ million)

	2000	2001	2002	2003	2004	2005	2006	2007
Germany	1866.63	1759.59	2028.11	2918.58	3868.31	4015.35	6023.63	12666.48
USA	3629.52	3015	3149.63	5034.86	6291.49	7001.35	9454.74	12604.70
Switzerland	2620.73	3160.14	2870.76	3312.75	5817.92	5939.92	6555.80	9115.26
UAE	2138.84	658.98	915.09	2059.85	4581.96	4641.10	4354.08	8639.01
Australia	1079.33	1062.76	1360.1	2649.24	3561.10	3824.53	4947.91	6835.91
Singapore	1506.44	1463.91	1304.09	2085.38	2582.16	2651.40	3353.77	5470.16
Korea (Rep.)	1210.12	893.76	1141.37	2829.19	3194.09	3508.77	4563.85	4778.68
Japan	2355.32	1842.19	2146.45	2667.69	3005.96	3235.13	4016.10	4590.84
U.K.	2727.86	3167.92	2563.21	3234.35	3431.35	3566.20	3930.30	4171.67
France	737.04	640.81	844.26	1090.23	1380.70	1894.10	4113.30	4155.72
Belgium	3474.89	2870.05	2763.01	3975.92	4566.29	4588.92	4725.14	4139.92
Italy	744.05	723.58	704.79	1071.04	1322.77	1373.10	1855.63	2681.07
Russia	617.47	516.66	535.51	959.63	1265.38	1322.74	2022.19	2114.06
Canada	380.51	396.30	529.43	566.29	725.89	775.72	919.87	1514.21
Netherlands	445.45	437.53	466.47	535.56	758.94	791.46	1049.55	1156.49

Source: India, Department of Commerce, system on foreign trade performance analysis (http://commerce.nic.in/ftpa/cnt.asp).

Table 7.2
Canada's Trade Missions to India, 1991–2007 (Partial List)

Date	Location	Involved parties	Details
2007	New Delhi, Bangalore, Mumbai, Punjab	Government of Ontario and business leaders	Mission to India and Pakistan to promote Ontario as a site for investment
2007	New Delhi, Hyderabad, Mumbai	Parliamentary Secretary to the Minister of International Trade Ted Menzies; Parliamentary Secretary to the Minister of Foreign Affairs Deepak Obhrai; and a high-level delegation from the Canadian Council of Chief Executives	Aims at strengthening Canada's relationship with India and increasing export and investment opportunities for Canadian companies
2006	Mumbai, New Delhi, Chandigarh, Amritsar	Manitoba Premier Gary Doer and 45 delegates from more than 34 companies and organizations	Largest Manitoba trade mission to date
2005	Mumbai and New Delhi	International Trade Minister Jim Peterson, Ted Menzies, Deepak Obhrai, and Health Minister Ujjal Dosanjh, as well as 65 representatives from over 50 Canadian businesses and various government departments and agencies	Energy, information, and communications technology and transportation
2005	India and Thailand	Led by the Earth Sciences Sector Assistant Deputy Minister Dr Irwin Itzkovitch	Earth Sciences Sector trade missions to promote Canada's capacity in natural disaster management and mitigation
2003	New Delhi	Agriculture and Agri-Food Minister Lyle Vanclief and several business and industry representatives	Bilateral meetings aimed at further opening the Indian market to Canadian agriculture and food products
2002	Mumbai and New Delhi	Trade Minister Pierre Pettigrew and over 130 representatives of Canadian businesses and government organizations	Six memoranda of understanding signed by Canadian firms in Mumbai
2000		Canada-India Business Council and 19 company representatives, 14 of whom were of South Asian origin	'Forging Synergies with India' mission
1999	New Delhi and Mumbai	Calgary MLA Shiraz Shariff and 8 company representatives	Canadian oil and gas mission.

Table 7.2   (*Continued*)

Date	Location	Involved parties	Details
1998	New Delhi, Mumbai, Chennai, Bangalore, and Chandigarh	Team British Columbia Trade and Investment Mission, led by then Attorney General Ujjal Dosanjh; 16/27 business participants were of South Asian origin	Government representatives MLA Harry Lalli and Special Advisor to the Premier Govind Sundram (Team British Columbia, 1998)
1997		Industry and Environment Canada and 20 business representatives, 12 of South Asian origin	Canada Environment business mission
1996	India, Pakistan, Malaysia	Prime Minister Jean Chrétien, 7 provincial premiers, and several business leaders; 2-week trade mission	Business deals worth Can $2 billion signed, and business links initiated (Canadian Newswire, 1996)
1994		International Trade Minister Roy MacLaren headed group of 40 Canadian business people	Largest Canadian trade mission to visit India at the time (Canadian Newswire, 1994)
1993		Prime Minister Joe Clark	Met with trade groups and officials
1991		International Trade Minister John Crosbie	
1983	New Delhi and Bombay	25 businesses focused on oil and gas	'The first private sector initiative of this sort' (*Toronto Star*, 1983)

Sources: Department of Foreign Affairs and International Trade (DFAIT) and relevant provincial departments of trade, and others listed on table.

government officials, and company representatives play, even if their portfolio is not directly linked to the event.

It took over a year for the minority Conservative government, elected in February 2006, to send a senior minister to India. One result of this visit was the Canada-India Foreign Investment Promotion and Protection Agreement (FIPA), concluded in June 2007, which provides 'a solid platform from which Canada and India can grow their commercial relationship in the future' (Canada, Department of Foreign Affairs and International Trade [DFAIT], 2007). Nevertheless, more jaded observers suggest the future growth of Canada's business linkages to India are more ominously characterized by Air Canada's decision to cancel all direct flights to India effective 1 May 2007. The president of the Canada-India Business Council (CIBC) articulated how this decision would be perceived: 'India might think we're talking out of both sides of our mouth, which is disheartening. On the one hand, we talk about trade promotion and yet at the same time, our national airline does this. Actions speak louder than words' (Yelaja, 2007).

Despite the concern over Canada's weak trading position with India, trade missions at the federal, provincial, and industrial sector levels have been promoted with the aim of creating export and investment links with India. Such state-led missions and export promotion act as a subsidization of international marketing efforts and contribute effectively to the export development of small and medium-sized enterprises (Wilkinson & Brouthers, 2006). The positive impact that interpersonal interaction has on trade is a central reason why economists and others suspect that immigrants possess important social and cultural credentials when it comes to trading with their source nations (Light, 2001; Light, Zhou, & Kim, 2002). They are seen as cultural interpreters for both the host and home country, and therefore as individuals who can positively influence outcomes. But what happens in situations where a large population of potential TEs exists, but trade relations remain underdeveloped? How can a focus on practice and the processes of the social construction of relevant agents illuminate what appears to be a seeming lack of effective TE behaviour?

Immigrants Transacting Trade in an Era of International Migration

Immigrant Traders

Within government and business circles, the benefits of immigration for trade development have been recognized – if not always explicitly, certainly in ways that encourage the use of immigrant entrepreneurs as sources of information and cultural acumen. In an attempt to understand the role that these associations play in contributing to trade, Canada's Department of Foreign Affairs and International Trade (DFAIT) commissioned research on the extent, nature, and activities of Asian ethnic business associations (AEBAs; Asia Pacific Foundation, 2004). The report found information on over 142 active AEBAs of varying sizes and mandates and suggested that the '"hidden advantage" of AEBAs for Canada's commercial interests in Asia remains largely underutilized' (ibid.: 8). The report recommended that the 'mainstreaming' of such organizations should be 'a future goal.'

Despite this apparent lack of engagement with AEBAs, a significant number of the business and political representatives listed as participants with Canadian trade missions to India (see Table 7.2) are of South Asian origin, lending support to the idea that South Asian immigrants possess important cultural capital or greater propensity when it comes to accessing the Indian market. In addition, the cultural capital these immigrant entrepreneurs are assumed to possess offers greater potential when the challenging nature of the Indian market is taken into consideration.

Henry (1991) argues that long-term commitment and cultural understanding are central to achieving success in the Indian market, and Vicziany (1993) has documented the necessity of such factors with regard to Australian companies trading with India. The DFAIT, echoing John Paynter's (1995) comments regarding the importance of people-to-people links, emphasizes Canada's possession of a domestic cultural resource when it comes to understanding and accessing India's markets: 'Why trade with India? The sheer size of its market and its resources; the commonality of Commonwealth traditions and the English language; its proven commitment to democratic principles; its potential as an emerging "Asian Tiger"; a massive pool of inexpensive but highly trained labour; *a large expatriate Indian population in Canada*; and tremendous infrastructural requirements all suggest that there is in fact enormous scope for Indo-Canadian commercial cooperation, both in the Indian market and jointly in the global economic village' (DFAIT, 1996a, emphasis added).

This heavy focus on personalized connections to facilitate and increase trade relations between India and Canada recognizes the potential of Indo-Canadians to initiate and facilitate trade between the two countries. But reaping the reward of this connection is still seen as underdeveloped, and in 2007 the India-Canada CEO round table report was still recommending that Canada 'maximize Canada-India people to people linkages through better leverage of the Indo-Canada community' (India-Canada CEO, 2007: 11).

In discussions with federal and provincial trade officials in Vancouver, Delhi, and Mumbai, the majority agreed that Indo-Canadians play an important role in creating trade connections for Canada, but their degree of confidence in this link was dependent upon personal experience. In Mumbai, one official at the Canadian Consulate told me that in his experience, 80 per cent of initial assessments that Canadians make of the Indian market, even those by large Canadian corporations, are made by Indo-Canadians (personal interview, 28 February 2000). He also advised me that about 80 to 85 per cent of those attending the 2000 mission of the Canada-India Business Council were Indo-Canadians, most of whom had been in Canada for over twenty years. Some officials recounted important examples of Indian immigrants responsible for developing an export market for Canada in India. One example is Hemant Shah, referred to as 'Mr India' by the Winnipeg press. He boasts immense success in connecting Manitoba businesses with opportunities in the Indian market.

Shah emigrated to Winnipeg in 1977, and after a few years of working at a variety of jobs – including parking attendant – to gain an understanding of business life in Canada, he went after his first contract. He cold-called at Kipp Kelly, a Winnipeg manufacturer of grain-cleaning equipment. Armed with a knowledge of India and a letter of introduction from his father, Shah was given permission to attempt to sell Kelly equipment in India. He financed the trip himself and eventually sold three pieces of equipment. 'I got my first deal using family contacts and political connections,' Shah says, 'and then one success led to another' (Bramwell, 1996: 15).

In 1986 Shah was in India on business. While visiting the new Canadian trade office in Mumbai, he was asked if he could facilitate a deal between a Winnipeg pulse exporter and a Western Indian importer interested in buying dried green peas. Shah met with the Indian importer, who coincidentally turned out to be an old family friend. This established instant trust and dispensed with the need for the usually long and arduous process of negotiation. The final result was the first export of green peas to India from Canada (official at Canadian Consulate, Mumbai, personal interview, 28 February 2000). Such chance meetings are not merely social minutiae, since they can and do contribute to reshaping trade flows. By early 2000, Canada became the single largest supplier of peas and pulses to India; Canada's export of peas and pulses to India was over 650,000 tonnes in 2001, an increase of 200 per cent from 1999 (DFAIT, 2003: 17). Shah is also credited with forming a memorandum of understanding between the Maharasta Chamber of Commerce and Industry in Pune and the Winnipeg Chamber of Commerce, an agreement that has been described by DFAIT (1996b: 50) as 'an excellent example of industry to industry co-operation.' Shah offers an ideal example of the trade-creating type of immigrant economists assume exists, and his trade value is in no small part linked to the cultural capital and status he maintains in a transnational context.

Despite the example of traders like Shah, some Canadian federal officials have voiced frustration with what they perceive to be the limited abilities of Indian immigrants to initiate trade, especially when compared with Chinese immigrant entrepreneurs. In geographically diverse settings (such as those created through immigration), comparisons are formulated in culturally specific and often essentialized ways. The following comments, made by a B.C. trade official in Vancouver, illustrate this frustration:

> China is about twelve years ahead of India purely because they liberalized twelve years before India. So it was really the Chinese community here which created the push. The difference is that the Chinese community are much more entrepreneurial than our East Indian community. East Indian community tends to be more the professionals; we are trained to be doctors, lawyers, mathematicians, scientists. (personal interview, 25 January 1999)

The structural and subjective contexts are conflated in this response; economic liberalization and occupational cultural traditions are both called upon to explain differences in Canada's trading relations with India and China. In this case the problem is that Indian immigrants are too professionalized. On the other hand, some responses posit that the immigrant is too exuberant in attempting to conduct trade, and in this way, can actually have a negative effect on the development of Canadian capacity to expand international trade:

> One of the reasons that people do not do business in China, in India, or in Iran, three huge markets with enormous potential, is that there has been a steady stream of newer immigrants coming over here with an eye to setting up a business link with their home countries. And they have gone into the major companies and they have said, 'my cousin is the so-and-so, my brother is the so-and-so.' They have given all of these pretences that they know who is doing what ... Now, what's happened is that you have all of these, we call them 'wannabes,' they are all coming over here with the pretence that they have all of these things that they can do for Canadian companies, can do to earn money. These companies go over there to check it out and have found it has been completely false, they spent a great deal of money and got absolutely nowhere, and now they refuse to deal with that country. (B.C. trade official, Vancouver, personal interview, 28 October 1998)

Conversion of symbolic capital demands that those in play recognize its value; without such recognition, symbolic capital is devalued. General trade patterns indicate where opportunities for immigrant entrepreneurs may lie. Goods such as food, textiles, and crafts dominate imports from India; all these industries are highly open to small operators who can easily coordinate and mobilize trade through social contacts. But with regard to exports, trade officials at the provincial level suggest that Canada's export programs tend to be directed at assisting larger corporations concentrated in central Canada and in highly capitalized industrial sectors, areas where immigrant entrepreneurs are not overly represented. This was also echoed by a member of the Canada-India Business Council, who argued that the Toronto-based head office of the CIBC was seen as distant from the needs of B.C. members and that Vancouver was rarely included on the itinerary of Indian business missions to Canada. This geographical imbalance was also apparent to trade officials in British Columbia:

> You have to remember, and temper any observations, that Vancouver is very much a branch office town, and there could be huge amounts of business being done with India, but it is being done out of Toronto and not out of Vancouver. We are getting the dregs of stuff, where you get Indian families coming over here and they set up little minor trading outfits with their mothers and their sisters and so on, where there really is some quite big stuff going on back east, machinery and that sort of thing. (Vancouver Trade Centre official, personal interview, 28 October 1998)

This classed, gendered, and regionalized representation of the Indian immigrant in Vancouver indicates the need to examine how immigration is not a homogeneous transfer process from one country to another; rather, it can be highly specific in terms of regional and class identity. But whereas one of the earlier quotes characterized Indian immigrants as too professional, this view suggests they are too embedded in kin networks. Such readings are produced not only by Canadian bureaucrats but also by Indian immigrants from regions other than Punjab, the traditional source of Indian immigrants to Canada:

> The type of immigrant that has been coming in, most of them may be from rural villages under the family class, who come here to work, but they are not much interested in, or they don't have the capacity to develop trade on a two-way basis. The new batch of immigrants that are coming in, there

are a lot of people coming in with business skills, a lot of people who would like to foster trade between India and Canada. In fact, there seems to be more trade associations, more trade groupings that have been set up. Four or five years back when I was new to Canada, I would go to these meetings and you know it would be the same crowd, the same stories and it would just sort of fizzle out, but I have seen more and more new faces coming into the picture now, so I think it is a very promising step. And the fact that these types of immigrants are coming in from India, I think it would certainly go a long way to fostering two-way trade. (Immigrant from Mumbai, personal interview, Vancouver, 13 March 1999)

Indeed the image of the 'new' Indian immigrant, educated, Western-ized, and linked into high-tech business, contrasts with the 'old' style migrants who made their way in life through hard labour in the re-source industries and built a community through family migration. Comments about the transformation of the 'quality' of immigrants, even from other Indian immigrants, reinforce the assimilationist im-migrant deficit rhetoric that has been associated with earlier waves of Indian immigrants (Rumbaut, 1997). This discourse of immigrant 'quality' illustrates how symbolic capital is complexly structured by the intersections of regional, religious, class, and gender identities. Map-ping how the migrant body is 'distributed ... according to the relative weight of the different kinds of capital in the total set of their assets' (Bourdieu, 1998: 230–1) demands that we comprehend the construction of identity within and between certain social groups. The contradic-tions of identity construction can also be amplified by interdepartmen-tal government policy perspectives.

Despite the reality of Indo-Canadians developing important trade links with India, Canada's federal departments exercise policies that still envision the immigrant trade entrepreneur in contradictory ways. While the DFAIT might envision the immigrant as a trade stimulator, Citizenship and Immigration Canada (CIC) still exercises its right to exclude invited business associates from India as security risks. This contradictory position was highlighted in one interview with an Indo-Canadian engineering director, who was also involved in the Can-ada-India Business Council, when I asked if he had experienced any problems between trade and immigration departments:

Yeah, we have one real serious problem ... A fellow here – he was with our mission – developed a contract, and he has two Subways [sandwich franchise] here ... he developed some contacts there, and they agreed, one in Delhi and one in Bombay, to open the franchise. After all this work on the contracts, everything was done, so they were coming here to see and sign the contract. They went to the [Delhi] Embassy, High Commission for the visa, and they refused the visa! They felt very insulted, you know, and they said we don't want this business, ok? So you know then the fellow called me and I gave the names of the people to contact right away. So he phoned B.C. Trade, Ministry of Investment, and he also phoned Industry Canada and the Department of Foreign Affairs, and those three people sent the faxes. You know. And then they [CIC] say ok ... but that is not the right way to approach, you know ... you should not have that kind of attitude ... But this is one of the issues which is really serious. (Engineering executive, personal interview, Vancouver, 25 November 1998)

The treatment these Indian citizens received from Citizenship and Immigration Canada contrasted with their supposed business value in the creation of new business linkages between India and Canada. I then asked if the problem was perhaps rooted in the general impressions certain immigration officials held with regard to India and Indians:

Exactly, exactly. They feel that all these are poor people who are coming here and they are going to burden us, and this is one of them. I don't know why they should think this way ... you feel ashamed as a Canadian ... Some of the families are multi-millionaires and good people. (Ibid.)

The Asia Pacific Foundation (2004) noted widespread concern regarding visa applications for visiting Asian trade delegations in their report on AEBAs and suggested that it was an area Citizenship and Immigration Canada should address more effectively. Such contradictions throw light on the struggle between the capitalist and nationalist motivations of the Canadian bureaucracy, and add further complexity to understanding the links between trade and immigration under conditions of rapid social and economic change. The important background to this issue is the tight regional linkages that exist between Canada and Punjab as well as the highly successful way in which immigrants in Canada have been able to effectively reproduce community by utilizing family migration routes (Walton-Roberts, 2003). In response to such demand, CIC officials have had to be vigilant in enforcing the regulations and maintaining the integrity of the system (Walton-Roberts, 2009), and their vigilance often ends up restricting the mobility seen as so central to the life of the TE agent. Viewing TEs as embedded only in business circuits also neglects the reality that TEs are socially embedded in diverse national contexts, and that this may inform their decision-making behaviours in ways that are in contrast to the rational homo economicus model. In many cases, immigrants' initial and primary transnational practice is investing in their home towns, villages, and family properties in India (Walton-Roberts, 2004). Indeed, one trade officer saw this cultural attachment and 'in-betweenness' as a precursor for their interest in developing trade:

> So what happens is that the first step is any trade with emerging markets, usually the funnel for that is Indo-Canadians, people like myself, who might be here and are really passionate about doing something ... It usually starts with importing; they bring something and then process it and people start coming and say, well this would be nice, if I can write off my next business trip, or my visit to India for business, what can I do? I can open something out, maybe I can think of exporting something in a small way. So you create usually an almost artificial business to help you write off some of the work you normally have, as an expense, because you want to go and see your family once a year or something like that. And that leads into, you know, 'hey you know, I am making some money; maybe if I invest a little bit more I can do something more.' So it builds up, and once the trade flow starts flowing and some of his problems are overcome by ... Indo-Canadian business people, then the mainstream usually goes in. (B.C. trade official, personal interview, Vancouver, 25 January 1999)

There are two connections this quote above introduces: the first is the link between imports and exports and the second is the one between the economic and non-economic. Economists have generally agreed that immigration is more strongly linked with imports than with exports (Baker & Benjamin, 1996; Globerman, 1995; Head & Ries, 1998). For the DFAIT this is not positive news, since their mandate is to encourage and support export ventures in order to bolster Canada's balance of trade. Missing in this scenario, however, is the recursivity that Olsson refers to: the realization that immigrants may begin with the importation of goods due to their immigrant community's cultural preferences, but after having developed this expertise, later identify and seize upon export opportunities. One Indo-Canadian entrepreneur I interviewed, though he imported fruit pulp from India, was involved in developing a mushroom-processing plant in Tamil Nadu that would

require significant exports of processing machinery and technical services from Canada (personal interview, Vancouver, 17 February and 13
July 1999). Another, though his business involved importing machinery
parts from his family's firms in India, was also re-exporting them to the
United States (personal interview, Vancouver, 19 February 1999).

Economic actions are often deeply grounded in cultural attachments
to place, and though this connection is often tacitly acknowledged, it is
rarely given explanatory power when it comes to the 'economic' representation of trade and immigration links. Such awareness is important
for changing the way we envision 'economic' processes as distinct and
separate from other processes of social and cultural interaction. The TE
is a powerful agent in the current era of global markets because he or
she utilizes cultural and social resources in order to achieve economic
success. Analysis of TE practice therefore also needs to employ both a
cultural and an economic lens.

The Canadian Business Community and the Economy

Of course, there are some cases where disappointment in the Canadian system also extends to the general business community in Canada,
which is seen as lacking the required business zeal, infrastructure, capitalization, and interest necessary to pursue Indian trade opportunities.
Recent studies have forcefully argued that inertia and ignorance are behind Canada's seeming inability – or reluctance – to take full advantage
of its multicultural talent in order to succeed in the global economy
(Mandel-Campbell, 2007; Dobson, 2006). This concern is also evident
in three other related issues: the high rate of Asian return migration
from Canada (Ley & Kobayashi, 2005; DeVoretz & Zhang, 2004), the
argument that non-immigrant Canadians do not possess the innovative risk-taking nature seen in immigrants (Mandel-Campbell, 2007;
Conference Board of Canada, 2007), and the constant concern regarding the dominance of Canada's trading relationship with the United
States (Burges, 2006). This issue of Canadian business conservatism
was broached in an interview with an Indian immigrant professional
working for a small engineering services company that was facing an
immense lack of Canadian interest in its attempts to raise financing for
a billion-dollar power generation project in northern India:

Q: I am getting the sense that you were fairly frustrated by the lack of
interest.

A: Um, X [company owner] would give you a very clear idea on that [laughter], he would really let off a lot of steam. But ... one can't really pin the blame on Canadian companies; they tend to be less adventurous when it comes to getting to overseas markets ... I think the tendency is for them to let others lead and they follow the markets when they feel they can do some business. (Recent immigrant from Mumbai, personal interview, Vancouver, 17 March 1999)

This point about the reluctance of the Canadian business establishment to get involved in difficult overseas markets was also made by several trade officials; the following statement is fairly representative of the thoughts many informants offered regarding the image of Canadian traders:

Canadians have not yet seen India as the sort of opportunity that others might, or if they have seen it, they are being typical of Canadian traders; 'I don't want to be first in,' and then three years from now when everyone else has gone in and cleaned up the market, they will be bitching because they can't make any profit there because they are last in. Canadians are terrible traders, they really are, they are so slow at getting off the mark, they have very little entrepreneurial spirit, they don't want to take a risk, everything they do has to be a sure-fire thing, and the result is that half the time, they miss the boat. (Vancouver Trade Centre official, personal interview, 28 October 1998)

This quote represents a fairly stable stereotype of the non-immigrant Canadian business community (Mandel-Campbell, 2007), an admission that it is not the Indian immigrant's inability to create international trade links but rather the Canadian trader's generally conservative and risk-averse behaviour that restrains the entrepreneurial efforts of the immigrant community. Canada's geographical proximity to the immense U.S. market and the relative ease of exporting to it explains why Canadian exporters might have little incentive to invest their energies into entering India, dubbed 'the bureaucratic bureaucracy' by the *Economist* magazine (Olive, 2007). Despite the image of India as an important emerging market demanding commitment and early access, the risks are still seen as too great:

The big problem that India suffers right now is that people don't see it as a safe place to do business. People don't feel comfortable that their money is safe, that they are going to get a return on investment, they can trust their partners and so on. It is a very, very uncertain market. Unless you have some absolutely blue-blood contacts there that you can trust with your life, most people won't do business with India. The time frames are too extracted; the concept of bribery, Canadians hate the thought of giving payments, of greasing palms. It is a way of doing business in Asia and they have got to get used to it; otherwise they will never get into the market. (B.C. trade official, personal interview, Vancouver, 28 October 1998)

In 2007 India placed over $300 billion worth of infrastructure projects out to tender, but only one Canadian firm expressed interest (Olive, 2007). In addition to the apparent lack of Canadian interest in India, there is also the general lack of Indian interest in Canada. Currently, it is more important for Indian businesses to connect with Asian, European, or U.S. companies. During an interview with a trade official at the consulate in Mumbai, he bemoaned the fact that most people did not even know there was a Canadian trade office in that city. Reinforcing this concern some years later, the India-Canada CEO round table report (2007) recommended that Canada work harder to promote a 'Canada brand' backed up by an enhanced Canadian government trade network in India. In building this brand and image of Canada overseas, it is not only entrepreneurs who can effectively forge the cultural linkages needed to smooth the market entry of interested parties; there is also an important role to be played by non-entrepreneurial figures in the guise of government and corporate officials.

The Non-entrepreneurial Immigrant and the Creation of Trade

The employment of Indian immigrants as Canadian government trade bureaucrats and as managers and professionals in large Canadian corporations trading with India also presents situations where immigrants can enhance trade opportunities. Over 90 per cent of those business leaders and government officials I interviewed in both Canada and India were Indo-Canadians. During one interview with three trade officials in Delhi, two of whom were Indo-Canadian, issues of selection due to ethnocultural background were specifically addressed. Individuals insisted that they had not been selected for particular government postings in South Asia because of their ethnocultural background, although they did comment on the under-representation of Indian-origin staff in Canada's High Commission in the United Kingdom (trade officials at the Canadian High Commission, Delhi, personal interview, 12 November 1999). In addition, Canadian officials made reference to the aggressiveness with which the U.S. Embassy in Delhi deployed its Indian-origin staff compared with the less evident role of British Indian staff in the U.K.'s offices.

During interviews with business personnel, several representatives of large corporations in Vancouver who had trade experience in India commented on the extent to which it helped to have employees of South Asian background to assist in developing projects in India:

> That helps, there is no question about that. It is not just the origin; it is … language and understanding the culture and knowing how to go about things. The North American who has lived in India in that same position, that person can do the same job, but … there are more of the Indians by origin here; therefore it becomes more and more practical to utilize those people in order to maximize your efforts in India … Indians, or Canadians of Indian origin, that are familiar, but they are very specialized people, you know. You just can't take somebody who is an engineer in civil structural to go and do project development. All that person can do is communication, that is it. Whereas there are other people who are very senior, they are incredible engineers, but they are very strong business people as well, and those are much more helpful to us. So sometimes we find that we don't have anybody within our company to help us in a specific case, so we are on our own. (Vice-president of an international engineering corporation, personal interview, Vancouver, 12 November 1998)

Similar comments arose in the following interview with an Indo-Canadian engineering director of a large corporation, who had been called upon to travel to India to assist in the development stage of large projects:

> We have one vice-president here who is Caucasian, you know. One of the projects we were talking about, he said … 'Why don't you accompany me?' I went with him and we went to a few places, and he said, 'I can't believe it.' What he was able to achieve, he said, 'I could not achieve in these few days what you achieve, you know, because of cultural issues.' He said, 'When you talk, there is the red carpet treatment, when I come, you know, they are a little bit shy to talk and very, very, conservative in their approach. (Engineering executive, personal interview, Vancouver, 25 November 1998)

Though such cultural positionality can be an important advantage when attempting to access overseas markets, ethnic difference plays a less benign role when it comes to the immigrant's location in the labour market. Although Indo-Canadians might be seen as valuable to corporations looking to develop links with India, their access to and visibility in the upper levels of the corporate structure has an important bearing on their ability to contribute to the creation of trade. The glass ceiling certainly does exist for Asian immigrants, who generally experience lower pay than non-immigrants and white immigrants with similar educational backgrounds (Pendakur & Pendakur, 1998). In a *Fortune* article (Warner, 2000) regarding Indians in Silicon Valley, Kanwal Rekhi, a highly successful technology entrepreneur and one of the founders of a networking organization called The Indus Entrepreneur (TiE), discusses the challenges faced with 'selling' an Indian-origin CEO to consumers and investors when the company goes public: 'We'd always hear that the company didn't have a "businessman," that there wasn't anyone with a marketing background or selling expertise. That's what they'd say. But the real issue was, will customers buy from an Indian? Indians were seen as damn good backroom operations people, but are they good in the front room, running the show and selling to customers?' (quoted in Warner, 2000: 356). This helps explain why, despite the wealth and success of Indian entrepreneurs during the early 2000s, there were relatively few Indian CEOs running high-tech companies. In many instances, venture capitalists (VCs) investing in an Indian-founded company have brought in a non-Indian CEO, relegating the founder to a technical role (Warner, 2000).

Links between immigration and trade do not depend on immigrants being constructed purely as traders. The skills and qualifications many immigrants possess with regard to accessing overseas markets do not have to be seen in isolation from their role within government departments and large corporations' efforts to access these markets. By identifying this aspect of immigration and trade creation, we are no longer making the immigrant the sole participant in the successful (or unsuccessful) development of trade. We undermine the implicit immigrant deficit model, instead turning our gaze to corporate and government hiring and promotion practices to determine whether opportunities for capacity building in international trade are being developed effectively through equitable hiring practices. This shift from the immigrant to the wider corporate and government systems reveals the implicit assumptions of econometric analysis of trade and immigration, where the responsibility for building links between immigration and trade lies somehow outside of core economic structures and processes.

Conclusion

In considering the ways in which immigrants contribute to creating trade networks between their home and host locations, the evidence of a positive relationship is compelling. Provincial and state government trade officials – those who see the people who visit their offices and create opportunities – consider immigrants to be important in internationalizing opportunities for Canadian corporations. Estimates regarding the size of this contribution and the magnitude of its success vary, and economists have had difficulty quantifying this relationship adequately, resulting in an impoverished image of socially nuanced processes. In this chapter I have considered primarily one aspect of immigrant-led transnational economic development, the promotion of international trade.

Quantifying how global trade is expanded by immigration is challenging for researchers since the relationship between the two processes is socially and spatially complex. Arguments that suggest the existence of a positive relationship between trade and immigration are perplexing in the case of Canada. Canada has a large Indian immigrant population but a constrained trading relationship relative to other nations. This constraint is due not to some limitation embodied within a particular immigrant community, as some trade officials might argue, but rather to the nature of the Canadian economy, its conservative ethos regarding overseas markets, the inertia effect of trade with the United States, and the uneasy diplomatic relations that have existed between Canada and India. In addition to the problems with the Canadian business mentality, we also need to highlight the disjuncture between the active economic citizenship of immigrants (their active participation in Canadian trade development) and their relatively ineffective inclusion into the corner offices of corporate Canada.

Stereotypical assumptions about immigrants and their propensity to trade directs our attention away from the problems located more broadly within wider economic structures. While the TE literature offers us an important research agenda, we must maintain a close watch on the structures within which TEs attempt to operate, as we look more closely at their grounded practices. Saxenian's work (2006) on the New Argonauts relates a particular type of agent, university-educated computer engineers, whose mobility and interconnectedness was facilitated within certain structural contexts, that is, a relatively liberal (pre-9/11) international student and temporary worker visa system and the extensive potential to network between home and host nations as well as within alumni networks. These structural factors were of vital significance to the formation of these 'Argonauts,' who were able to create the regional advantage Saxenian details.

In this chapter I have identified how the structural dimensions of India-Canada relations offer a combination of specifically embedded India-Canada migratory circuits, immense trade inertia, and related Canadian business conservatism, and how all these conspire to restrain trade relations with the challenging Indian market. The importance of immigration to the creation of trade therefore cannot be considered in isolation from general economic and cultural geography, nor can we ignore the processes by which different actors construct images of markets and players through highly cultural, racial, spatial, and classed stereotypes. Ongoing research into the role of TEs needs to focus on the trade and immigration dimension in specific contexts, both geographical and sectoral, by combining a deft eye for cultural practice with a strong structural sensibility.

ACKNOWLEDGMENTS

An earlier draft of this chapter was presented at the April 2007 meeting of the Association of American Geographers (AAG) in San Francisco, California, in the 'Economic Geographies of Migrant Transnationalism' session and at the Transnational Entrepreneurship Conference at Wilfrid Laurier University, Waterloo, Ontario. I would like to thank Ivan Light, Valerie Preston, and three anonymous reviewers for their helpful comments on earlier versions of this chapter. Funding for this research was provided by the Social Sciences and Humanities Research Council of Canada, the Shastri-Indo Canadian Institute, and the Vancouver Metropolis Centre for Research on Immigration and Integration in the Metropolis.

REFERENCES

Amin, A., & Thrift, N. (1995). Globalisation, institutional thickness and the local economy. In P. Healy, S. Cameron, S. Davoudi, S. Graham, & A. Madani-Pour (Eds.), *Managing Cities: The New Urban Context*, 91–108. Chichester: Wiley.

Asia Pacific Foundation of Canada. (2004). The role of Asian ethnic business associations in Canada. *Canada Asia Commentary*, 35 (April). http://www.asiapacific.ca/analysis/pubs/listing.cfm?ID_Publication=345. Accessed 9 April 2007.

Assanie, N., & Woo, Y.P. (2004). *Canada in Asia: What Works, What Doesn't in the Indian Market*. Vancouver: Asia Pacific Foundation Canada.

Baker, M., & Benjamin, D. (1996). Trade links and immigration in Asia Pacific Region. In R. Harris (Ed.), *The Asia Pacific Region in the Global Economy: A Canadian Perspective*, 303–348. Calgary: University of Calgary Press.

Barnes, T. (1996). *Logics of Dislocation: Models, Metaphors, and Meanings of Economic Space*. London: Guilford.

Bauder, H. (2003). 'Brain abuse' or the devaluation of immigrant labour in Canada. *Antipode*, 35(4): 699–717.

Bhachu, P. (2004). *Dangerous Designs: Asian Women Fashion in the Diaspora Economies*. New York and London: Routledge.

Bolan, K. (2005). *Loss of Faith: How the Air India Bombers Got Away with Murder*. Toronto: McClelland and Stewart.

Bourdieu, P. (1998). *Practical Reason: On the Theory of Action*. Palo Alto: Stanford University Press.

Bramwell, R. (1996). India connect: Hemant Shah feels India/Canada trade holds significant potential. *Manitoba Business*, 18(10): 15.

Briggs, X. d. S. (2004). Civilization in color: The multicultural city in three millennia. *City and Community*, 3: 311–342.

Burges, S. (2006). Canada's postcolonial problem: The United States and Canada's international policy review. *Canadian Foreign Policy*, 13(1): 97–113.

Canada. Department of Foreign Affairs and International Trade (DFAIT). (1996a, March). *Canada India Trade Overview*. Ottawa: DFAIT.

Canada. Department of Foreign Affairs and International Trade (DFAIT). (1996b). *Focus India*, 45. Ottawa: DFAIT.

Canada. Department of Foreign Affairs and International Trade (DFAIT). (2003). *South Asia Trade Action Plan*. http://www.infoexport.gc.ca/ie-en/DisplayDocument.jsp?did=66681. Accessed 9 Jan. 2008.

Canada. Department of Foreign Affairs and International Trade (DFAIT). (2007). *Canada and India Conclude Investment Agreement*. News release, No. 82, 16 June. Ottawa: DFAIT.

Canada. Multiculturalism Secretariat. (1989). *Multiculturalism Means Business: A Directory of Business Contacts*. Ottawa: Multiculturalism and Citizenship Canada.

Canada. Oil and Gas Mission. (1999). *Canadian Oil and Gas Mission to India*. Ottawa: Author.

Canadian Press Newswire. (1994, 19 Oct.). Quick Facts [India's trade booms].

Canadian Press Newswire. (1996, 8 Jan.). Team Canada trade mission heads to India. *Canadian Press Newswire Electronic Text.*

Castells, M. (1996). *The Information Age: Economy, Society and Culture,* vol. 1, *The Rise of the Network Society.* Massachusetts: Blackwell.

CIC (Citizenship and Immigration Canada). (2005). *Landing Immigrant Data System.* Ottawa: CIC.

Coe, N., & Bunnell, T.G. (2003). 'Spatialising' knowledge communities: Towards a conceptualisation of transnational innovation networks. *Global Networks,* 3(4): 437–456.

Collins, J. (2003). Cultural diversity and entrepreneurship: Policy responses to immigrant entrepreneurs in Australia. *Entrepreneurship and Regional Development,* 15(2): 137–149.

Conference Board of Canada. (2007). *How Canada Performs 2007: A Report Card on Canada.* June. Ottawa. http://www.conferenceboard.ca/documents. asp?rnext=2047. Accessed Sept. 2007.

Crick, D., Chaudhry, S., & Batstone, S. (2001). An investigation into the overseas expansion of small Asian-owned U.K. firms. *Small Business Economics,* 16(2): 75–94.

Delvoie, L.A. (1998). Canada and India: A new beginning? *Round Table,* 345: 51–64.

DeVoretz, D. (1996). Comment. In R. Harris (Ed.), *The Asia Pacific Region in the Global Economy: A Canadian Perspective,* 348–355. Calgary: University of Calgary Press.

DeVoretz, D., & Zhang, K. (2004). Citizenship, passports and the brain exchange triangle. *Journal of Comparative Policy Analysis: Research and Practice,* 6(2): 199–212.

Dobson, W. (2006). The Indian elephant sheds its past: The implications for Canada. *C.D. Howe Institute Commentary* 235 (June). Toronto: C.D. Howe Institute.

Dunlevy, J.A. (2006). The influence of corruption and language on the pro-trade effect of immigrants: Evidence from the American states. *Review of Economics and Statistics,* 88(1): 182–186.

Dwyer, C. (2004). Tracing transnationalities through commodity culture: A case study of British-South Asian fashion. In P. Jackson, P. Crang, & C. Dwyer (Eds.), *Transnational Spaces,* 60–77. London: Routledge.

Dwyer, C., & Crang, P. (2002). Fashioning ethnicities: The commercial spaces of multiculture. *Ethnicities,* 2(3): 410–430.

Dwyer, C., & Jackson, P. (2003). Commodifiying difference: Selling EASTern fashion. *Environment and Planning D: Society and Space,* 21: 269–291.

Environment and Industry Canada. (1997). *Canada Environment Business Mission*. Ottawa: Environment and Industry Canada.

Fawcett, J., & Gardner, R. (1995). Asian immigrant entrepreneurs and non-entrepreneurs: A comparative study of recent Korean and Filipino immigrants. *East-West Center Reprints: Population Series*, 316: 26.

Gallegos, G.A. (2004). Border matters: Redefining the national interest in U.S.-Mexico immigration and trade policy. *California Law Review*, 92(6): 1729–1778.

Girma, S., & Yu, ZH. (2002). The link between immigration and trade: Evidence from the United Kingdom. *Weltwirtschaftliches Archiv – Review of World Economics*, 138(1): 115–130.

Globerman, S. (1995). Immigration and trade. In D. J. DeVorertz (Ed.), *Diminishing Returns: The Economics of Canada's Recent Immigration Policy*, 243–267. Vancouver: C.D. Howe Institute.

Gould, D.M. (1994). Immigrant links to the home country: Empirical implications for United States bilateral trade flows. *Review of Economics and Statistics*, 76(2): 302–316.

Granovetter, M. (1995). The economic sociology of firms and entrepreneurs. In A. Portes (Ed.), *The Economic Sociology of Immigration: Essays on Networks, Ethnicity, and Entrepreneurship*, 128–165. New York: Russell Sage Foundation.

Gupta, S. (2006). Foreign direct investment in India: Policy reform and politics. *Canadian Foreign Policy*, 13(2): 19–36.

Hardill, I., & Raghuram, P. (1998). Diasporic connections: Case studies of Asian women in business. *Area*, 30(3): 255–261.

Head, K., & Reis, J. (1998). Immigrants and trade creation: Econometric evidence from Canada. *Canadian Journal of Economics*, 31(1): 47–62.

Head, K., Ries, J., & Wagner, D. (1998). *Immigrants and the Trade of Provinces*. RIIM Working Paper Series No. 98-21, Research on Integration and Immigration in the Metropolis (RIIM), Vancouver, B.C.

Helliwell, J. (1997). National borders, trade and migration. *Pacific Economic Review*, 2(3): 165–185.

Henry, D. (1991). Technology transfer, old myths and new realities. In N.K. Choudhry (Ed.), *Canada and South Asian Development: Trade and Aid*, 97–109. New York: E.J. Brill.

Hiebert, D. (2002). The spatial limits to entrepreneurship: Immigrant entrepreneurs in Canada. *Tijdschrift voor Economische en Sociale Geografie*, 93(2): 173–190.

Hsing, Y. (2003). Ethnic identity and business solidarity: Chinese capitalism revisited. In L. Ma & C. Cartier (Eds.), *The Chinese Diaspora: Space, Place, Mobility, and Identity*, 221–236. Lanham: Rowman and Littlefield.

Hummels, D., (1999). *Towards a Geography of Trade Costs*. Mimeo. University of Chicago.

Hyndman, J. (2003). Aid, conflict and migration: The Canada-Sri Lanka connection. *Canadian Geographer*, 47(3): 251–268.

India-Canada CEO Round Table Meeting. (2007, March). *India-Canada Closer Engagement Deeper Ties*. March. New Delhi. http://www.ceocouncil.ca/en/view/?document_id=570&area_id=8. Accessed Jan. 2008.

India Canada News. (2001, March). Canada's pulse industry looks for value-addition in Indian market. New Delhi: Canadian High Commission.

Keely, C. (2003). Globalization transforms trade-migration equation. *International Migration*, 41(1): 87–92.

Kim, K.C., & Hurh, W.M. (1985). Ethnic resources utilization of Korean immigrant entrepreneurs in the Chicago minority area. *International Migration Review*, 19(1): 82–111.

Kloosterman, R.C. (2003). Creating opportunities: Policies aimed at increasing opening for immigrant entrepreneurs in the Netherlands. *Entrepreneurship and Regional Development*, 15(2): 167–181.

Kohli, U. (2002). Migration and foreign trade: Further results. *Journal of Population Economics*, 15(2): 381–387.

Kothari, K. (2006). Spatial practices and imaginaries: Experiences of colonial officers and development professionals. *Singapore Journal of Tropical Geography*, 27: 235–253.

Kotkin, J. (1992). *Tribes: How Race, Religion and Identity Determine Success in the New Global Economy*. New York: Random House.

Krugman, P. (1991). *Geography and Trade*. Cambridge: MIT Press.

Kyle, D. (1999). The Otavalo trade diaspora: Social capital and transnational entrepreneurship. *Ethnic and Racial Studies*, 22(2): 422–446.

Lever-Tracy, C., Ip, D., & Tracy, N. (1996). *The Chinese Diaspora and Mainland China: An Emerging Economic Synergy*. London: Macmillan.

Ley, D. (2003). Seeking homo economicus: The Canadian state and the strange story of the business immigration program. *Annals of the Association of American Geographers*, 93(2): 426–441.

Ley, D. (2005). Shaky borders? In H. van Houtum, O. Kramsch, & W. Zierhofer (Eds.), *B/ordering Space*, 61–73. Aldershot: Ashgate.

Ley, D. (2006). Explaining variations in business performance among immigrant entrepreneurs in Canada. *Journal of Ethnic and Migration Studies*, 32(5): 743–764.

Ley, D., & Kobayashi, A. (2005). Back to Hong Kong: Return migration or transnational sojourn? *Global Networks*, 5(2): 111–127.

Light, I. (2001). Globalization, transnationalism and trade. *Asian and Pacific Migration Journal*, 10(1): 53–80.

Light, I., & Bonacich, E. (1988). *Immigrant Entrepreneurs: Koreans in Los Angeles.* Los Angeles: University of California Press.

Light, I., Zhou, M., & Kim, R. (2002). Transnationalism and American exports in an English-speaking world. *International Migration Review*, 36(3): 702–725.

Maas, M. (2005). Transnational entrepreneurship: Exploring determinants and impacts of a Dutch-based Filipino immigrant business. *Asian and Pacific Migration Journal*, 14(1–2): 169–191.

MacQueen, K., & Geddes, J. (2007, 28 May). Air India: After 22 years, now the time for truth. *Maclean's*, 16–20.

Mandel-Campbell, A. (2007). *Why Mexicans Don't Drink Molson: Rescuing Canadian Business from the Suds of Global Obscurity.* Toronto: Douglas and McIntyre.

McCullough, M. (2000, 21 Sept.). High-tech guru opens Vancouver chapter. *Vancouver Sun*, D1, D2.

Morley, D., & Robins, K. (1995). *Spaces of Identity.* London: Routledge.

Mosk, C. (2005). *Trade and Migration in the Modern World.* New York: Routledge.

Nayyar, D. (1994). *Migration, Remittances and Capital Flows: The Indian Experience.* Delhi: Oxford University Press.

Ohmae, K. (1999). *The Borderless World: Power and Strategy in the Interlinked Economy.* New York: Harper Collins.

Olive, D. (2007, 8 March). Big wheel starts to roll. *Toronto Star*, K3.

Olsson, G. (1975). *Birds in Egg.* Michigan Geographical Publication No. 15. Ann Arbor: Department of Geography, University of Michigan.

Page, J., & Plaza, S. (2006). Migration remittances and development: A review of global evidence. *Journal of African Economies*, 15: 245–336.

Paynter, J. (1995). Canada-India diplomatic relations. In J.R. Wood (Ed.), *Genuine Mutual Interest: Proceedings of the Plenary Session of the Silver Jubilee Conference of the Shastri Indo-Canadian Institute*, 39–48. New Delhi: Shastri Institute.

Peberdy, S. (2000). Mobile entrepreneurship: Informal sector cross-border trade and street trade in South Africa. *Development Southern Africa*, 17(2): 201–219.

Peberdy, S., & Crush, J. (2001). Invisible trade, invisible travellers: The Maputo Corridor spatial development initiative and informal cross-border trading. *South African Geographical Journal*, 83(2): 115–123.

Pendakur, K., & Pendakur, R. (1998). The colour of money: Earnings differentials among ethnic groups in Canada. *Canadian Journal of Economics*, 31(3): 518–548.

Plüss, C. (2005). Constructing globalized ethnicity: Migrant from India in Hong Kong. *International Sociology*, 20(2): 201–224.

Portes, A. (1995). Economic sociology and the sociology of immigration: A conceptual overview. In A. Portes (Ed.), *The Economic Sociology of Immigration: Essays on Networks, Ethnicity, and Entrepreneurship*, 1–41. New York: Russell Sage Foundation.

Portes, A., & Guarnizo, L. (1991). Tropical capitalists: U.S.-bound immigration and small enterprise development in the Dominican Republic. In S. Diaz-Briquets & S. Weintraub (Eds.), *Migration, Remittances and Small Business Development in Mexico and Caribbean Basin Countries*, 101–131. Boulder: Westview Press.

Portes, A., Guarnizo, L.E., & Haller, W.J. (2002). Transnational entrepreneurs: An alternative form of immigrant economic adaptation. *American Sociological Review*, 67(2): 278–298.

Prakash, B.A. (1998). Gulf migration and its economic impact: The Kerala experience. *Economic and Political Weekly*, 33(50): 3209–3213.

Raghuram, P. (2004). Initiating the commodity chain: South Asian women and fashion in the diaspora. In A. Hughes & S. Reimer (Eds.), *Geographies of Commodity Chains*, 120–136. London: Routledge.

Raghuram, P., & Strange, A. (2001). Studying economic institutions, placing cultural politics: Methodological musings from a study of ethnic minority enterprise. *Geoforum*, 32(3): 377–388.

Rath, J., & Kloosterman, R. (2000). Outsiders' business: A critical review of research on immigrant entrepreneurship. *International Migration Review*, 34(3): 657–681.

Rubinoff, A.G. (2002). Canada's re-engagement with India. *Asian Survey*, 42(6): 838–855.

Rumbaut, R.G. (1997). Paradoxes (and orthodoxies) of assimilation. *Sociological Perspectives*, 40(3): 483–511.

Russell, S., & Teitelbaum, M. (1992). *International Migration and International Trade*. World Bank Discussion Paper No. 160, Washington, DC: World Bank.

Sayer, A. (1997). The dialectic of culture and economy. In R. Lee & J. Wills (Eds.), *Geographies of Economies*, 16–26. London: Arnold.

Saxenian, A. (1999). *Silicon Valley's New Immigrant Entrepreneurs*. San Francisco: Public Policy Institute of California.

Saxenian, A.L. (2002). Transnational communities and the evolution of global production networks: The cases of Taiwan, China and India. *Industry and Innovation*, 9(3): 183–202.

Saxenian, A.L. (2006). *The New Argonauts: Regional Advantage in a Global Economy*. Cambridge: Harvard University Press.

Schoeberger, E. (1996). *The Cultural Crisis of the Firm.* Oxford: Blackwell.

Schmutzler, A, (1999). The new economic geography. *Journal of Economic Surveys,* 13(4): 355–379.

Scott, A.J. (2004). A perspective of economic geography. *Journal of Economic Geography,* 4(5): 479–499.

Stampnitzky. L. (2006). How does 'culture' become 'capital'? Cultural and institutional struggles over 'character and personality' at Harvard. *Sociological Perspectives,* 49(4): 461–481.

Stanton, P., & Lee, J. (1996). Australian cultural diversity and export growth. *Journal of Multilingual and Multicultural Development,* 16(6): 497–511.

Swamy, S. (2007, 10 Aug.). *Recent Economic Progress in India and China and Its Implications for Canada.* Presented at Finance Seminars and Brown Bag Lunch Series, Wilfrid Laurier University, Waterloo, Ontario.

Teixeira, C., Lo, L., & Truelove, M. (2007). Immigrant entrepreneurship, institutional discrimination, and implications for public policy: A case study in Toronto. *Environment and Planning C: Government and Policy,* 25(2): 176–193.

Toronto Star. (1983, 5 April). 'Historic' mission seeks to strengthen Canada-India trade. F2.

Trickey, M. (2001, 20 March). Canada thaws relations with India. *Vancouver Sun,* A8.

van Apeldoorn, B. (2004). Theorizing the transnational: A historical materialist approach. *Journal of International Relations and Development,* 7(2): 142–176.

Vicziany, M. (1993). Australian companies in India: The ingredients for successful entry into the Indian market. In M. Vicziany (Ed.), *Australia-India, the Economic Links: Past, Present and Future,* 24–84. Nedlands, Western Australia: Indian Ocean Centre for Peace Studies and South Asia, Research Unit, University of Western Australia.

Wagner, D., Head, K., & Ries, J. (2002). Immigration and the trade of provinces. *Scottish Journal of Political Economy,* 49(5): 507–525.

Walton-Roberts, M. (2003). Transnational geographies: Indian immigration to Canada. *Canadian Geographer,* 47(3): 235–250.

Walton-Roberts, M. (2004). Returning, remitting, reshaping: Non-resident Indians and the transformation of society and space in Punjab, India. In P. Crang, C. Dwyer, & P. Jackson (Eds.), *Transnational Spaces,* 78–103. London: Routledge.

Walton-Roberts, M. (2009). *India-Canada Trade and Immigration Linkages: A Case of Regional (Dis)advantage?* Metropolis British Columbia Working Paper Series No. 09-04. Vancouver: Metropolis British Columbia Centre of Excellence for Research on Immigration and Diversity (MBC).

Walton-Roberts, M., & Hiebert, D. (1997). Immigration, entrepreneurship, and the family: Indo-Canadian enterprise in the construction industry of Greater Vancouver. *Canadian Journal of Regional Science*, 20(1–2): 119–140.

Walton-Roberts, M., & Pratt, G. (2005). Mobile modernities: A South Asian family negotiates immigration, gender and class in Canada. *Gender, Place and Culture*, 12(2): 173–196.

Warner, M. (2000, 15 April). The Indians of Silicon Valley. *Fortune*, 356.

Waters, J. (2002). Flexible families? 'Astronaut' households and the experiences of lone mothers in Vancouver, British Columbia. *Social and Cultural Geography*, 3(2): 117–134.

White, B. (1994). *Turbans and Traders: Hong Kong's Indian Communities*. Oxford: Oxford University Press.

Wilkinson, T., & Brouthers, L.E. (2006). Trade promotion and SME export performance. *International Business Review*, 15(3): 233–252.

Wong, L.L. (2004). Taiwanese immigrant entrepreneurs in Canada and transnational social space. *International Migration Review*, 42(2): 113–152.

Wong, L.L., & Ng, M. (2002). The emergence of small transnational enterprise in Vancouver: The case of Chinese entrepreneur immigrants. *International Journal of Urban and Regional Research*, 26(3): 508–530.

Wood, J. (1999). Canada-India relations: The current issues. In U. Thakkar & M. Kulkarni (Eds.), *India in World Affairs: Towards the 21st Century*, 139–156. Mumbai: Himalaya Publishing House.

Yelaja, P. (2007, 16 Feb.). Air Canada ripped for cutting India trips. *Toronto Star*.

Zahra, S.A., & George, G. (2002). International entrepreneurship: The current status of the field and future research agenda. In M. Hitt, D. Ireland, D. Sexton, & S. Camp (Eds.), *Strategic Entrepreneurship: Creating an Integrated Mindset*, 255–288. Cambridge: Blackwell.

8 Legal and Social Institutions for Transnational Entrepreneurship: A Multiple Case Study in the Spanish Context

DAVID URBANO, NURIA TOLEDANO, AND DOMINGO RIBEIRO-SORIANO

In recent years technological, social, and economic changes have enhanced the practice of transnationalism around the world (Wong & Ng, 2002). Typical examples of these transformations include such innovations as high-speed jet travel, inexpensive long-distance telephone communication, e-mail, and the Internet, all of which help to enable easy, cheap, and fast contact over long distances, as well as transnational business practices (Castells, 1996; Levitt, 2001; Roberts, Frank, & Lozano-Ascencio, 1999; Vertovec, 1999).

Transnationalism also represents a topic of growing interest in the academic field, witnessed by the proliferation of scholarly articles, university seminars, and conferences devoted to exploring its nature and contours. In addition, there are diverse disciplines, for example, anthropology, sociology, or business management, that include transnationalism-related topics in their field of study (Casson, 1990; Faist, 2004; Glick-Schiller, Basch, & Szanton-Blanc, 1995; Levitt & Dehesa, 2003; Livesay, 1995; Portes, 2001; Vertovec, 1999; Westhead & Wright, 2000). However, as Vertovec (1999: 447) notes, 'most of this burgeoning work refers to quite variegated phenomena.' On the one hand, a significant body of research has emphasized the strategies adopted by particular businesses that operate across national boundaries. In these cases, transnational entrepreneurship (TE) is considered to be synonymous with international entrepreneurship (IE), and is studied from the economic and organizational points of view within management studies (Castells, 1996; Dicken, 1992; Reuber & Fischer, 1997; Sklair, 1995; Wolff & Pett, 2000). On the other hand, a second perspective of TE highlights its relationship with ethnic entrepreneurship (EE) (Guarnizo, 2003). Recent studies have documented the existence of a vast array of specific TE activities undertaken by migrants (Guarnizo, 2003; Itzigosohn & Giourguli, 2002; Zhou, 2004). Two main approaches to the study of TE can be discerned: the 'transnationalism from above' of corporations and states and the 'transnationalism from below' of international migrants (Smith & Guarnizo, 1998). While the former has been widely considered in entrepreneurship literature (Madsen & Servais, 1997; McDougall & Benjamin, 2000; Moen, 2002; Oviatt & McDougall, 1997; Rialp et al., 2005), the latter has received much less attention (Guarnizo, 2003; Kelly, 2003; Kyle, 1999; Landolt, 2001; Light, Zhou, & Kim, 2002; Morawska, 2004; Portes, Guarnizo, & Haller, 2002; Vertovec, 1999; Wong & Ng, 2002; Zhou, 2004).

The present study expands on that existing literature, bringing to light the cases of 'transnationalism from below' and the institutional factors that influence their emergence into the same analytical framework. We examine four cases of transnational entrepreneurs (TEs) with different origins or ethnic identities – North African, Latin American, Eastern European, and Asian – who have started their own business in Spain, specifically in Catalonia, a region in the northeastern corner of Spain. We pay particular attention to the role that legal and social institutions have had on TE. To facilitate understanding, we turn to an institutional perspective (North, 1990, 2005) by arguing that TE can be both facilitated and constrained by the institutional framework. Specifically, institutional forces may be defined by legal and social structures.

After this introduction, the study is structured as follows. First, we present institutional theory as the theoretical framework for analysing TE. In the following section, the research design and data method are described. Subsequently, we focus on describing the case studies and analysing the main results. Finally, the chapter ends with the main conclusions and implications for future research.

Transnational Entrepreneurship from an Institutional Perspective

Transnational activities undertaken by migrants have opened a new dimension in the study of immigrant entrepreneurship (Itzigsohn & Gioruli, 2002; Portes, Haller, & Guarnizo, 2001; Wong & Ng, 2002). According to Guarnizo (2003: 675), 'this emergent transnational entrepreneurship appears to be a distinct mode of transnational economic action, clearly distinguishable from the more common and well-studied immigrant entrepreneurship path (i.e., ethnic entrepreneurship) undertaken by migrants in the country of reception.'

The emerging literature on the relationship between transnationalism and entrepreneurship has covered a wide variety of experiences among entrepreneurs of diverse ethnic identities (Portes, Guarnizo, & Haller, 2002). In different versions, authors such as Itzigsohn et al. (1999), Kyle (1999), and Landolt, Autler, and Baires (1999) have focused on the entrepreneurial process of TEs, describing how immigrants build and conduct businesses in both their country of origin and their place of reception. More recently, a new set of researchers has compared different cases in order to create typologies of transnational practices (Itzigsohn & Giorguli, 2002; Morawska, 2004; Portes, Escobar, & Walton, 2007) and analysed the factors that explain these practices (Landolt, 2001; Portes, 2000; Portes & Landolt, 2000; Wong & Ng, 2002).

Many of the past inquiries indicate that networks are important to TE, and a great part of their understanding has been built on the theory of social capital (Portes, 2000; Portes & Landolt, 2000; Portes, Haller, & Guarnizo, 2001). There are also, however, increasing questions about the influence of the political structures of the host city/country where the TEs reside and the home country/region they originate from (Gold, 2001; Landolt, 2001; Min, 1987; Morawska, 2004; Portes, Haller, & Guarnizo, 2001; Yoon, 1995; Zhou & Tseng, 2001). Portes, Haller, and Guarnizo, for example, explain that 'transnational entrepreneurship lies at the intersection of immigrant enterprise and the broader field of transnationalism which includes political and socio-cultural activities as well' (2001: 7). Although we have learned a great deal from the previous research based on social capital theory, it does not emphasize the role of legal context in TE. Moreover, there are also other theoretical foundations that can be used to explore the phenomenon. Particularly, an institutional perspective can add legal elements to the social factors and provide a clearer explanation of the different factors that have an influence on TE. In recent years, this perspective, especially institutional economics, has been used by a great number of academics to explain different topics relative to entrepreneurship and small and medium-sized enterprises (Aidis, 2005; Anderson, 2000; Díaz, Urbano, & Hernández, 2005; Djankov et al., 2002; Kalantaridis, 2007; Lerner & Haber, 2001; North, Smallbone, & Vickers, 2001; Urbano, 2006; Stephen, Urbano, & van Hemmen, 2009; Wai-Chung, 2002). The adoption of this approach is supported by the basic belief that the decision to create a new enterprise is conditioned by the existing institutional framework, which conditions the actions of different agents that participate in society through a structure of incentives and opportunities.

Institutional economics develops a very wide concept of 'institutions.' North (1990: 3), one of the major authors in this field, points out that 'institutions are the rules of the game in a society, or more formally, institutions are the constraints that shape human interaction.' Since the main function of institutions in a society is to reduce uncertainty by establishing a stable structure for human interaction, North (1990, 2005) attempts to explain how institutions and institutional frameworks affect economic and social development.

Institutions can be either formal – such as political rules, economic rules, and contracts – or informal – such as codes of conduct, attitudes, values, norms of behaviour, and conventions: in short, the culture of a determined society. According to North (1990), formal institutions are subordinate to informal ones in the sense that they are the deliberate means used to structure the interactions of a society in line with the norms and cultural guidelines that make up its informal institutions. Furthermore, whereas a governing body can influence the evolution of a society's formal institutions in a rather direct way, informal institutions are much less tangible and usually fall outside the direct influence of public policy. They can be moulded, but tend to resist change and take time to evolve towards new social norms.

Hence, based on North's (1990, 2005) works, for newly forming organizations, the institutional environment defines, creates, and limits entrepreneurial opportunities and thus affects the speed and scope of entrepreneurial activity (Díaz, Urbano, & Hernández, 2005; Urbano, 2006). In the TE arena, formal institutions may favour the emergence and development of transnational activities in supporting immigrant entrepreneurs and eliminating some of the obstacles that hinder the start-up process. Informal institutions may also contribute to encouraging TE among immigrants.

Research Design

Since the role that legal and social institutions play in TE in Spain remains a complex and underexplored area, we adopted an inductive multiple-case research design (Eisenhardt, 1989, 2007; Yin, 1984).

Case study research involves the examination of a contemporary phenomenon in its natural setting (Yin, 1984). It is especially appropriate for research in new topic areas, and it is frequently used both in the field of entrepreneurship (e.g., Chetty, 1996; Corbett, Neck, &

DeTienne, 2007; Godel, 2000; Leung, Zhang, Wong, & Foo, 2006; Neergard & Ulhøi, 2006; Rialp et al., 2005) and in transnational immigrant research (e.g., Chin, Yoon, & Smith, 1996; Durand, Parrado, & Massey, 1996; Grasmuck & Pessar, 1991; Itzigsohn et al., 1999; Landolt, Autler, & Baires, 1999; Mahler, 1995; Toledano, Urbano, & Ribeiro, 2009), particularly for early theory. Multiple cases – compared with single case studies – are also generally regarded as more robust, providing the observation and analysis of a phenomenon in several settings. Particularly, the multiple-case design allowed us to treat the different cases as a series of independent experiments and to follow replication logic (Yin, 1984). In addition, in this research, the logic of inductive inquiry was utilized, which helped us both to build on past literature and to provide contextually grounded new insights that can generate theory amenable to subsequent testing in future research.

Case Selection

As was noted above, this research comprises a detailed field study of four TEs who come from different countries and created their businesses in Catalonia, Spain. While this area has a long history of migration, in recent years it has become the gateway to Europe for many groups and has received a large flow of immigrants from many countries. Currently, Moroccan, Ecuadorian, Chinese, and Rumanian immigrants are some of the most numerous groups located in Catalonia. For this reason, our theoretical sample (Eisenhardt, 1989; Yin, 1984) was selected from transnational entrepreneurs who come from these countries.

The selection process began with an analysis of the different immigrant associations of the groups studied, namely, the Association of Moroccan Workers and Immigrants in Spain (ATIME), the Bayt Al-Thagafc Private Foundation, the Association for Latin American Integration in Catalonia, the Rumanian Association in Catalonia (ASOCROM), and the Union of Chinese Associations in Catalonia. In each of them, informal contacts were maintained in order to achieve more data about TEs. In the second stage of the process, twenty immigrant entrepreneurs – five from each ethnic identity – were informally interviewed, with a view to obtaining additional information about the firms. These interviews helped us to design the study protocol that we would use later in our fieldwork. Finally, to maximize the diversity of the cases selected, entrepreneur firms that varied in activity sector were included in this study. Nevertheless, they also shared some common characteristics, such as their recent creation (all the firms were less than seven years old) and the consideration of 'transnationalism' in the terms used by Portes, Guarnizo, and Haller (2002: 284), which means 'entrepreneurs travelling abroad at least twice a year and whose firms depend on regular contact with foreign countries.' Entrepreneurs willing to collaborate in this study were also helpful in selecting the final case studies.

Data Collection and Data Analysis

Data were gathered using different methods and tools, applying the concept of triangulation proposed by Yin (1984). We collected data using personal interviews, observations, and secondary sources.

The data were collected over an eighteen-month period (January 2006 to June 2007). During the period of study, we visited and interviewed the entrepreneurs for each selected case several times. The contacts were highly personalized and they varied in duration, from two hours to much longer periods, while the direction and the length of the interviews were determined by the form of the emerging data. To this end, we used semi-structured interviews and a single protocol for all of the cases, and it was adapted as new aspects of interest were introduced into the research. This allowed us to develop a better understanding of how entrepreneurs organized their transnational activities from Catalonia, and what and how institutional factors influenced them. Some employees and/or family of each entrepreneur were also interviewed to complete the information about the nature of transnational activities. Additionally, to achieve greater richness and multiple perspectives of the phenomenon (Eisenhardt, 1989), interviews with relevant organizational members both in terms of entrepreneurship – people in charge of mainstream new business support – and immigrants – leaders of immigrant communities in Catalonia – were conducted. In total, thirty-two in-depth interviews were carried out, with Spanish being the language used.

Secondary sources were consulted prior to carrying out the interviews, and included some archival material on the firms as well as published newspaper or journal articles.

Data analysis and data collection were iterative. Therefore, the findings from the initial data led to the inclusion of new prompts in the interview guide for later sessions, so that emerging ideas could be pursued. We designed an inventory of open codes, based on the topics established through the different interviews and categories suggested by the theoretical framework used in this chapter. Particularly, the literature on transnationalism, entrepreneurship, and institutional theory offered us terminology and conceptual references that helped to develop labels for the identified emerging variables. The existing literature also gave us the basis for interpreting our data in order to facilitate the emerging propositions.

The Case Studies

Brief descriptions of the main characteristics and basic profiles of the four cases are summarized in Table 8.1. For reasons of confidentiality, the names of all people have been disguised. Although the TEs have a similar age, they vary in level of education and motivation to start their transnational businesses.

Discussion

Our data, based on interviews, observations, and secondary sources, suggest that formal institutions, such as legal, economic system, and support mechanisms for new businesses, and informal institutions, such as social networks, have had an influence on the emergence and development of TE in Spain. However, while formal institutions contributed to the increase of transnational activities, informal institutions were revealed as an important push factor on both the creation and development of TE in Spain. Moreover, the data showed that, whereas formal institutions affected all the case studies in a similar way, the contribution of informal institutions varied depending on the ethnicity of the transnational entrepreneurs. We consider these aspects in the following paragraphs.

The Role of Legal or Formal Institutions in TE

The low influence of legal institutions on creating transnational enterprises, or formal institutions according to North's (1990, 2005) perspective, was evidenced throughout the cases. Particularly, in all the cases we studied, the Spanish legal system for regulating the situation of immigrants was seen to be an important factor that influenced the immigrants' decision to settle in Spain but not their decision to become transnational entrepreneurs. We note that the legal system in Spain is

Table 8.1
Four Case Studies of Transnational Entrepreneurs, Barcelona, Catalonia, Spain

	Case Study 1	Case Study 2	Case Study 3	Case Study 4
Nature of business, year established	Restaurant and cultural activities, 2000	Meat trade, 2002	Textile industry, 2000	Communications industry, 2005
Profile of entrepreneur	Female, age 40, Ecuador	Male, age 43, Morocco	Male, age 39, China	Female, age 35, Rumania
Background/experience prior to start-up	Low formal education, but years of professional experience in several restaurants in Barcelona; always had links with the culture of her country of origin	Above-average levels of education and professional preparation; some previous business experience in another commercial activity in his country of origin	Above-average levels of education and experience prior to start-up; worked for other Chinese in Spain before creating his own business in Barcelona	High level of formal education, professional training (including language skills, legal knowledge), and some professional experience in her country of origin
Reason for starting a new firm in Catalonia	To improve her economic and social situation	Difficulty in finding employment	Wished to set up his own business	Cultural values; rejects the low prestige of the employee, whom she considers to be 'conformist,' without the drive for success or ambition
Business history (antecedents and key characteristics)	Started as a restaurant specializing in Latin American cuisine; following positive reaction to its specialities, 2 years after opening, owner decided to broaden the firm's activities and began to promote and publicize art and culture from Latin American countries, offering artistic Latin American cabaret-type performances	Started from a focus on traditional products and services to the Moroccan community; after 1 year, entrepreneur expanded his market domain, offering products and services to a broader group of clients, outside his own ethnic group (local population and other ethnic groups)	Chinese clothing wholesaler, started as a retailer to customers of his own ethnic community; increasing numbers of immigrants from his country of origin, and the creation of new ventures in the same line of business by many of them, enabled this entrepreneur to become a large importer of textiles to supply these new businesses	Started with the distribution of brief news items about Rumania; firm now puts out a magazine and runs a Rumanian radio station in Barcelona, as well as other activities; the business provides emotional, useful, and up-to-date information – thus, the *Rumanian Review* has become a cornerstone of nostalgia for expatriate Rumanians

made up of a complex structure of regulations at the international, European Union, national, and regional government levels. Within this legal structure, the Spanish Constitution is the obligatory starting point, wherein it is stated that, in principle, foreigners enjoy the same basic rights as Spanish citizens; the next regulatory area that affects the legal immigration framework is that of the treaties, international agreements, and regulations of the European Union. Nevertheless, the data from our research also indicate that the legal system played an important role in the decision to expand the number of transnational activities, and consequently it could be considered a push factor of the high levels of TE in Spain in recent years. As one of the transnational entrepreneurs told us during an interview, 'a major entry of immigrants into Spain, and Catalonia, meant for me a large number of people involved in travelling through host and origin countries, and a greater amount of potential customers, employers or suppliers' (Case 1).

Similarly, while the Spanish economic system was not recognized as relevant to initiating the transnational activities, it was considered important in facilitating the increased number of them after businesses had initiated their transnational operations. For example, in Case 3, the TE pointed out that the growth that had taken place in the Spanish economy in recent years, along with the globalization of the market particularly with the Chinese Pacific economies of Taiwan, Hong Kong, and China, has had an important impact on the economic organization of his small business, and currently transnationalism itself forms a part of his firm's business strategy. In the transnational activities development phase, technological transformations in economic markets (e.g., innovations such as jet travel, inexpensive long-distance telephone calls, fax, e-mail, and the Internet) were also seen as a major help in facilitating the transnational business practices, consistent with the findings of previous studies (Portes, Guarnizo, & Landolt, 1999; Smith & Guarnizo, 1998; Wong & Ng, 2002).

Likewise, the data demonstrated that, whereas the mainstream business support had no influence on the creation of the businesses, the number of transnational activities increased with these public support measures. Therefore, as has been previously noted by some authors (Lerner & Haber, 2001; North, Smallbone, & Vickers, 2001; Portes, 2003), there is a low use of support for creating new businesses among the immigrant population. We found that TEs initially perceived that mainstream business support cannot be used by immigrants. As one interviewed TE stated, 'Your specific situation is never considered by support institutions' (Case 2). This suggests that the low propensity to use mainstream business support is not due to a lack of awareness of the existence of business support, but to a lack of confidence and trust in the capacity of institutions to solve their specific problems as TEs, and their problems in general as immigrant citizens. Interestingly, from the business support agencies' point of view, the perception of the situation was different. Our key informants considered that some support mechanisms may meet the needs of ethnic and transnational firms. For example, one of the representatives of mainstream new business support commented: 'Some needs of ethnic entrepreneurs reflect the lack of experience-related characteristics of entrepreneurs, especially in market decisions, and consequently our support measures may help them in their entrepreneurial decisions.' However, although there are different perceptions about the role that entrepreneurship business support could play in the emergence of TE, all the key informants (entrepreneurs and people in charge of business support) considered the support mechanisms to be supportive of the increase in transnational activities among immigrants.

Therefore, from the above explanation, and in the light of institutional theory (North, 1990, 2005), we suggest the following propositions:

Proposition 1: Formal institutions will be relatively more important for increasing the number of transnational activities among immigrants than promoting the emergence of TE.

Proposition 1a: A regulative environment in developed countries (e.g., Spain) that favours the arrival of immigrants will motivate immigrant entrepreneurs to increase their transnational activities.

Proposition 1b: An economic and technological environment that facilitates contacts and exchanges will motivate immigrant entrepreneurs to increase their transnational activities.

Proposition 1c: An entrepreneurial environment that supports the creation and consolidation of new firms will motivate immigrant entrepreneurs to increase their transnational activities.

The Role of Social or Informal Institutions in TE

As was noted earlier, prior research has suggested that social networks have a great importance to TE (Portes, Haller, & Guarnizo, 2001; Wong

& Ng, 2002). In traditional immigrant literature, networks are examples of ethnic resources that are conceptualized as sociocultural and demographic features of the whole group that co-ethnic entrepreneurs actively use in business or from which their business passively benefits (Wong & Ng, 2002). The data from our research indicate a similar view for TEs in Spain. In particular, the TEs we interviewed noted that social networks became an important resource not only in transnational activities but also in the creation of the firms. Personal relationships based on family, friendship, and community were stressed in all of the cases. Nevertheless, differences in the context of immigrants as well as in the cultural values that predominate in the ethnic groups involved in our study resulted in variations in the characteristics of these networks. According to our data, transnational family networks were used in Cases 2 and 3. In Case 3, the entrepreneurial culture that exists among Chinese immigrants facilitated the use of family networks. These networks included businesses that nurture and assist transmigrant connections and businesses that were physically located in only one part of the transnational social field, but which were dependent on influxes of goods or capital from transmigrant connections. One Chinese entrepreneur (Case 3) commented that 'the use of family networks is considered very common in my community.' As the entrepreneur explained, 'Many Chinese entrepreneurs have transnational family networks that are intricately woven into the firm's sites and interfirm relations.' Therefore, in this case, not only wives and brothers but also uncles and in-laws were the family members involved in transnational business.

These kinds of networks that involve extended families as an integral part of transnational business operations are consistent with the findings of Wong and Ng (2002). These networks were considered of crucial importance for linking other business connections in the form of suppliers, clients, importers, and the like. However, the immigrant entrepreneur assumed the central role in transnational activities and for this reason he travels frequently to China. In this sense, the entrepreneur reported that 'it is common for Chinese entrepreneurs to go to China two to four times per year to find clients, suppliers, or check the situation with partners.' With regard to Case 2, the Moroccan entrepreneur along with other key informants of this case (family members) also highlighted the importance of the family in transnational activities. His brother, for instance, reported that the trust that exists between the family – in this case extended families – had facilitated the development of transnational activities. Therefore, similarly to Case 3, the transnational nature that characterizes this enterprise was influenced by the exploitation of social and family networks in order to recruit human resources, develop supply and distribution activities, and even create publicity about their activities in different places.

In contrast, although networks were important to the creation and development of TE in Cases 1 and 4, the family was not involved in these social networks. Both of these cases illustrate a network typology based on professional links. In these cases, the creation of networks with family members had become much more difficult because of the smaller number of immigrants from these countries in Catalonia and the presence of ethnic enclaves. Particularly, while the recent arrival to Catalonia of Rumanian immigrants explained the difficulties in creating family networks, the wide dispersion of Latin Americans throughout Spain justified the major importance of professional networks. Although the composition of networks varies in our case studies, social networks emerge as a potent factor that explains to a great extent the creation and growth of TE in Spain.

Hence, in the framework of institutional theory (North, 1990, 2005), our discussion suggests the following proposition:

Proposition 2: Informal institutions will be relatively important for facilitating the emergence of transnational enterprises as well as increasing the number of transnational activities among immigrants.

Proposition 2a: Social networks will motivate immigrant entrepreneurs to create and develop their own transnational businesses.

Proposition 2b: Due to differences in the contexts of immigrants, transnational entrepreneurs will use their social networks in different ways to develop transnational activities.

Conclusion

The important role that TE is currently playing in the economy of the host countries has increased the interest of academics and researchers in the study of this phenomenon (Itzigsohn & Gioruli, 2002; Portes, Haller, & Guarnizo, 2001; Vertovec, 1999; Wong & Ng, 2002; Zhou, 2004). However, to date, little is known about the factors that influence the decisions included in the transnational process in the Spanish context. In this research, using a multiple-case study approach and taking institutional economics (North, 1990, 2005) as a theoretical framework,

Figure 8.1: Theoretical model of TE from an institutional perspective

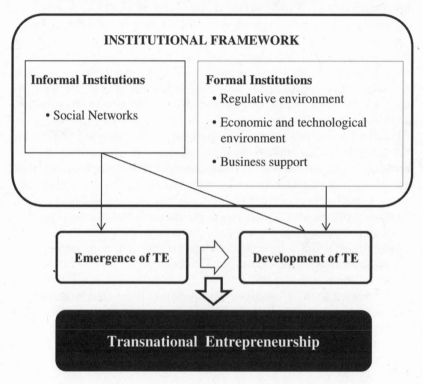

four case studies have been explored in depth in order to study the influence that legal and social institutions have on TE in Spain (Catalonia) (see Figure 8.1).

Our study suggests that formal institutions – using the terminology employed by North (1990, 2005) – play an important role in increasing transnational activities. Nevertheless, informal institutions are the most important determinants of TE because they not only facilitate the increase of these activities but also contribute to their emergence. These differences between the institutions are in part a function of the lack of trust that TEs have in foreign institutions. In contrast, members of their community are the main support for all their entrepreneurial decisions.

From an academic point of view, our research also provides support for the institutional theory and its implementation in the field of entrepreneurship. In this sense, North's (1990, 2005) ideas on formal and informal institutions used in this research contribute to a better understanding of TE. According to this theory, the actions of TE may be the responses not only to the social capital – social institutions – of immigrant entrepreneurs, but also to the legal or formal institutions existent in the host society. In this sense, the resulting propositions should help direct future TE research, and may establish a first step for future work to explore the influence of different institutions on diverse transnationalism among immigrants.

Finally, the propositions developed here also have significant implications for policy-makers. In particular, taking into account the low impact of legal institutions on the creation of transnational enterprises and the lack of consideration of immigrant entrepreneurs by business support mechanisms, future entrepreneurial policies should facilitate the flow of people and capital in order to increase the business opportunities and stimulate TE. In doing so, it might be interesting to consider the examples of U.S. business migration programs, where the immigration policy is much more advanced. On the other hand, due to the Catalonian multiculturalism and its high levels of business activity being in part related to the emergence of transnationalism among immigrant entrepreneurs, it would be interesting to continue promoting business activity to increase entrepreneurship rates not only among the local population but also among the immigrant population.

ACKNOWLEDGMENTS

The authors acknowledge the financial support from the Projects SEC2006-06017 and SEJ2007-60995 (Spanish Ministry of Education and Science) and 2005SGR00858 (Catalan Government's Department for Universities, Research and Information Society).

REFERENCES

Aidis, R. (2005). Institutional barriers to small- and medium-sized enterprise operations in transitions countries. *Small Business Economics*, 25(4): 305–18.
Anderson, A. (2000). Paradox in the periphery: An entrepreneur reconstruction? *Entrepreneurship and Regional Development*, 12(2): 91–109.
Casson, M. (1990). *Entrepreneurship*. Aldershot: Edward Elgar.
Castells, M. (1996). *The Rise of the Network Society*. Oxford: Blackwell.

Chetty, S.K. (1996). The case study method for research in small and medium sized firms. *International Small Business Journal*, 15(1): 73–85.

Chin, K., Yoon, I., & Smith, D. (1996). Immigrant small business and international economic linkage: A case of the Korean wig business in Los Angeles, 1968–1977. *International Migration Review*, 30(2): 485–510.

Corbett, A.C., Neck, H.M., & DeTienne, D.R. (2007). How corporate entrepreneurs learn from fledgling innovation initiatives: Cognition and the development of a termination script. *Entrepreneurship, Theory and Practice*, 31(6): 829–852.

Díaz, C., Urbano, D., & Hernández, R. (2005). Teoría económica institucional y creación de empresas. *Investigaciones Europeas de Dirección y Economía de la Empresa*, 11(3): 209–230.

Dicken, P. (1992). *Global Shift*. London: Paul Chapman.

Djankov, S., La Porta, R., Lopez-de-Silanes, F., & Shleifer, A. (2002). The regulation of entry. *Quarterly Journal of Economics*, 67: 1–37.

Durand, J., Parrado, E.A., & Massey, D.S. (1996). Migradollars and development: A reconsideration of the Mexican case. *International Migration Review*, 30(2): 423–444.

Eisenhardt, K.M. (1989). Building theories from case study research. *Academy of Management Review*, 14(4): 532–550.

Eisenhardt, K.M. (2007). Theory building from cases: Opportunities and challenges. *Academy of Management Journal*, 50(1): 25–32.

Faist, T. (2004). Towards a political sociology of transnationalization. *European Journal of Sociology*, 45(3): 19–54.

Glick-Schiller, N., Basch, L., & Szanton-Blanc, C. (1995). From immigrant to transmigrant: Theorizing transnational migration. *Anthropological Quarterly*, 68(1): 48–63.

Godel, S. (2000). Klaus B: The success story of an entrepreneur, a case study. *European Journal of Work and Organization Psychology*, 9(1): 89–92.

Gold, S.J. (2001). Gender, class, and networks: Social structure and migration patterns among transnational Israelis. *Global Networks*, 1(1): 19–40.

Grasmuck, S., & Pessar, P. (1991). *Between Two Islands: Dominican International Migration*. Berkeley and Los Angeles: University of California Press.

Guarnizo, L.E. (2003). The economics of transnational living. *International Migration Review*, 37(3): 666–699.

Itzigsohn, J., & Giorguli, S. (2002). Immigrant incorporation and sociocultural transnationalism. *International Migration Review*, 36(3): 766–798.

Itzigsohn, J., Cabral, C.D., Medina, E.H., & Vazquez, O. (1999). Mapping Dominican transnationalism: Narrow and broad transnational practices. *Ethnic and Racial Studies*, 22(2): 316–339.

Kalantaridis, C. (2007). Institutional change in post-socialist reimes: Public policy and beyond. *Journal of Economic Issues*, 41(2): 435–442.

Kelly, C.B. (2003). Globalization transforms trade-migration equation. *International Migration*, 41(1): 87–92.

Kyle, D. (1999). The Otavalo trade diaspora: Social capital and transnational entrepreneurship. *Ethnic and Racial Studies*, 22(2): 422–446.

Landolt, P. (2001). Salvadoran economic transnationalism: Embedded strategies for household maintenance, immigrant incorporation, and entrepreneurial expansion. *Global Networks*, 1: 217–242.

Landolt, P., Autler, L., & Baires, S. (1999). From 'Hermano Lejano' to 'Hermano Mayor': The dialectics of Salvadoran transnationalism. *Ethnic and Racial Studies*, 22(2): 290–315.

Lerner, M., & Haber, S. (2001). Performance factors of small tourism ventures: The interface of tourism, entrepreneurship and the environment. *Journal of Business Venturing*, 16(1): 77–100.

Leung, A., Zhang, J., Wong, P.K., & Foo, M.D. (2006). The use of networks in human resource acquisition for entrepreneurial firms: Multiple benefit considerations. *Journal of Business Venturing*, 21(5): 664–686.

Levitt, P. (2001). *The Transnational Villagers*. Berkeley and Los Angeles: University of California Press.

Levitt, P., & Dehesa, D.R. (2003). Transnational migration and the redefinition of the state: Variations and explanations. *Ethnic and Racial Studies*, 26(4): 587–611.

Light, I., Zhou, M., & Kim, R. (2002). Transnationalism and American exports in an English-speaking world. *International Migration Review*, 36(3): 702–725.

Livesay, H.C. (1995). *Entrepreneurship and the Growth of Firms*. Aldershot: Edward Elgar.

Madsen, T.K., & Servais, P. (1997). The internationalisation of born globals: An evolutionary process? *International Business Review*, 6(6): 561–583.

Mahler, S.J. (1995). *American Dreaming: Immigrant Life on the Margins*. Princeton: Princeton University Press.

McDougall, P.P., & Benjamin, M.O. (2000). International entrepreneurship: The intersection of two research paths. *Academy of Management Journal*, 43(5): 902–906.

Min, P.G. (1987). Filipino and Korean immigrants in small business: A comparative analysis. *Amerasia Journal*, 13(1): 53–71.

Moen, O. (2002). The born globals: A new generation of small European exporters. *International Marketing Review*, 19(2): 156–175.

Morawska, E. (2004). Immigrant transnational entrepreneurs in New York:

Three varieties and their correlates. *International Journal of Entrepreneurial Behaviour & Research*, 10(5): 325–348.

Neergard, H., & Ulhøi, J.P. (2006). Government agency and trust in the formation and transformation of interorganizational entrepreneurial networks. *Entrepreneurship Theory and Practice*, 30(4): 519–539.

North, D.C. (1990). *Institutions, Institutional Change and Economic Performance*. Cambridge: Cambridge University Press.

North, D.C. (2005). *Understanding the Process of Economic Change*. Princeton: Princeton University Press.

North, D.C., Smallbone, D., & Vickers, I. (2001). Public support policy for innovative SMEs. *Small Business Economics*, 16(2): 303–317.

Oviatt, B.M., & McDougall, P.P. (1997). Challenges for internationalisation process theory: The case of international new ventures. *Management International Review*, 37(2): 85–99.

Portes, A. (2000). The resilient significance of class: A nominalist interpretation. *Political Power and Social Theory*, 14: 249–284.

Portes, A. (2001). Introduction: The debates and significance of immigrant transnationalism. *Global Networks*, 1(3): 181–194.

Portes, A. (2003). Theoretical convergencies and empirical evidence in the study of immigrant transnationalism. *International Migration Review*, 37(3): 874–892.

Portes, A., Guarnizo, L.E., & Landolt, P. (1999). The study of transnationalism: Pitfalls and promise of an emergent research field. *Ethnic and Racial Studies*, 22(2): 217–237.

Portes, A., & Landolt, P. (2000). Social capital: Promise and pitfalls of its role in development. *Journal of Latin American Studies*, 32: 529–547.

Portes, A., Haller, W.J., & Guarnizo, L.E. (2001). *Transnational Entrepreneurs: The Emergence and Determinants of an Alternative Form of Immigrant Economic Adaptation*. Working Paper No.WPTC-01-05, ESRC Research Programme, Oxford University.

Portes, A., Guarnizo, L.E., & Haller, W.J. (2002). Transnational entrepreneurs: An alternative form of immigrant economic adaptation. *American Sociological Review*, 67(2): 278–298.

Portes, A., Escobar, C., & Walton, R. (2007). Immigrant transnational organizations and development: A comparative study. *International Migration Review*, 41(1): 242–281.

Reuber, R., & Fischer, E. (1997). The influence of the management team's international experience on internationalization. *Journal of International Business*, 28(4): 807–825.

Rialp, A., Rialp, J., Urbano, D., & Vaillant, Y. (2005). The born-global phenomenon: A comparative case study research. *Journal of International Entrepreneurship*, 3: 133–171.

Roberts, B.R., Frank, R., & Lozano-Ascencio, F. (1999). Transnational migrant communities and Mexican migration to the U.S. *Ethnic and Racial Studies*, 22(2): 239–266.

Sklair, L. (1995). *Sociology of the Global System*. (2nd ed.). London: Prentice-Hall.

Smith, M., & Guarnizo, L. (1998). *Transnationalism from Below*. New Brunswick, NJ: Transaction Publishers.

Stephen, F.H., Urbano, D., & van Hemmen, S. (2009). The responsiveness of entrepreneurs to working time regulations. *Small Business Economics*, 32: 259–276.

Toledano, N., Urbano, D., & Ribeiro, D. (2009). Creación de empresas e immigración. El caso del empresario venezolano en España. *Revista Venezdana de Gerencia*, 14(45), 9–23.

Urbano, D. (2006). *New Business Creation in Catalonia: Support Measures and Attitudes towards Entrepreneurship*. Barcelona: Col. lecció d'estudis CIDEM.

Vertovec, S. (1999). Conceiving and researching transnationalism. *Ethnic and Racial Studies*, 22: 447–462.

Wai-Chung, H. (2002). Entrepreneurship in international business: An institutional perspective. *Asia Pacific Journal of Management*, 19: 29–61.

Westhead, P., & Wright, M. (2000). *Advances in Entrepreneurship*. Cheltenham: Edward Elgar.

Wolff, J., & Pett, T. (2000). Internationalization of small firms: An examination of export-strategy approach, firm size, and export performance. *Journal of Small Business Management*, 38: 34–47.

Wong, L.L., & Ng, M. (2002). The emergence of small transnational enterprise in Vancouver: The case of Chinese entrepreneur immigrants. *International Journal of Urban and Regional Research*, 26(3): 508–530.

Yin, R. (1984). *Case Study Research*. Beverly Hills: Sage.

Yoon, I. (1995). The growth of Korean immigrant entrepreneurship in Chicago. *Ethnic and Racial Studies*, 18(2): 315–335.

Zhou, M. (2004). Revisiting ethnic entrepreneurship: Convergences, controversies, and conceptual advancements. *International Migration Review*, 38(3): 1040–1074.

Zhou, Y., & Tseng, Y. (2001). Regrounding the 'ungrounded empires': Localization as the geographical catalyst for transnationalism. *Global Networks*, 1(2): 131–153.

9 A Review of Related Streams of Immigration and Global Entrepreneurship Research

BENSON HONIG AND ISRAEL DRORI

The scholars brought together in this volume have used multiple perspectives to examine one of the most ubiquitous, yet understudied phenomena of the day – the increase in labour and entrepreneurial mobility accompanying globalization that has created a new class of active agents of change and economic development. These 'citizens of the world,' living next door to us in countries rich and poor, present both a challenge and a dilemma for policy-makers. Concerns, many addressed in this volume, range from understanding immigration and institutional frameworks, through science and legal policies, to learning how individuals develop networks and leverage their bicultural characteristics. It is our hope that by reviewing existing literature on the subject, we are able to help policy-makers and scholars untie the Gordian knot facing them regarding the very complex interrelationships that characterize transnational entrepreneurship (TE). In this chapter, we review existing literature towards the goal of differentiating overlapping yet complementary fields of study, research questions, and units of analysis, providing a useful map for scholars and policy-makers attempting to grapple with this complex yet important field.

It has been noted in the chapters of this book that the transnational position in both home and host societies is contingent on the sociocultural, political, and economic resources at the disposal of transnational entrepreneurs (TEs). Business strategies and chances of success are also associated with the multiple contexts of social and cultural realms that may accompany economic and other resources. In a globalized world, the ability to operate as a transnational entrepreneur implies a distinct opportunity structure that enables those who found and maintain businesses to benefit from their bifocal modus operandi. As the various chapters of this book illustrate, multiple contexts are a constitutive feature of transnational entrepreneurs and a prime contributor to their strategy of seeking and exploiting business opportunities.

Transnational entrepreneurship is one of the few streams of research that attempts to understand the entrepreneurial activities of migrants on the backdrop of a globalized world. In this book we introduce various studies that addresses the scope, boundaries, and theoretical lenses of TE research, as they relate to a set of issues including: what is the meaning of operating in multiple contexts; what are the key determinants of transnational entrepreneurs who operate in the field of science; what is the nature of network building or the importance of contingency and locality in attempting to explain immigration in terms of a multiplicity of economic relationships? To develop a better understanding of transnational entrepreneurship, it is worthwhile to consider the different types of entrepreneurship activities that stem from migration and globalization and compare them with transnational entrepreneurship. To this end, this chapter examines the distinctions between two other relevant but different streams of research: international entrepreneurship (IE) and ethnic entrepreneurship (EE). Thus, we review IT and EE as an integrated part of the global context, which together with TE, have led to a number of insights into the immigrant and global entrepreneurship processes.

International Entrepreneurship Research

International entrepreneurship refers to the discovery, enactment, evaluation, and exploitation of opportunities across national borders to create future goods and services (McDougall & Oviatt, 1997, 2000; Oviatt & McDougall, 1994, 2005; Zahra, 1993). The emergence of international entrepreneurship is associated with the process of globalization and increased competition in markets. The IE process draws from the internationalized environment and, in particular, relates to the innovation and risk-taking that firms undertake as they expand in the international realm (Zahra & George, 2002; Zahra, 2005). Scholarly interest in IE reflects the influence of globalization regarding corporate entrepreneurship (Knight & Cavusgil, 1996) as well as 'born global' ventures, namely, young enterprises that seek international markets early in their life cycle (McDougall & Oviatt, 2000; Oviatt & McDougall, 1994, 2005; Zahra & George, 2002).

The analytical focus of international entrepreneurship centres around a variety of themes such as the comparative international context of entrepreneurial activities across boundaries (Yeung, 2002), the influence of networks and learning on the prospects of emergence and sustainability (McDougall & Oviatt, 2000), and the advancement of causal models of various organizational and strategic aspects of IE and the consequences of different political and economic environments (Zahra & George, 2002; Young, Dimitratos, & Dana, 2003).

For decades IE research has been associated with the 'born global' construct. Empirical research has drawn on two basic explanatory frameworks: resource-based and social network theories (Young, Dimitratos, & Dana, 2003). The former explains how new and/or young international ventures are able to activate the necessary resources to achieve a competitive advantage in international markets (Bloodgood, Sapienza, & Almeida, 1996; McDougall, Shane, & Oviatt, 1994). The latter examines the nature of the venture's location within networks to better understand survival in the competitive international environment (Oviatt & McDougall, 1994). Thus, IE research is primarily concerned with the innovative, proactive, and risk-taking behaviour of firms in an uncertain international business environment (McDougall & Oviatt, 2000; Zahra & Garvis, 2000), and it is largely unconcerned with issues of ethnicity and multiple affiliations.

Ethnic Entrepreneurship Research

Ethnic entrepreneurship is another research stream related to the study of transnational entrepreneurship. Ethnic entrepreneurs (EEs) are individuals whose group membership is tied to a common cultural heritage or ethnic origin, and who are known to those outside the ethnic group as having such traits (Rath & Kloosterman, 2000; Yinger, 1985). Since EEs are intrinsically entwined in particular social structures in which individual behaviour, social relations, and economic transactions are constrained (Aldrich, Zimmer, & McEvoy, 1989; Aldrich & Waldinger, 1990), varied ethnic resources such as internal markets, access to capital (Wilson & Portes, 1980), or ethnic solidarity have provided the impetus for entrepreneurship. The EE literature analytically distinguishes between two main types of EEs: middleman minorities and enclave entrepreneurs (Bonacich, 1972; Light & Gold, 2000). Middleman minorities are those entrepreneurs who take advantage of ethnic resources such as language, networks, and skills to trade between their host and origin societies, while retaining their ethnic identity and non-assimilation stance as an integral part of their business strategy. Examples of middlemen minorities include Jews, Armenians, and Chinese (Light & Gold, 2000). Enclave entrepreneurship activities, in contrast, are bounded by a certain location and are usually populated by co-ethnics. Chinese communities in San Francisco, Cubans in Miami, and the Korean community in Atlanta are notable examples of enclave communities (Min, 1988, 1990; Portes, 1987; Portes & Jensen, 1989; Wong, 1998). These entrepreneurs rely primarily upon local resources and ethnic networks (Light & Bonacich, 1988; Light & Gold, 2000; Waldinger, Aldrich, & Ward, 1999). Thus, EE activities are deeply embedded in community networks, and are characterized by an inward orientation and a distinctive intercommunity social and economic context.

Transnational Entrepreneurship Research

In contrast to the ethnic entrepreneurship paradigm, the locus of reference for transnational entrepreneuship is the international theatre, where TE research focuses explicitly on the significance and opportunity of cross-border business activities (Portes, Guarnizo, & Haller, 2002). In particular, TE promotes international trade by taking advantage of globalization and the entrepreneurs' cosmopolitan way of life, enabling the more timely acquisition of the resources required for operating cross-national businesses. Furthermore, TEs multiply ethnic resources that facilitate operating beyond the boundaries of their ethnic environment (Light & Gold, 2000; Yeung, 2002). Thus, TE reflects the widespread diffusion of a distinct elite – a binational, non-assimilating group originating from migrant communities.

Transnational entrepreneurs function by mastering key resources and becoming international business leaders, thereby largely superseding the outdated middleman minorities in the theatre of international commerce. Consistent with this perspective, TE activities have been conceptualized more recently as a mechanism of adaptation to the host society, replacing earlier modes described in terms of activities and assimilation associated with ethnic groups (Morawska, 2004).

The transnational EE, who started off as a migrant, may arrive either 'from above' or 'from below.' Some countries, such as Canada, New Zealand, and the United States, give privileged access to entrepreneur immigrants in hopes of stimulating economic growth (Sassen, 1994; Wong, 2003), by setting aside non-quota immigration priority to persons who pledge to start businesses or invest in business in the host society. This increasingly common practice leaves immigrant populations with state-prioritized entrepreneurs who were selected for admission precisely because of their existing business skills and financial capital. Entrepreneurs who have arrived 'from above' have class-related resources that their non-entrepreneur co-ethnics normally lack, but they nonetheless increase the percentage of self-employed citizens within their immigrant group.

Transnational EEs can also 'arrive from below' as economic immigrants who are independently founding their businesses using social capital and networks, and exploiting opportunities in both their new home and former country. Transnational entrepreneurs engage in cross-national activities due to the very basic fact that immigration to another country is part of their personal history. Notable examples include the varied Chinese transnational entrepreneurs, Indian entrepreneurs, and the Taiwanese in their numerous diasporas (Saxenian, 2002; Wong & Ng, 2002; Wong, 2004; Yeung, 1999), as well as various immigrant groups in the United States such as the Dominicans (Itzigsohn et al., 1999), Colombians, and Salvadorans (Guarnizo, 1994; Guarnizo & Luz, 1999).

Conclusion: Demarcating the Stream of TE Research

Both IE and EE present research traditions that overlap facets of transnational entrepreneurship, although each highlights perspectives that circumvent certain critical elements of transnational entrepreneurial activity, failing to fully account for the dynamic complexity of multiple cultural perspectives. TE and IE share a focus on the institutional factors that shape and constrain the entrepreneurial process, including consideration of national culture and local institutions during internationalization; Rosenzweig and Singh (1991), for example, examine multinational corporations (MNCs) with respect to the dual institutional pressures that exist between an MNC subsidiary's institutional environment and its local environment. Nevertheless, an important conceptual demarcation exists between IE and TE. Yeung carefully maps out the distinctions between TE and IE from an institutional theory perspective, pointing out that transnational entrepreneurship activities have to cope with and adapt to the institutional relations in *both* home and host countries through 'the social and business networks, in which these transnational entrepreneurs are embedded, political-economic structures, and dominant organizational and cultural practices in the home and host countries' (2002: 30).

Yeung's discussion of the relationship between IE and TE suggests that international business activities pose a challenge in adapting to the host country's social, economic, and political systems, thus requiring 'exceptional qualities in the process of creating and sustaining particular business ventures across national boundaries by social actors' (2002: 31). In taking an institutional view, Yeung focuses on the necessity of understanding the influence of multiple institutional environments on TE activity. He points out that institutions form the 'rules of the game' that govern TE decision-making, and argues that transnational entrepreneurs operate by 'enrolling' in cross-border institutional structures. EE, in contrast, focuses primarily on the issues related to ethnicity and social structure, but largely avoids examining the kinds of global business and resource factors unique to transnational entrepreneurship. Finally, unlike the IE research stream, which emphasizes the firm as a central unit of analysis, the TE stream emphasizes transnational entrepreneurs as embedded agents whose lines of action are determined within the multiple institutional structures in which they operate and by which they are sometimes constrained (see Sewell, 1992).

While Yeung (2002) focuses on understanding the influence of multiple institutional environments on TE activity, he does not address the central issues pertaining to embeddedness in multiple cultural perspectives that account for the dynamic creation of new structures or the adaptation of existing institutions. For Yeung, global and national institutions are more or less given structures, and so he fails to address transnational entrepreneurship agency, as well as the role of cultural identities in formulating TE opportunities. For example, the Chinese transnational entrepreneur in Northern Ireland discussed in chapter 1 played an active role in modifying an existing national small business agency to undertake research and support specifically for external tourism – an arena previously overlooked by that agency.

Table 9.1 compares and contrasts the three orientations with respect to definitions, unit of analysis, and primary research questions. As is shown, the epistemological frameworks reflected in the IE, EE, and TE research streams are not mutually exclusive; various concepts, constructs, and analytical understandings of transnational entrepreneurship are shared by all three. All three approaches focus on activities that reflect the basic entrepreneurial process of discovery, enactment, evaluation, and exploitation of market opportunities and value creation across borders, but within the international business environment (Baker, Gedajlovic, & Lubatkin, 2005; McDougall & Oviatt, 2000). At

Table 9.1
Comparison of TE, IE, and EE Research Streams

	International Entrepreneurship	Ethnic Entrepreneurship	Transnational Entrepreneurship
Definition	Entrepreneurial activities (the discovery, enactment, evaluation, and exploitation of opportunities) across national borders to create future goods and services	Entrepreneurial activities that involve individuals whose group membership is tied to a common cultural heritage or origin and are known to outgroup members as having such traits	Entrepreneurial activities that involve individuals who migrate from one country to another, concurrently maintaining business-related linkages with their former country of origin and currently adopted countries and communities
Unit of analysis	Firm-level actions of an export firm or internationally oriented organization, usually a multinational corporation; also an early stage firm's role and position within a network of cross-border relationships	Individual actions of an immigrant, often with distinctive language and customs, engaged in formal, informal, or illegal self-employment and/or businesses in adopted country; also entrepreneur's role and position within an ethnic community network	Individual actions of an immigrant engaged in two or more socially embedded environments, maintaining global relations, enhancing creativity, and maximizing his or her resource base; also entrepreneur's role and position within a network of transnational relationships
Primary research questions	How do entrepreneurial outlooks and capabilities account for the evolution of new international markets? How do entrepreneurs help firms overcome liabilities of newness and foreignness? How and why do some firms exploit entrepreneurial vision and knowledge in recognizing opportunities to engage in early stage international growth?	What processes account for the evolution of ethnic enclaves that result in entrepreneurial activities? How do entrepreneurs overcome institutional constraints, and language and cultural barriers in their adopted environments? How do entrepreneurs develop immigrant institutions, structures, and social capital networks that support entrepreneurial activities?	What processes account for the evolution of entrepreneurial businesses in two or more environments? How do entrepreneurs overcome dual sets of institutional constraints, and languages and cultural barriers? How do entrepreneurs develop and maintain institutional, structural, and social capital networks in more than one country?

the same time, the challenges imposed by a transnational context draw attention to the need for transnational entrepreneurs to be aware of the multiple institutional, structural, and cultural factors that influence the creation and growth of their businesses.

While the analytical framework of transnational entrepreneurship suggested by Yeung (2002) helps highlight the multiple institutional forces faced by transnational entrepreneurs, it is largely focused on the factors that influence the extent to which the various sources of isomorphic pressure prevail. As a result, it fails to explain how TEs are able to distance themselves from institutional norms and create novel solutions and strategies. Further, TEs not only learn how to balance the tensions between home and host country-related factors, but they also decide whether to pay attention to social objectives over economic ones. For example, TEs may elect to provide employment opportunities in their country of origin regardless of the comparative economic rate of return. Thus, both agency and practice appear to be particularly important when unpacking the process of seeking and exploiting business opportunities within multiple social structures.

Future research may also explore the notion of institutional work referring to the practices and processes by which transnational entrepreneurs define a social boundary, distinguishing between social domains, which themselves reflect the need to establish legitimacy and control in the social and economic spheres. For example, an institutional perspective may be used for examining the integration of macro- and microstructures (Morawska, 2004) within the immigrant community and its associations. It may provide insight into the mode of integration into society and the economy at large (Waldinger, Aldrich, & Ward, 1999; Light & Rosenstein, 1995), explaining how TEs achieve legitimacy, power, skill, and sociocultural resources essential to the venture's success. Transnational entrepreneurs' institutional settings are also influenced by the specific contextual configuration of social actors and their choices. The scope and magnitude of TE activities are closely related to the actions and orientations of individuals. They are influenced over time by social and historical circumstances such as cultural and social capital, the civil-political environment (both in their spaces of operation and globally), and the availability of resources.

REFERENCES

Aldrich, H., & Waldinger, R. (1990). Ethnicity and entrepreneurship. *Annual Review of Sociology*, 16: 111–135.

Aldrich, H., Zimmer, C., & McEvoy, D. (1989). Continuities in the study of ecological succession: Asian business in three English cities. *Social Forces*, 67: 920–944.

Baker, T., Gedajlovic, E., & Lubatkin, M. (2005). A framework for comparing entrepreneurship processes across nations. *Journal of International Business Studies*, 36: 492–504.

Bloodgood, J., Sapienza, H., & Almeida, J.G. (1996). The internationalization of new high-potential U.S. ventures: Antecedents and outcomes. *Entrepreneurship Theory and Practice*, 20: 61–76.

Bonacich, E. (1972). A theory of middleman minorities. *American Sociological Review*, 38: 583–594.

Guarnizo, L. (1994). Los Dominicanyorks: The making of a binational society. *Annals of the American Academy of Political and Social Sciences*, 533: 70–86.

Guarnizo, L., & Luz, M. (1999). Transnational migration: A view from Colombia. *Ethnic and Racial Studies*, 22: 397–421.

Itzigsohn, J., Dore, C., Hernandez, E., & Vasquez, O. (1999). Mapping Dominican transnationalism. *Ethnic and Racial Studies*, 22: 316–339.

Knight, G.G., & Cavusgil, S.T. (1996). The born global firm: A challenge to traditional internationalization theory. *Advances in International Marketing*, 8: 11–26.

Light, I.H., & Bonacich, E. (1988). *Immigrant Entrepreneurs: Koreans in Los Angeles*. Berkeley: University of California Press.

Light, I., & Gold, S. (2000). *Ethnic Economies*. San Diego: Academic Press.

Light, I., & Rosenstein, C. (1995). *Race, Ethnicity and Entrepreneurship in Urban America*. New York: Aldine de Gruyter.

McDougall, P., & Oviatt, B. (1997). International entrepreneurship: Literature in the 1990's and directions for future research. In D.S. Sexton (Ed.), *Entrepreneurship 2000*, 291–320. Chicago: Upstart Publishing.

McDougall, P., & Oviatt, B. (2000). International entrepreneurship: The intersection of two research paths. *Academy of Management Journal*, 43: 902–908.

McDougall, P., Shane, S., & Oviatt, B. (1994). Explaining the formation of international new ventures: The limits of theories from international business research. *Journal of Business Venturing*, 9: 469–487.

Min, P.G. (1988). *Ethnic Business Enterprise: Korean Small Business in Atlanta*. New York: Center for Migration Studies.

Morawska, E. (2004). Immigrant transnational entrepreneurs in New York: Three varieties and their correlates. *International Journal of Entrepreneurial Behavior and Research*, 10: 325–348.

Oviatt, B., & McDougall, P. (1994). Towards a theory of international new ventures. *Journal of International Business Studies*, 25: 45–64.

Oviatt, B., & McDougall, P. (2005). The internationalization of entrepreneurship. *Journal of International Business Studies*, 36: 2–8.

Portes, A. (1987). The social origins of the Cuban enclave economy of Miami. *Sociological Perspectives*, 30: 340–372.

Portes, A., & Jensen, L. (1989). The enclave and the entrants. *American Socio-logical Review,* 54: 929–949.

Portes, A., Guarnizo, L.E., & Haller, W.J. (2002). Transnational entrepreneurs: An alternative form of immigrant economic adaptation. *American Sociologi-cal Review,* 67: 278–298.

Rath, J., & Kloosterman, R. (2000). A critical review of research on immigrant entrepreneurship. *International Migration Review,* 34: 657–681.

Rosenzweig, P., & Singh, J. (1991). Organizational environments and the mul-tinational enterprise. *Academy of Management Review,* 16: 340–361.

Sassen, S. (1994). Economic internationalization: The new migration in Japan and the United States. *Social Justice,* 21: 62–82.

Saxenian, A. (2002). Transnational communities and the evolution of global production networks: The cases of Taiwan, China and India. *Industry and Innovation,* 9: 183–202.

Sewell, W. (1992). A theory of structure: Duality, agency, and transformation. *American Journal of Sociology,* 98: 1–29.

Waldinger, R., Aldrich, H., & Ward, R. (1999). *Ethnic Entrepreneurs in Industrial Society.* Newbury Park: Sage.

Wilson, K., & Portes, A. (1980). Immigrant enclaves: An analysis of the labor market experiences of Cubans in Miami. *American Journal of Sociology,* 86: 295–319.

Wong, B. (1998). *Ethnicity and Entrepreneurship: The New Chinese Immigrants in the San Francisco Bay Area.* Boston: Allyn and Bacon.

Wong, L.L. (2003). Chinese business migration to Australia, Canada and the United States: State policy and the global migration marketplace. *Asian and Pacific Migration Journal,* 12: 301–335.

Wong, L.L. (2004). Taiwanese immigrant entrepreneurs in Canada and trans-national social space. *International Migration,* 42: 113–152.

Wong, L.L., & Ng, M. (2002). The emergence of small transnational enterprises in Vancouver: The case of Chinese entrepreneur immigrants. *International Journal of Urban and Regional Research,* 26: 508–530.

Yeung, H. (1999). The internationalization of ethnic Chinese business firms from Southeast Asia: Strategies, processes and competitive advantage. *Inter-national Journal of Urban and Regional Research,* 23: 103–127.

Yeung, H. (2002). Entrepreneurship in international business: An institutional perspective. *Asia Pacific Journal of Management,* 19: 29–61.

Yinger, M.J. (1985). Ethnicity. *Annual Review of Sociology,* 11: 151–180.

Young, S., Dimitratos, P., & Dana, L.P. (2003). International entrepreneurship research: What scope for international business theories? *Journal of Interna-tional Entrepreneurship,* 1: 31–42.

Zahra, S.A. (1993). Conceptual model of entrepreneurship as firm behavior: A critique and extension. *Entrepreneurship Theory and Practice*, 14: 5–21.

Zahra, S.A. (2005). A theory of international new ventures: A decade of research. *Journal of International Business Studies*, 36: 20–28.

Zahra, S.A., & Garvis, D.M. (2000). International corporate entrepreneurship and company performance: The moderating effect of international environmental hostility. *Journal of Business Venturing*, 15: 469–492.

Zahra, S.A., & George, G. (2002). International entrepreneurship: The current status of the field and future research agenda. In M. Hitt, D. Ireland, D. Sexton, & S. Camp (Eds.), *Strategic Entrepreneurship: Creating an Integrated Mindset*, 255–258. Oxford: Blackwell.

Contributors

Barbara Carmichael is Professor of Geography and Environmental Studies and the Director of the NeXt Research Centre (Centre for the Study of Entrepreneurship and Nascent Technology) at Wilfrid Laurier University, Waterloo, Ontario. Her work in entrepreneurship focuses on tourism entrepreneurship, transnational entrepreneurship in tourism, and lifestyle motivations.

Betty Conklin is a new venture consultant with Excellerator, LLC, and she has assisted in the development of several successful new ventures. She received an MBA with an emphasis in Entrepreneurship at the University of Louisville, Kentucky, and a BA in Cultural Anthropology from the University of California, Davis. Her research interests include transnational entrepreneurship and new venture strategy.

Israel Drori is Professor at the School of Business, College of Management, Rishon Le Zion, Israel. He is an organizational ethnographer (PhD, University of California, Los Angeles), and his current research is focused on the emergence of new industries (high-tech, nanotechnology) and the organization of work.

Paula Danskin Englis is Associate Professor at the Campbell School of Business, Berry College, and a Research Fellow at the Nikos Institute of Knowledge Intensive Entrepreneurship at the University of Twente, The Netherlands. She has published in the entrepreneurship areas of knowledge management, networks, global start-ups, and value chains.

Ari Ginsberg is Professor of Management and Entrepreneurship at

New York University Stern School of Business, where he has held the positions of chairman of the management department and director of the Berkley Center for Entrepreneurial Studies. He is a recipient of the Citibank Excellence in Teaching Award, the Peter Drucker Fellowship, and the Harold Price Chair in Entrepreneurship and Innovation.

Peter Groenewegen is Professor of Organization Science at the Faculty of Social Sciences of the Vrije Universiteit, Amsterdam. He has published on social networks in and around organizations, environmental policy, and institutional theory.

Benson Honig (PhD, Stanford University) holds the Teresa Cascioli Chair in Entrepreneurial Leadership at McMaster University in Hamilton, Ontario, and is past president of the Canadian Council for Small Business and Entrepreneurship. He is the recipient of the 2009 Grief Research Impact Award, and an editor of *Entrepreneurship Theory and Practice*. His research interests include social entrepreneurship, transnational entrepreneurship, organization studies, business planning, and social capital.

Gerry Kerr (PhD, York University) is Associate Professor of Strategy and Entrepreneurship at the Odette School of Business, University of Windsor, Ontario. His research interests involve both areas of study, and his articles have appeared in *Business Horizons, Journal of Management History, Frontiers in Entrepreneurship Research,* and *Journal of Small Business and Entrepreneurship*, among other publications.

Ivan Light is Professor Emeritus of Sociology at the University of California, Los Angeles. He is the author of numerous articles and six books in the areas of immigration, entrepreneurship, and urban sociology.

Xiaohua Lin (PhD, Oklahoma State University) is Professor of International Business and Entrepreneurship and the Director of the International Research Institute at the Ted Rogers School of Management, Ryerson University, Toronto, Ontario. He is the founder of the Canadian Entrepreneurship & Innovation Platform, a non-profit organization that promotes and facilitates Canada-based transnational entrepreneurship.

Kathleen Montgomery (PhD, New York University) is Professor of

Organizations and Management at the Anderson Graduate School of Management at the University of California, Riverside. She uses institutional theory to study changes in the system of professions and issues of professional-organizational relationships. Her recent work focuses on issues of professional trust and integrity.

Amalya L. Oliver (PhD, University of California, Los Angeles) is Professor at the Department of Sociology and Anthropology and Chair of the Library Authority at the Hebrew University, Jerusalem. She studies networks for learning, interorganizational networks and collaborations in biotechnology, processes of change in the professions, scientific entrepreneurship, and scientific misconduct.

Pankaj C. Patel is Assistant Professor of Management at Ball State University in Muncie, Indiana. His current research interests include the role of transnational social networks in enhancing venture performance. He is also interested in the role of country-level trade networks in exploiting migrants' abilities to engage in transnational entrepreneurship.

Domingo Ribeiro-Soriano is Professor of Management at the University of Valencia, Spain. He is currently participating in various Spanish and European research projects. He has publications in several international journals and has also served as reviewer. He is the editor of the *International Entrepreneurship and Management Journal* and *Service Business: An International Journal*.

Francine K. Schlosser (PhD, University of Waterloo) is Associate Professor in Management at the University of Windsor, Ontario. She researches individual and interpersonal factors influencing strategy related to marketing, human resources, entrepreneurship, and the adoption of technology. This interfunctional focus has allowed her scholarly contribution to cross traditional boundaries between business areas. Her articles have been published in the *Journal of Organizational Behavior, Journal of Strategic Marketing, Journal of Business Research,* and *Journal of Managerial Psychology*. Dr Schlosser is also the Director of the Centre for Business Advancement and Research (CBAR), a student outreach centre providing market research and business plan development.

Nuria Toledano is Associate Professor in Entrepreneurship at the

University of Huelva, Spain, and is currently visiting professor at the Autonomous University of Barcelona. Her research interests include entrepreneurship policy, immigrant entrepreneurship, and universities' spin-offs. She participates in several European research projects and has several publications in international scholarly journals.

David Urbano is Associate Professor in Entrepreneurship at the Autonomous University of Barcelona, Spain. His research is focused in the conditioning factors to entrepreneurship in different contexts using an institutional approach. He is currently participating in various Spanish and European research projects and has several publications in international scholarly journals.

Ingrid Wakkee is Assistant Professor at the Faculty of Social Sciences and the Center for Entrepreneurship at the Vrije Universiteit, Amsterdam. Her research interests involve renascent entrepreneurship, born global firms, and market-driven social ventures. Her work has appeared in journals such as *International Review of Entrepreneurship, International Small Business Journal, International Entrepreneurship and Management Journal,* as well as in edited volumes published by Edward Elgar.

Margaret Walton-Roberts is a human geographer with a focus on international migration. Her research has operated on two broad tracks: the first is on Indian emigration and transnational migrant networks, and the second on immigration to second- and third-tier cities in Canada. Currently she is Associate Professor in the Geography and Environmental Studies Department and the Director of the International Migration Research Centre at Wilfrid Laurier University in Waterloo, Ontario.